T0054638

Praise for *Prine on Prine*

"This book is a stunner! Only the glorious Holly Gleason could assemble such a magnificent collection to celebrate the life and world-changing artistry of her friend John Prine. Perhaps the most joyful history book you'll ever read. His music explodes from the pages."

—**Tom DeSavia**, coauthor of *Under the Big Black Sun:*
A Personal History of LA Punk and *More Fun in the New World:*
The Unmaking and Legacy of LA Punk

"Listening to John Prine instantly jolts me to a higher vibration and feels like I'm walking on holy ground, free, fearless, and naked as the eyes of a clown. He shakes me, wakes me, conjuring up emotions I didn't know I had, reminding me that tenderness is a virtue. His words make me want to be a better person, to recognize myself in everyone's eyes, to hold all of humanity in high esteem—because we're all in it together. Praise be to Holly Gleason for this oh-so-important, exquisitely curated collection. John Prine improved the world by being alive. Let's do our best keep that big, beautiful ball rolling."

—**Pamela Des Barres**, author of *I'm With the Band* and
Let's Spend the Night Together

"Nobody wrote songs like John Prine, filled with humor, humanity, and perfectly cockeyed detail. But what this elegantly curated collection— culled from interviews, TV and radio appearances, and even recipes— reveals is that . . . well, that's just who the guy was. Whether he's at the Library of Congress or in the pages of *Hot Rod* magazine, Prine's wit and fierce independence constantly shine through."

—**Alan Light**, author of *The Holy or the Broken: Leonard Cohen, Jeff*
Buckley, and the Unlikely Ascent of "Hallelujah"

"I worked at Atlantic when John was signed, and I was so blown away by the power of his lyrics that I played the album nonstop. At a young age I realized what true songwriting was all about and the master was named John Prine! Prine's songs speak to your heart, your mind and your soul. The brilliant genius of John Prine was not only the magic he had in writing about everyday life for everyday people; just as important was that his lyrics provoked you into thinking about everyday things that you may never have given much thought to. And after he woke up those feelings, you realized you couldn't have said it any better. The respect, admiration, and love for Prine and his songs that Holly Gleason has is obvious not only in her eloquent introduction but in the interviews she selected to pay proper homage to him."

—**Linda Moran**, president and CEO, Songwriters Hall of Fame

"As close to an autobiography as we're going to get from John Prine, *Prine on Prine* captures the inimitable, whimsical voice of one of our greatest songwriters, from the beginning of his career to his final days, evolving from the shy, self-effacing, uncertain youngster film critic that Roger Ebert discovered to the wise, cunning veteran who left a body of work probably second only to Dylan. Nashville legend Holly Gleason knew the man and assembled this brilliant collection with a knowing eye and loving heart."

—**Joel Selvin**, author of *Fare Thee Well: The Final Chapter of the Grateful Dead's Long, Strange Trip* and other books

"Holly Gleason has always been one of our greatest music journalists, but this book solidifies the fact that she's much more than that: she's one of the great preservers of the stories that make up American music. Here the esteemed writer has meticulously gathered the best interviews, features, and reviews in which Prine offered insights into his process as one of the all-time best songwriters. She's found the work of writers such as Studs Terkel, Roger Ebert, Ronni Lundy, Cameron Crowe, and many others who deftly show us the man behind the music. In doing so, Gleason provides the fullest picture of Prine we've ever had, and it's one that enriches our understanding of him as an artist and as a person. *Prine on Prine* is a must-read for anyone who loves John Prine or anyone who loves great music."

—**Silas House**, Kentucky Poet Laureate and author of *Lark Ascending*, *Clay's Quilt*, *The Coal Tattoo*, and *Southernmost*

"This carefully curated set of interviews shines a light on why this man and these songs are deeply, deeply embedded in our collective memory. It's the magic of how a USPS mail carrier became the first songwriter to read at the Library of Congress at the behest of America's Poet Laureate—and the way we've all spent decades marking life's moments with John Prine records. In reading these pieces, it becomes clear: the interviews are the man—and the insight that Holly, who knew Prine well, brings to them shows John Prine truly was that man. His songs are powerful and spot on, and they seem to come from a very regular guy, albeit one with great compassion and wisdom. In reading *Prine on Prine*, he comes across that way and more."

—**Greg Harris**, president and CEO, Rock & Roll Hall of Fame

"With a deep understanding and knowledge of John Prine—the man and his music—Holly Gleason has searched every nook and cranny to curate a thoughtful biography of one of our greatest singer-songwriters. Her insightful text sets the scene as we experience Prine, the unfiltered raconteur, via five decades of media coverage, from major magazines to niche publications, television scripts to a recipe book, talk show appearances, movie roles and his PEN Award presentation. *Prine on Prine* is both revelatory and entertaining."

—**Holly George-Warren**, author of *Janis: Her Life and Music* and *A Man Called Destruction: The Life and Music of Alex Chilton*

PRINE
ON PRINE

INTERVIEWS AND ENCOUNTERS WITH JOHN PRINE

EDITED BY HOLLY GLEASON

CHICAGO
REVIEW
PRESS

Copyright © 2023 by Holly Gleason
All rights reserved
Published by Chicago Review Press Incorporated
814 North Franklin Street
Chicago, Illinois 60610
ISBN 978-1-64160-630-1

Library of Congress Control Number: 2023940199

A list of credits and copyright notices for the individual pieces in this collection can be found on pages 329–332.

Cover design and typesetting: Jonathan Hahn
Cover photo: Slick Lawson

Printed in the United States of America

For Cupid & BooBoo,
who opened all of the windows and so many doors . . .

"The sun can play tricks with your eyes on the highway
The moon can lay sideways 'til the ocean stands still
But a person can't tell his best friend he loves him
'Til time has stopped breathing you're alone on the hill . . ."

—John Prine, "He Was in Heaven Before He Died"

CONTENTS

PART IV · "I *AM* A RECORD COMPANY" B/W WELCOME TO NASHVILLE CITY LIMITS

PART V · COMING INTO HIS OWN

Even though Einstein left the music business and opened a beloved East Nashville bakery with his wife Ellen, his passion for the stories, moments, and adventures never flagged. So in many ways, *Prine on Prine* is a testament to Einstein as well as the journalists who reached into Prine's life to understand what shaped his songs.

To all the writers, reporters, creators, and publishers, thank you for giving someone considered a "cult figure" the space at a time when space truly was finite, curated, and being published meant something. Recognizing it's not always about the "product sold" can be its own reward—and liability when justifying the space to higher-ups. But telling Prine's story well meant that generations of people who needed these songs *knew* he was out there, playing around America—and it allowed him to keep working in those years when there was no radio scare or new Oh Boy project to report.

Robert Hilburn was the first of the writers who developed an ongoing dialogue with Prine. He was encouraging about this project, wrote right into the heart of Prine's coming of age. Dave Hoekstra and later Randy Lewis were also critical voices who maintained an evolving conversation with the man. Thanks to all three, plus Craig Marks and Ralph Drew at the *Los Angeles Times* for help navigating the permissions, as well as Steve Warmbir at the *Chicago Sun-Times* and the gracious folks at the *Illinois Entertainer.*

Small, local entertainment publications truly matter. The *Illinois Entertainer*, the Tri-State area's *Aquarian*, and New Orleans's *OffBeat* speak to the vibrant entertainment culture of those places. All three foster vibrant writing, takes that reflect local taste and provide a sense of community in an increasingly alienated world.

So many great journalists have covered Prine over the years. I am especially grateful to these contributors for agreeing to be a part of this book: Poet Laureate Ted Kooser for the idea to have John "read" at the Library of Congress; Dean of Rock Critics Robert Christgau for coming to dinner; Cameron Crowe's sister for bringing the young writer for his interview, as well as Billy Bob Thornton, Mike Leonard, Cynthia Sanz, Bob Mehr, Paul Zollo, Benjy Eisen, Dave Cobb, Ronni Lundy, Jesse Kornbluth, Gil Asakawa, Alex Rawls, Chris Willman, Lloyd

Sachs, Andy Ellis, Michael McCall, Bob Millard, Dave Wallace Jr., Jay Saporita, Bruce Pollack, and the late Roger Ebert and Studs Terkel. You *understand* art and its importance. Gratitude also to Jeremy Tepper, Steve Blatter, and so many other kind souls for their help with attaining the permissions.

Enough can't be said for Chaz Ebert, Roger Ebert's wife and collaborator, and Allison Schein Holmes at the WFMT Studs Terkel Radio Archive Foundation for allowing the earliest signs of Prine to be included in this compilation. Those works set into motion a career that was never intended but took wing on the quality of simple songs that sketched visceral moments.

For refuge, Margot McCormack and the entire staff of Margot Café & Bar in East Nashville, Howley's "Cooked in Sight, Must Be Right" and Dontee's Diner in West Palm Beach, the Sunset Marquis in West Hollywood, the library of the Society of the Four Arts in Palm Beach, l'Albatros in Cleveland, and Presti's Bakery on Murray Hill.

For emotional support and inspiration: Parnassus Books and Grimey's New & Preloved Music & Books in Nashville; Visible Voice Books and the Cleveland Museum of Art in Cleveland; Cuff's for the conversations and bottles of wine in Chagrin Falls, Ohio; Alex Bevan, anywhere he may play; and the Country Music Hall of Fame for absolutely everything.

A few superheroes should also be recognized. George Dassinger, of Dassinger Creative Services, who served as the publicist for *The Missing Years* and *Lost Dogs and Mixed Blessings*, not only stewarded a fairly reluctant Prine through the process of promoting his records, but also was meticulous with his files and generous when I called. As someone with an eye for the story, his archives from those years were exceptional and his friendship to a young writer was as pivotal as Prine's own faith in me during those early Florida years.

Charlie Pickett, who trafficked the permissions and kept the workflow going, brought a set of fairly virgin eyes to the endeavor. A punk rocker who'd missed Prine's various incarnations, his reactions to the man he watched come to life reminded me that the humanity of the creators is truly as important as the art.

Mike Leonard, who spent a great deal of time with John doing his television profiles and became a friend, was a bellwether of the late mid-career Prine forward. The conversations about that time of starting labels and Contemporary Folk Grammys were heady; his sense of detail reinforced my own memories.

At a time in John's life when a little spark was needed, Billy Bob Thornton started a bonfire with a movie part written basically *to* who John was—and a song people will get married to as long as crooked kettles are finding lids to fit.

Rick Bolsom, editor of *Country Song Roundup*, dug through a basement's worth of issues to find that story. Always a champion of the writers and "good artists," Bolsom understood what being in *Country Song Roundup* meant, because of Prine's Kentucky roots.

Barney Hoskyns, who runs Rocksbackpages.com, which serves as the most universal clearinghouse of writing about pop, rock, rap, country and other contemporary musics in the world, had several key pieces, and the site and its podcast were a great reinforcement of why these books matter.

Michael McCall knew John as a member of the Nashville community. As an ongoing reader, sounding board, occasional resource, and longtime friend, he shared observations and insights that were invaluable in maintaining the authenticity of who John was in any given era. For all the phone calls, texts, e-mails, I'm sorry—but I'm not. This book is better for your encouragement and talking through the speed bumps, roadblocks, and tangles along the way.

Kathie Orrico, who listened, and Jake Basden, who read, were also part of the process of building a man through the various mediums and media. There is an odd rhythm to compiling pieces when the subject's story rarely changes, made even more challenging as all newcomers to the telling feel the need to repeat the already known facts because they're new to them. As both weeders in the garden and enthusiasts in the stories, you both kept my triple guessing to a minimum.

Kara Rota, at Chicago Review Press, thank you for your patience—and willingness to wait. Having seen what this could be, I appreciate you wanting the best and not merely the most expedient. In a world where the Internet seems to be gospel, those who wrote in the days when newspapers had morgues—often brown envelopes or manilla folders of actual clippings—and research meant sorting through stacks of paper have been lost to a system where not being deemed valuable enough to digitize and tag often means being lost in the stuff that "didn't matter." Consolidation is the enemy of good reporting. One contacted publication wasn't aware that the story they owned even existed—then wanted entirely too much money for inclusion. And so it goes. Kara Rota, Chicago Review Press: thank you for making sure these artists and their words, the stories and moments, are collected for all to see.

Hardcore fans already know about JPShrine.org. As a source of all things Prine, there is no other. To avoid sidetracking or falling into another's picture of John, I did not consult or go there. But for those who crave more, know it is a wonderful place to venture. You will not only find plenty of "the Prine kind," you will join a community of people who find rapture and connection through the cracks in the dream Madison Avenue sells us.

Mostly, hopefully, you will find my friend. All of the facets and dimensions, edges and soft spots that made him so much more than a compelling American songwriter.

INTRODUCTION

John Prine hated interviews. Hated them. Hated talking about himself, hated taking apart the songs. Hated every speck of self-aggrandizement or fawning reporter repartee. It's not that he wasn't gracious. Nor did he think he was above it. But putting the attention on him made him feel awkward, even a little strange. Pulling apart the songs, he almost felt like he was cutting up his children in ways that didn't serve them. He didn't mind, once you got him talking, but it was just painful. Something to endure—for many years—to sell tickets to the shows his legion of faithful would pour into, hungry to hear the tales of the oddballs, the outcasts, the unseen, and the thrown away over his classic folk, almost Appalachian fingerpicking.

He didn't set out to *be* the patron saint of the unwanted and the unlikely, but his candy heart couldn't help noticing the pathos in those people's lives. He couldn't stand injustice in any way—seeing what had happened to his family's hometown in Paradise, Kentucky, or the state of his friends who'd been sent to active duty in Vietnam, who when they returned were shunned, shamed, and abandoned. Even microinjustices really struck him. People who'd lived their lives the best they could and didn't get a break or hit a bad set of circumstances—when they slid into the recesses, Prine couldn't help noticing. Or writing songs about it.

"Donald and Lydia." "Six O'Clock News." "Quiet Man." "Hello in There." "Sam Stone." "Angel from Montgomery." Plus, the sly humor of the ironic patriotic skewer "Your Flag Decal Won't Get You into Heaven

Anymore," the dancer and draftee's life plan "Spanish Pipe Dream," even the quite possibly contraband "Illegal Smile."

All on his first album. A twenty-three-year-old kid, struggling with the inequities he saw around him. All written with such tenderness and truth. Kris Kristofferson—who was riding high on *two* Song of the Year awards in the same year, for "Sunday Mornin' Comin' Down" from the Country Music Association and "For the Good Times" from the Academy of Country Music—was so slack-jawed when he heard Prine's songs in an after-hours set he'd been dragged to at the Earl of Old Town that he asked the dark-headed young man to play them again.

Kristofferson became an ally and champion. When Prine and his best friend Steve Goodman came to New York City a few weeks later and realized their new pal was playing the Bottom Line with Carly Simon as his opening act, they went straight from the airport to the club. Seeing the two young Chicago songwriters, the soon-to-be movie star had a plan.

Kristofferson called Prine up to play a few songs during his set, knowing Atlantic Records' Jerry Wexler was in the audience. The next day, Prine had a record deal with the home of Aretha Franklin; Arif Mardin was attached as his producer. Not bad for a mailman from Maywood, Illinois.

His self-titled debut was a sensation; Prine earned a 1972 Best New Artist Grammy nomination. Bob Dylan, off the radar following his motorcycle wreck, sang Prine's songs back to him at a friend's apartment *before* the self-titled debut album was released. The songs weren't just songs; they were sketches, portraits of moments, short stories. The sense of detail, the corkscrew twist of emotions prompted Karin Berg in *Rolling Stone* to define Prine's sweet spot as "a poetic tumble of keen nostalgia, insights to loneliness and isolation, the pain of seeing one's self in emotional nakedness and the running ahead of that pain—but it sometimes catches up."

For all the "new Dylan" raving, that loneliness—later captured with the phrase "out there running just to be on the run" in *German Afternoons'* "Speed of the Sound of Loneliness"—was a theme that underscored many of the songs. Prine, who had many, many friends, understood that isolation, self-imposed or merely from being unseen, was one of the cruelest realities of them all. With compassion, he picked those lonely people out, held them up, and made sure they knew someone recognized the echo in their soul; it created a fan base unlike any other.

Vietnam veterans were especially passionate about the man who grappled with their own yo-yoing reality, returning from a war no one could explain while being vilified by their peers. "Saigon" and "Take the Star Out of the Window" supplemented the traumatized GI of "Sam Stone" and his harrowing end with explorations of the life confronting those vets who didn't slide into drug addiction as they coped with atrocities the hippies could not compute.

The same could be said for women cast aside by society. Long before *Aimless Love*'s "Unwed Fathers," cowritten with future Country Music Hall of Famer Bobby Braddock ("He Stopped Loving Her Today," "D-I-V-O-R-C-E"), captured the fate of pregnant young women abandoned by their impregnators, and "The Oldest Baby in the World," which lovingly caressed a middle-aged barfly failing at finding a partner, Prine was showing the world the women who fell out of focus with the unwed mother in "Six O'Clock News," the lost soul in "Come Back to Us Barbara Lewis Hare Krishna Beauregard," and the now-classic "Angel from Montgomery."

Mortality. Ecology. Counterculture truths. Should've-been country classics. Tender romantic engagements. Hilarious tales. Christmases in prison. Dear Abby's column. Iron Ore Betty. Small treasons and cultural betrayals. And then there's the use of metaphor and his word play.

What doesn't get nearly enough attention is his seeking musical restlessness. Intimate folk records. Grinding ravers. Soul-undertowed songwriter fare. Summer campfire standards. Myriad dance rhythms. Old-school Southern gospel. Horn blasts. Steel guitar that melts over the tracks. Electric guitars that both buzz and twirl. Cissy Houston for punctuation on "Sweet Revenge." Truly country- and western-sounding timbres—and not the more modern country.

As the Rolling Stones were gathering torque, Prine, who'd grown up on Hank Williams Sr. and Chuck Berry, leaned into the roots edge without folk's sweetness. He wasn't a suburban kid playing hillbilly or jug music; he was the city-dwelling spawn of generations of Bluegrass

Staters. That tentativeness of life gives even the vocals on hushed ballads like "One Red Rose" or "If You Don't Want My Love" a bit of extra need.

I met John Prine in 1985. Informed he didn't talk to college papers, there was no interview when I inquired. They didn't care, weren't interested. *Aimless Love* had been released; they seemed to want to let the album to do the talking.

Then, an assignment for the *Miami Herald*—at that time one of the nation's top ten daily papers—to advance a South Florida concert. Interview scheduled, with the stern admonishment: "He doesn't like talking to reporters." When he finally called, we talked for two-and-a-half hours. About everything. Songs. Life. Food, especially home cooking. Country music. Johnny *and* Rosanne Cash. Old cars. The Midwest. Steve Goodman.

Due to my switch to a full-time job at a competitor, the *Herald* story never ran. The *Palm Beach Post*, who'd just hired me, had me review his show at the Carefree Theater, an old movie house that hosted concerts for people like B. B. King, the Band, and . . . Prine. Waiting after the show to apologize for the wasted interview, to explain what happened to his beautiful little story, I felt I'd let him down.

Never mind that he'd stepped over the monitor during his set-opening "Lulu Walls" and said, "Hey, Holly," causing me to yelp. I should've known he was just naughty enough to not care about a damned newspaper story but was someone who *really* enjoyed living the Ferris Bueller life.

When I started to apologize for the spiked story, he waved it off. He wanted to tell me about *Tribute to Steve Goodman*, a mostly Chicago folkie compilation to honor his "City of New Orleans" writing best friend, who'd died after an extended battle with leukemia. *Tribute* would win the very first Best Contemporary Folk Grammy, but in that moment, Prine was more concerned about making sure his friend's legacy was seen. He actually laughed about the piece being spiked, made some comment like, "Well, then it was just like two friends talking and not even business."

Not even business. Yes, John Prine is in the Songwriters Hall of Fame, won the PEN Song Lyrics of Literary Excellence Award, and was the first songwriter to perform at the Library of Congress. He had a number-one country hit with George Strait's version of "I Just Want to Dance with You," which was nominated for the Country Music Association Song and Single of the Year. He was nominated in 2018 for the Rock & Roll Hall of Fame, as well as being nominated for an International Bluegrass Music Award for his Mac Wiseman collaboration *Standard Songs for Average People*. Yes, he's left a mark on other artists, too. He created an enduring rock classic with Bonnie Raitt's version of "Angel from Montgomery" and a torch song and bathhouse standard in Bette Midler's *The Divine Miss M* recording of "Hello in There." He informed—and played—a character in Billy Bob Thornton's *Daddy and Them* (2001). *And* more recently, he's served as a beacon to several waves of indie-minded, song-driven roots artists, from My Morning Jacket's Jim James and Bon Iver's Justin Vernon to Jason Isbell and Sturgill Simpson, to Kacey Musgraves, Brandi Carlile, and Margo Price, plus signing Todd Snider, the Bis-Quits, Shawn Camp, Dan Reeder, Arlo McKinley, Emily Scott Robinson, Tre Burt, and Kelsey Waldon.

Yes, he started his own record company in the middle 1980s, when viable artists just didn't do that. With his managers Al Bunetta and Dan Einstein, he blazed a trail for other artists to follow. In the days before Oh Boy Records had distribution, before there was an Internet, let alone a GoFundMe opportunity, Prine's fans sent in checks, saying, "When the record's done, send it to me."

It was never business, just doing the right thing. For the music, but also for the kind man who just thought the ego of it all was . . . awful. When a major Nashville label dangled seven figures in the late '80s to buy Oh Boy, the notion of a record company offering all that money swept Music Row; Prine went to an event with the brass, changed his mind.

"There's more to life than money, Holly," he informed a wide-eyed young woman. He was right.

In this anthology, amid the stories, scripts, speeches, and conversations, there are many tales of how they happened. In some ways, what *wasn't* written in the pieces is even more insightful and delicious than the work assembled here. It's why I'm grateful for the subtitle *Interviews and Encounters*. It's why the introductions to some of these pieces are longer than just the standard *where*, *when*, *how*, and *what* of Prine's career.

Prine's graciousness to Cameron Crowe's sister, his evolving conversations with those journalists with multiple entries, his impact on fellow heartland songwriter John Mellencamp, and his acute curiosity, basic decency, and introspection, far deeper than many people realized—all these and more show a respect and generosity to those people who penetrated the border.

In reading the various entries across Prine's very to-thine-own-muse-be-true career, two things became clear: his story rarely changed, and he used certain moments and narratives from his life to give interviews while still maintaining his distance. The amount of repetition is obviously the wages of an almost half-century career, as new writers feeling the need to catch up coupled with the fact he was an authentic working-class poet. Like Bukowski at the post office, Prine had grown up in the working world and was watching humanity as he kept so many people connected through the cards, letters, and packages he delivered daily.

Several interviewers developed deeper interactions. Instead of the purely transactional fan dance of celebrity, trading the illusion of intimacy for the flogging of whatever one is selling, Prine would open his heart—and his truth—to a select coterie. It's why several contributors have multiple entries, here. They were the ones who fell into those deeper conversations and explored Prine's heart as much as his career.

PART I

The Singing Mailman Emerges

SINGING MAILMAN WHO DELIVERS A POWERFUL MESSAGE IN A FEW WORDS

Roger Ebert | October 9, 1970 | *Chicago Sun-Times* / RogerEbert.com

John Prine may well be one of the greatest songwriters to ever live. Bob Dylan sang songs from Prine's unreleased debut back to him when they first met, later raving to the Huffington Post in 2009, "Prine's stuff is pure Proustian existentialism. Midwestern mindtrips to the nth degree. . . ."

But long before Steve Goodman dragged Kris Kristofferson to see his good friend perform, there was a buzz around the postal worker raised on Appalachian music, his older brother's guitar lessons, and what he'd picked up at the Old Town School of Folk Music. Having jumped onstage on a dare at the Fifth Peg's weekly hoot night, where anyone could get up and play, the shaggy-haired kid from Maywood, Illinois, shocked the crowd silent with "Sam Stone."

When the crowd went wild, the owner offered Prine a weekly slot. It paid better than carrying the mail, let him sleep in; Prine didn't have a plan, but this felt okay. Back from West Germany, he didn't need a plan just yet.

But when the *Chicago Sun-Times* film critic Roger Ebert went on the lam from a truly dreadful movie, it was as if fate went looking for a beer. The storied newspaper man ducked into the very gin joint where Prine was playing—and taking in the songs, Ebert opted to write a full feature about what he heard in Prine's music instead of panning a garbage movie. Once that happened, the momentum built—and the shows were packed. Suddenly, John Prine was in play.

As he told the *Chicago Tribune*'s Greg Kot in 2010, Prine turned down an offer from Delmark's Bob Koester to make an album. Prine didn't have any notion of what he wanted, but knew, "By me saying no, that's when it clicked: I must have something in mind that I'm not telling myself."

Beyond putting the country/folk songwriter in play, Ebert would remain a friend through both men's lives. Not only would Ebert show up and visit when Prine faced his neck cancer, the internationally renowned film critic would also encourage Prine through his physical therapy and process finding his way back after treatment.

Survivors as well as writers, the two men and their wives would see each other for dinner whenever they were in the same city.

For a man who invested such poignant humanity in his songs, the idea that his career began with a "meet cute" is hard to fathom. Yet for an artist who could sing, "How lucky can one man get," sometimes destiny is a bad movie that requires a cold beer to wash the taste out of one's mouth. —Ed.

Through no wisdom of my own but out of sheer blind luck, I walked into the Fifth Peg, a folk club on West Armitage, one night in 1970 and heard a mailman from Westchester singing. This was John Prine.

He sang his own songs. That night I heard "Sam Stone," one of the great songs of the century. And "Angel from Montgomery." And others. I wasn't the music critic for the Chicago Sun-Times, but I went to the office and wrote an article. And that, as fate decreed, was the first review Prine ever received.

While 'digesting Reader's Digest" in a dirty book store, John Prine tells us in one of his songs, a patriotic citizen came across one of those little American flag decals. He stuck it on his windshield and liked it so much he added flags from the gas station, the bank and the supermarket, until one day he blindly drove off the road and killed himself. St. Peter broke the news: "*Your flag decal won't get you into heaven anymore; It's already overcrowded from your dirty little war.*"

Lyrics like this are earning John Prine one of the hottest underground reputations in Chicago these days. He's only been performing professionally since July, he sings at the out-of-the-way Fifth Peg, 858

W. Armitage, and country-folk singers aren't exactly putting rock out of business. But Prine is good.

He appears on stage with such modesty he almost seems to be backing into the spotlight. He sings rather quietly, and his guitar work is good, but he doesn't show off. He starts slow. But after a song or two, even the drunks in the room begin to listen to his lyrics. And then he has you.

He does a song called *The Great Society Conflict Veteran's Blues*, for example, that says more about the last 20 years in America than any dozen adolescent acid-rock peace dirges. It's about a guy named Sam Stone who fought in Korea and got some shrapnel in his knee.

But the morphine eased the pain, and Sam Stone came home *"with a Purple Heart and a monkey on his back."* That's Sam Stone's story, but the tragedy doesn't end there. In the chorus, Prine reverses the point of view with an image of stunning power:

There's a hole in Daddy's arm
Where all the money goes. . .

You hear lyrics like these, perfectly fitted to Prine's quietly confident style and his ghost of a Kentucky accent, and you wonder how anyone could have so much empathy and still be looking forward to his 24th birthday on Saturday.

So you talk to him, and you find out that Prine has been carrying mail in Westchester since he got out of the Army three years ago. That he was born in Maywood, and that his parents come from Paradise, Ky. That his grandfather was a miner, a part-time preacher, and used to play guitar with Merle Travis and Ike Everly (the Everly brothers' father). And that his brother Dave plays banjo, guitar and fiddle, and got John started on the guitar about 10 years ago.

Prine has been writing songs just as long, and these days he works on new ones while delivering mail. His wife, Ann Carole, says she finds scraps of paper around the house with maybe a word or a sentence on them and a month later the phrase will turn up in a new song.

Prine's songs are all original, and he only sings his own. They're nothing like the work of most young composers these days, who seem to specialize in narcissistic tributes to themselves. He's closer to Hank Williams than to Roger Williams, closer to Dylan than to Ochs. "In my songs," he says, "I try to look through someone else's eyes, and I want to give the audience a feeling more than a message."

That's what happens in Prine's *Old Folks*, one of the most moving songs I've heard. It's about an elderly retired couple sitting at home alone all day, looking out the screen door on the back porch, marking time until death. They lost a son in Korea: *Don't know what for; guess it doesn't matter anymore.* The chorus asks you, the next time you see a pair of *"ancient empty eyes,"* to say *"Hello in there. . .hello."*

Prine's lyrics work with poetic economy to sketch a character in just a few words. In *Angel From Montgomery*, for example, he tells of a few minutes in the thoughts of a woman who is doing the housework and thinking of her husband: *How the hell can a person go to work in the morning, come back in the evening, and have nothing to say?*

Prine can be funny, too, and about half his songs are. He does one about getting up in the morning. A bowl of oatmeal tried to stare him down, and won. But *"If you see me tonight with an illegal smile—It don't cost very much, and it lasts a long while—Won't you please tell the Man I didn't kill anyone—Just trying to have me some fun."*

Prine's first public appearance was at the 1969 Maywood Folk Music Festival: "It's a hell of a festival, but nobody cares about folk music." He turned up at the Old Town School of Folk Music in early 1970 after hearing Ray Tate on TV. He did a lot of hootenannies at the Fifth Peg and at the Saddle Club on North Ave., and the Fifth Peg booked him for Sunday nights in July and August.

In those two months, the word got around somehow that here was an extraordinary new composer and performer. His crowds grew so large that the Fifth Peg is now presenting him on Friday and Saturday nights; his opening last weekend was a full house by word-of-mouth. He had a lot of new material, written while he was on reserve duty with the Army in September.

There's one, for example, called *The Great Compromise*, about a girl he once dated who was named America. One night at the drive-in movie, while he was going for popcorn, she jumped into a foreign sports car and he began to suspect his girl was no lady. *"I could of beat up that fellow,"* he reflects in his song, *"but it was her that hopped into his car."*

INTERVIEW WITH STUDS TERKEL

Studs Terkel | 1975 | *The Studs Terkel Show*, **WFMT-FM**

Studs Terkel was a well-established voice of culture, politics, and social issues when a young folk singer on the verge of his debut album went to the studios of WFMT-FM, where the one-hour *The Studs Terkel Show* was broadcasted daily since 1952. Martin Luther King Jr., Tennessee Williams, Frank Zappa, Dorothy Parker, Leonard Bernstein, Big Bill Broonzy, and another folk singer named Bob Dylan had preceded the former mailman creating a local sensation.

Nicknamed "Studs" after the character Studs Lonigan, from a trilogy of novels by James T. Farrell about a young Irish Catholic from Chicago's rough South Side, Terkel came by his affinity for real life honest. When he was young, his parents ran a boarding house across from Bughouse Square, the nickname granted to Chicago's Washington Square Park for its role as an unofficial forum where people from all walks of life could speak their minds.

With Prine's father being both a diemaker and "ward healer" in politically charged Chicago, Terkel recognized the depth of Prine's working-class bona fides and was intrigued by the gravitas and humanity of the young postal worker's songs. For all the local heat Prine had generated at the Fifth Peg and the Earl of Old Town—as well as the buzz on his upcoming Atlantic debut release—Terkel's hunger for headier topics like where art comes from, how empathy is formed, and the truest meaning of home guided their conversation.

At this point, the twenty-three-year-old songwriter was many things. An ex-soldier; a postal worker; a grandson of a carpenter and part-time preacher from Paradise, Kentucky; the apple of his mother and grandmother's eyes; husband to his high school sweetheart Ann Carole Menaloscino; and a kid who learned to play guitar from his older brother, love bluegrass from summers in Kentucky, and listen to "The Opry" from his dad, Prine embodied the blue-collar truth of the Southern expats who migrated to the Midwest for work.

In Terkel's studio, the conversation was brisk. The men talked over each other, excited to share details and insights. Prine played several songs and even stayed after the radio show to record several songs to capture this time in his life.

Honored to be recognized by a such an impactful force in social commentary, Prine told Terkel all about his father, Bill Prine, when the show wrapped. "He was really interested in speaking to my father, because of what he did for a living," Prine told me once in a conversation about Terkel's *Working* and *My American Century*. "We were going to try to make that happen, because of all the oral history work he did, and then my father died. . . ." —Ed.

Studs Terkel: Biting, biting commentary. John Prine, the singer/writer of that song. Somehow thinking of that song and think in the headlines too these days with the exposé now of the deceitfulness of the administration, the previous one the continuation of a *New York Times* exposé of a song you sing. How are you? First of all, we think of a lot of country western songs being very militarily inclined, you know, *The Fighting Side of Me* and others, you know. And yet, do you sense in that world of song, of which you're so much the part, changes occurring there, too? Questionings?

John Prine: I'm kind of based in country music. I like Hank Williams a whole lot, and it's just the subject I chose to write about. I wrote that one when I was a mailman. I was delivering *Reader's Digest*, and they put out an issue one month that that gave everybody a free American flag decal. That was just about the same time there was all this talk going on about the silent majority and everything. I thought we've kind of cheated a lot of people out of being able to say, people that just hadn't said anything yet, and they got their flag decals. Just about everybody was taking *Reader's Digest*, and just about everybody stuck them right on their front door, right next to the mailbox. The next day when I come up, I saw them all sitting there, and I was kinda thinking of the Reverend Carl McIntyre, too, a little bit.

Terkel: Is that how you get the idea—you worked as a mailman for a while, right here in Chicago?

Prine: Oh, I was working in Maywood, but I was out in Westchester delivering mail.

Terkel: So the idea comes along. Who is John Prine, where are you from?

Prine: Well, I'm from Maywood, but my family is from western Kentucky. All my brothers are from up here.

Terkel: Western Kentucky.

Prine: Right.

Terkel: Is it a mining region?

Prine: Yeah. It's down Muhlenberg County. I come from this little place called Paradise, sits down on the Green River. They had like those names. Paradise was, I like to go down there. There's a whole lot of my relatives down there. It's just a real small town. Just about everybody is somebody they could figure out some kind of relation they had to you.

It was out of the way, you had to go out of the way to get there. I mean, you couldn't pass through the town. You had to be going to the town to get there.

Terkel: And it's called Paradise, Kentucky?

Prine: Yeah. I guess what it was, I don't know, but I guess around 150 years ago, somebody was coming down Green River; they were going someplace else. I don't remember where, but they stopped there. There was a good place, I guess, to stop, and they just stayed there, you know, and they just named it Paradise.

Terkel: Did you find it like paradise when you were a little kid?

Prine: Oh, yeah, it was, in a way. There was always something different about the town. I could go to another town, maybe five miles away, and there's just that much difference between Paradise. It was set aside from everything else.

Terkel: The mines run dry or?

Prine: They've been mining down here a long time. A lot of them. My grandfather was a miner for a while, and a whole lot of people down there, they worked the mines. I guess they found out they'd get more mining if they strip-mined the country.

So they bought up just about everybody, a little at the time, living in Paradise. It was mostly old people. The young ones didn't stay in Paradise. And because all there was was two stores there, pretty soon they ended up buying everybody out. They tore the whole town down. There's one house left standing, I'm told. I'm going to go down there in a couple of months, there's a house they forgot about that's off hidden behind the woods; some people moved into or were just passing through, some old woman and one of her sons moved into it. My father was down a couple months ago; he was gonna go on up and talk to 'em, but he said the young fellow looked real mean.

Terkel: It's funny. This music that influenced you has been the music of the region then, too. Country music.

Prine: Yeah. My father always listened to country music, you used to listen to Grand Ole Opry on Saturday nights, and sit in the kitchen, listening.

Terkel: Of course, just as when you were a mailman carrying *Reader's Digest* gave you the idea for the flag decal song, so I supposed Paradise in Kentucky has given you the bases of so many songs. You mentioned *Old People*, too. There's a song called *Paradise*, isn't there?

Prine: Yeah, this is about the—I got one about the town itself and what they did. It was Peabody Coal Company that strip-mined it all. Peabody's the head of some sort of environmental commission now, or the head of Peabody. I don't know if there's any Peabodys left in Peabody Coal Company, but they were involved in an environmental commission.

They passed some state laws a couple years back down in Kentucky, concerning strip-mining. I guess they weren't real rigid. Anyway, they didn't do a whole lot about it; they said like within 20 years, maybe the land would be able to hold cattle without 'em sinking in the ground. So, that's why there's a line in a song about the air smelling like snakes down there.

I always felt like most of my songs explain themselves, but that particular line, I'd kinda like to explain it. When I was a little kid, there's this old Civil War prison, and the only way you'd get to it was down the river. We'd go down there every once in a while. When we go down to Paradise, we go down to the prison and just knock around down there. It was just a nice place to go when you're a little kid. We were going down there once, and this aunt of ours told us if we were going over there, we'd better take a pistol because there are snakes all over Adry Hill, she says, "and if you smell anything that smells like cantaloupe, you'd better start shooting." She says that's just exactly what they smell like. We wasn't very old, maybe eight or nine. It took about 40 minutes to get over to the prison; by the time we got over there, just about everything up there smelt like cantaloupe to us. We was that scared, you know?

Terkel: That's ironic. Here's where Paradise becomes very ironic, indeed, the name. I'm thinking also, John Prine, why you're so effective a songwriter, poet, really. Is your memory of childhood—says everything tasted, smelled like cantaloupe, you recall the color of the little, almost miniature-looking train of Peabody, too. It's these childhood memories that are so strong, aren't they?

Prine: Yeah. I don't know. I could go to different places and just right away get different feelings. Paradise was always the same. I go back to a lot of other places and a lot of them never look like what you remembered them to be, but that's what I always got a kick out of down in Paradise, 'cause it was always, as soon as I got there, it was just like I remembered

Terkel: It didn't look smaller? Very often when you return after you reach young manhood, or manhood, and you remember the little kid, it looks so much smaller.

Prine: Maybe approaching the town, it looks smaller, but once I get in it and just the idea of being in there is like being in a big house, almost. Because it was just like one street with eight or nine houses lined one side and on the other side, too.

Terkel: I'm thinking about your eye, and your ear and your one other thing I'd call the understanding heart. You spoke of old people. You spoke of the older people leaving. You have a song about old—What made you write the song—It's called *Old People*. We have the other name for it.

Prine: *Hello In There.*

Terkel: What led you to write . . .

Prine: There's a lot of reasons. When I was little, old people used to take to me real fast, for some reason. I used to take to them real fast. I always spent a lot of time with my grandfather. He's a carpenter. For a while. I delivered papers in an old people's home. It was just very depressing, and it was supposedly one of the better. . .

Terkel: One of the better homes.

Prine: Yeah.

Terkel: And that depressed you . . . the idea of the segregation of old people, the putting them away.

Prine: Yeah. They just sat around and I imagine they had recreation for 'em; some of them would, but most of them seemed like they were kind of just waiting around to die.

Terkel: Out of it came—

Prine: I very rarely write a tune before I write the lyrics to it. Usually they both just come at the same time, but I had this tune and I was going to write a love song. And I sat down and just wrote a song about old people.

Terkel: I don't know what to say. I think that's going to be a classic just in hearing it. You have everything in it, don't you? A complete shutting out of old people, the feelings they undoubtedly have you were able to evoke an experience, quite remarkable.

Prine: I believe I'd hate to sing that song for old people.

Terkel: Oh, yeah

Prine: One of the first concerts I ever did was for some old people over at the YWCA on Dearborn. I wasn't writing too much then. I just did it to help out my brother. It was kind of strange because they really enjoyed every song; they enjoyed the whole show. We did every kind of music you could think of. Five or six years ago, at least.

Terkel: I don't know how very old people feel, but I think somehow they'd find that song theirs. The idea is to be recognized; you're saying,

"Hello, in there," you know? It's that nonrecognition, being thrown away like a used orange rind as Willy Loman said in *Death of a Salesman*. Or as the old grandmother battled, in Edward Albee's *American Dream*, the play. Remember that? She refused to be taken away, but they took her away in that cart. She fought it all the way, you know?

Prine: I watched that three times when they had it on recently. They had it on television last year.

Terkel: It's a powerful song, oh, boy. Everything. They're talking about also lost manhood. Meeting his friend from the factory, what's new, the same old news, too. It's almost a picture, it's almost, almost a powerful short story that you have.

Prine: I didn't want to pick strange names, I just wanted to pick names now that if you're born long ago that you might be named, because names usually get popular.

Terkel: Fashions in names change.

Prine: But I didn't want to make the names too strange.

Terkel: No, you got Fred, and you got daughter Loretta and son-in-law.

Prine: Rudy's the dog, lives across the street.

Terkel: Yeah.

Terkel: My guest is, John Prine who is, as you can probably guess by now, about the most imaginative and moving of American songwriters and singers today. You say you had a melody all set, but you had a love song all set for it.

Prine: But I didn't have any words. I figured that tune was pretty enough for a love song, and I sat down to write one and instead I wrote about old people.

Terkel: What else do the people like, when you sing for them? Because there's so many of your songs—at least ten [*laughs*] . . . we'll hear a bit of those; I want to save "Sam Stone" for a moment.

Prine: This is a short one I wrote when I was 14. I call it *A Frying Pan*. I liked Roger Miller a whole lot then; he was writing all that stuff. [*Sings.*]

Terkel: You were 14 when you wrote that, you say? So it's the Roger Miller influence, but also was things you observed and saw, you know. The breaking up of homes, too, running away, and I suppose you may have seen that, too, as a kid? Here again, the combination of influences on you, I suppose.

Prine: Yeah. I don't know where that went from. It's that sometimes I write a little bit faster than I think, and I have to sit back and see what I wrote.

Terkel: You were 14. When did you start?

Prine: My brother taught me a couple of chords on the guitar, and I started writing right away. I wrote a song one night. My first song took me about three hours; I went downstairs and I told my mother I wrote a song. She sat down to listen to it, and I got about halfway through; I was picking it, and she started singing *Will The Circle Be Unbroken*. I got so embarrassed, I don't even know a word to that song today! I just threw the lyrics away and didn't write anything for a little while after that. I didn't know, I thought I had my own tune.

Terkel: Oh, it was *Will The Circle Be Unbroken*? Your mother—Did your family sing?

Prine: Oh, my mother? Her father lived down in Paradise. He used to play guitar a lot. Merle Travis is from, you know, in Byrd County, and so is Ike Everly, the Everly Brothers' father. A whole lot of people used to pick down around there.

Terkel: I'm talking to John Prine. You'll soon be hearing his songs on Atlantic, and undoubtedly John will be known throughout the country, too, as rightfully he should be, as one of the most imaginative of America's songwriters today and singers.

We take a slight pause, and we'll return with John and of course, *Sam Stone* among other songs, how he came to write these songs, too.

Terkel: John, as we pick up the conversation, it's quite a distance from Paradise, Kentucky—distance and time—yet not too many years ago to Chicago, where you've been living for some time now.

Prine: My family comes from Paradise. And we just used to always go back down there during the summer.

Terkel: Does your family still think, even though you were born here, your family, being Kentuckians, still think of that as home?

Prine: First thing my father used to tell everybody. He's the last of a dying breed. Kentuckian. Pure Kentuckian.

Terkel: It's funny, Appalachian people, mountain people, and black people from the Deep South invariably speak of home as where they came from, not where they are, at this moment in Chicago. So, we come to the Great Society.

Prine: *Conflict Veteran's Blues.*

Terkel: "Veteran's Blues," or "Sam Stone." We'll talk about it after you do it.

Prine: [*Sings.*]

Terkel: That song really says it all. You wrote that song, how long ago now?

Prine: Three years ago.

Terkel: Three years and since then, information has come to our country, and to people about the . . . heroin, the addicts in Vietnam. That's it, too, isn't it? A certain kind of writer of songs, and a certain kind of poet, is also able to judge and prophesy, too. Can tell the feelings you heard, is that it?

Prine: Well, more or less. I didn't sit down to write a song about a veteran on heroin. It was just the two things. Heroin usually doesn't end any place, and there was kind of just a futile feeling when you're in the service.

I wasn't in Vietnam; they sent me to Germany for two years. Throughout the whole army, when you were over in Germany you didn't feel like you're doing too much there, like you had no business. And it was that, plus the image of somebody on heroin. That's the only reason I combined the two, it was more than trying to write a song about a veteran on heroin. It was kind of strange it ended up. Now there's a lot of heroin.

Terkel: It's funny how it worked out. You had the image, the idea in mind, the symbol in mind. And the reality came into being. Irony. It's funny, as I listen to "Sam Stone," then to "Old People," there's a connecting thread here in which both are counting for nothing in the way, whether it's the young soldier or whether it's the old couple. In your songs you are, by implication, without any soapbox saying, you know, "look at me."

This song, what a use of lines. Use of "little pitchers have big ears." You using old homilies, too, and often they become very ironic.

Prine: I was surprised how many people had never heard that before, 'cause stuff we'd say. I just thought everybody used that.

Terkel: "Sweet old songs don't sound the same on broken radios."

Prine: "Sweet songs never last too long on broken radios."

Terkel: I love that line: "There's a hole in Daddy's arm where the money goes."

Prine: I had those two lines, that's what started the whole song off. I had that "sweet songs never last too long on broken radios" and "there's a hole in Daddy's arm where all the money goes." I was thinking like some political cartoon, like the humor they use. I had kind of a picture of a fellow shooting money into his arm, with like a rainbow of money falling down into his arm. And that's where I got that line.

Terkel: That's how it works then. There are a couple of images you have, and out of it, your observation, experience, hearing . . .

Prine: If the image is strong enough, then the rest of the song will develop out of it. If the first couple ideas of the song, then I don't have as hard a time. Like that was one of the easiest songs I ever wrote.

Terkel: Really?

Prine: Because after I had that, those two lines, the rest [of] the song just poured out of me.

Terkel: That's how it works sometimes, just flows sometimes; sometimes more difficult.

Prine: If the idea is kind of sketchy in the first place, then the song usually takes me a lot longer because every line after is a little sketchy—and I don't want to get too far away from the original thought.

Terkel: You have the monkey on the back, too. I suggest, Nelson Algren, I remember who first used that Purple Heart in "The Man with the Golden Arm."

John, so it's the city. It's the city plus the mountain country; both have had their impact on you. An observation, because the songs just flow. How many songs have you written? Have you kept track?

Prine: Somewhere between 25 and 30 . . . I use most all of them. I run into a lot of people, they say, they've written 500 songs or something. But you never hear more than about 40 of them at the most.

Terkel: Should point out that Kris Kristofferson, while visiting Chicago and playing at The Quiet Knight, heard John Prine and, as you probably could guess, flipped and urged he come to The Bitter End in New York where Kristofferson was playing, and during a couple of . . . nights.

Prine: Stevie Goodman . . . helped out, he was playing with Kris.

Terkel: And Steve Goodman, too.

Prine: He brought Kris over to see me over at The Earl, kept telling him to come over. He got him over there the last night he was in town.

Terkel: At The Earl of Old Town. And that was it. And of course, what happened in New York to you guys. Critics, others came to hear John. So you'll be soon hearing and buying, I trust, his recordings on Atlantic. He's going to Muscle Shoals, Alabama.

Prine: I hope so. It's kind of a toss-up between there and New York. I hope to end up down in Muscle Shoals.

Terkel: This is an interesting development? In Muscle Shoals, Alabama where the dam is, as you point out, halfway.

Prine: There's a big TVA dam. . . . And they've got one at Paradise, that was before they strip-mined it. They built a TVA dam. I was looking through my grandmother's trunk about five or six years after she had passed away. I ran across a postcard between her and her cousin that was talking about this. Back in the late '30s or so, talking about how they were going to ruin the whole—building this TVA dam, you know. It was really strange the way it was so up to date with the strip-mining they were doing, too.

Terkel: The TVA, of course, had a wholly different purpose in mind, providing power for the . . .

Prine: There were a lot of people that lived right around there, didn't want it at the time.

Terkel: Strip mining, of course, a wholly different purpose.

Prine: A lot of jobs came out of there for a lot of people.

Terkel: Come back to the songs. Go ahead, name your poison.

Prine: Well, this is a song about when I was in the Army. I was down in Louisiana most of the time. Just about every army camp in the States has a small town right near it where all the soldiers go. Usually the whole thing's made up of saloons, maybe five or six saloons and a beauty parlor. That's about it. The people in these towns always seemed just a little different. It seemed like they had to put up with almost like a tourist town, except offseason or something. The soldiers would come to town, but they never, none of them ever wanted to be there. They really raised hell, you know, all the time.

I got to thinking about the people living in these towns. So I wrote this as a love story. I usually say it's about couple of lovers that never met, is what it is. It's about two people I picked, and they don't meet in this song at all. And it's partially about masturbation, too, because I thought both these people were alone. I mean, mentally, too, they spend a lot of times just with themselves. [*Sings "Donald and Lydia."*]

Terkel: John, more and more it appears your songs are so powerful, they really are dramas, too. This could easily be, this powerful, aching sort of short story of these two people, of loneliness, of course, and all of that unfulfilled, of dreaming and a fantasy. Lydia, Donald and love.

Prine: I tried a couple of times. I used to liked to write. I could never write anything longer than a short story. I just couldn't, I want to get everything right away.

Terkel: Well, you do. That's the point. The short story, so it's also a poem. I suppose poetry and short stories get to things immediately, too. Also, you said it was just the Army town, the town near a barracks and the feeling you get. You capture middle America, smalltown America, yet also people in the big cities, too. Along with everything, Lydia and Donald also are here, too . . . what you capture in that one place.

So the song comes to you then, almost any source [can be] the basis of the song you write.

Prine: I'm getting to where now I almost like to pick some sort of theme and work around it, you know? Get some kind of foundation and work around it. Now, more or less to see what I can do with it. What's that— "Blow up your TV, throw away your paper, if possible, play."

Terkel: The sign there, yeah.

Prine: That's one I added to these two lines I had, "She was a level-headed dancer on the road to alcohol and I was just a soldier on my way to Montreal." I wanted to mix politics and romance, up together, see what come out of it. It's kind of like the American Dream is in a way what came out.

Terkel: Yeah, a soldier on the way to Montreal tells us quite a bit!

Prine: I call it a "Spanish Pipedream." [*Sings.*]

Terkel: That's not a bad recipe at all.

Prine: That song was a whole lot of fun to write.

Terkel: Now these are songs we get a great kick hearing, too; the humorous songs and the light at the same time making that point. How does that line go again, that "she was a dancing girl on the road to alcohol"?

Prine: "She's a level-headed dancer on the road to alcohol. . . ."

Terkel: "And I was a soldier. . . ."

Prine: "And I was just a soldier on the way to Montreal." I figure if I can't get a song out of that, I couldn't write any more.

Terkel: That's a beauty, though. And found Jesus on their own, too. That's interesting, too. Well, you know, there's so much to John Prine, that all we do is just hear a bit of him during an hour. We look forward, of course, to the album; no doubt there'll be several albums. We're just meeting today, at least I am, for the first full hour. I heard I think, someone who is a quite powerful and important songwriter in America today. And John, what's a good way, aside from wishing you good luck down in Muscle Shoals, and Atlantic and the songs, what's a good song to say goodbye with for the moment?

Prine: Oh, boy.

Terkel: So many. It need not be a farewell song, just a song. You have "Quiet Man," "Far [from] Me," and "Illegal Smile."

Prine: I got one. It's called "The Flashback Blues."

Terkel: "Flashback Blues." And so as John Brown sings—John Brown! I like that, too, it's not . . .

Prine: Well, I might change it.

Terkel: Hey, John Brown, too, is a powerful man. John Prine sings that! I thank you very much indeed. Best of luck.

PART II

The First New Dylan

THE POSTMAN SINGS TWICE

Cameron Crowe | February 9, 1973 | *Los Angeles Free Press*

My sister and I did interviews together in the beginning. This worked well, because she loved music and also because she drove and I didn't. She was a flight attendant and looked like a cross between Sally Field and Linda Ronstadt. She still does. She also knows her music. We both loved John Prine.

We did the interview in his L.A. hotel room; I believe it was at the Sunset Marquis.

He had bedhead and was still waking up. He had a charming, sparkly smile and told a story like he was sharing his secrets only with you. He loved that we were both fans. I loved his first album and had seen him playing at San Diego State around the time of that initial record. The feeling around him was still a kind of shock that he had emerged at a world-class level of songwriting. It was almost like he had performed a magic trick, as Springsteen might say, but by the time of our interview it was already obvious that it was no trick. The first album was no fluke. He was an artist to be cherished, and was just at the beginning of a huge body of work. . . .

His voice was a little scratchy from the road.

My sister was charmed by him. He had kind eyes, she said. He was a deep well with a wonderful sense of humor, not too dry and not too easy. Just perfect. And yes, shy. But not too shy to want to know about us, to make our session a conversation.

I only ran into him a couple times after that, once at a party at Bonnie Raitt's house. Coincidentally, my sister was also there, and he remembered us both. We picked up right where we left off.

And a handful of decades after that, I found my way to him on the floor of the Grammy Awards and reintroduced myself to him again.

I thanked him for our interview, which I told him he probably wouldn't even remember.

"Of course I do," he said, with the same smile. His wife Fiona was looking on.
"Your sister was there too. . . . Tell her I said hi."
I rushed home and called her. She was knocked out. We both were. Still are.
Here's a little piece of the conversation. . . . —Cameron Crowe

Two years ago, John Prine was a Chicago postman. Now he's embarking on his first headlining concert tour, a point in a folk singer's career that is intensely anticipated from the very beginning. He still looks at the world through a postman's eyes—an asset that just may have basis for his *deserved* acceptance as a singer/songwriter.

Over the past year, Prine has been making the grueling rounds of America's clubs. Fourteen shows a week (three shows a night on weekends), he has spent much time singing into the spotlights and standing on miniature wood platforms passing for stages.

The story of Prine's discovery by Kris Kristofferson (a janitor at Columbia Recording Studios, New York, six years back) and Paul Anka (now Prine's manager) is well-known. Today, after two brilliant albums, *John Prine* and *Diamonds in the Rough*, Kristofferson now takes pride in calling him, "the best singer/songwriter in America today."

I spoke with John recently about his various projects, relationship with Dylan and his work on record.

———————

Do you feel that you've been ignored by the radio stations?

Well, I never have gotten a whole lot of airplay. I don't know, in some areas, I get a lot of airplay, but as a whole, I never come near to getting enough airplay on the AM stations or the country stations. At first I thought that was because it was hard to program me, now . . . I don't know. There were a lot of guys who got into my first album maybe seven months after it was released, and by then, the program director has dropped it from the playlist. Then they had to wait until the next album came out til they could play my stuff and still be timely.

Did you have a lot of material available when you went into the studio for Diamonds in the Rough?

Yeah, we did. We ended up having to cut stuff off the album. See the way it is, I didn't finish a song unless I plan on using. I can tell whether the song's any good or not before I finish it.

I don't understand when guys say they've written four hundred songs. I don't see how. I figure there really must be some awful ones in there. I've only written, at the most, forty. Maybe thirty-five songs . . . I write in clumps. Recording doesn't worry me, though, I can always get enough songs together to record.

Have the tunes on (the new album) been around awhile?

About half of them were tunes that I couldn't put on my first album. They only let me put thirteen cuts on each album. I wanted to put it on the first one, but they couldn't do it. The record company said that it would pack the grooves too close and it would run right into the label.

How many songs have you written in the past year?

Five. I had some other songs I wanted to finish for the second album. I set a deadline for myself to finish the tunes for *Diamonds in the Rough.* The deadline came and went, and I only finished half of the songs I wanted to. All the songs on the first album were ballads and stories.

I put all these together and I left out all my other songs purposely for the next one. I'm writing a little bit differently now than before. I'm trying not to write so many ballads. They're too easy. I mean, if I don't watch it, I'll be turning out ballads about the coffee. . . . I'm trying to be a little more broad.

Why don't you have a back-up band?

I've always considered it. But I'd have to run into the right guys. I'll probably find them in a Holiday Inn somewhere . . . somebody who could cover different people's stuff really well and have no desire to play their own music. There aren't many guys I can play with on songs without being inhibited. I don't know how to lead a band. If somebody strays, I go right with him. David Bromberg and the guys he plays with . . . I never seem to have much trouble playing with them, though.

You play a lot with Steve Goodman.

Yeah. That's because we hung out together a lot. I imagine sooner or later, I'll add a back-up band. I didn't feel like I really need one. Though I imagine that I'll run into some guys that are really into my kind of music and are eager to play with me. Have you seen Jessie Collin Young's new band? That's the kind of band that I'd like to have.

Are you responsible for the arrangements on the tunes on the album?

Yeah, on the second album I am. On the first album, they had charts and everything when I went in 'cause the musicians were studio musicians. On the second album, I didn't even tell the record company what songs I was gonna do. I didn't tell them anything. I just told them when I was coming into the studio . . . and to be ready. We had the studio booked from ten until midnight, 'cause Bromberg had to cut out for the west coast. We only had him for about three days. And . . . we got drunk and just let the tape roll . . . and everybody I'd brought in with me already knew the songs, and we just sat around playing them. It was so much easier than the way we did the first one.

Didn't the first album come easily for you?

It was kind of painful, but only because I'd never been into a studio before . . . I was afraid to tell the musicians because they all played better than I played. They've been playing for years, and I was afraid to tell them, "Hey, that doesn't sound right." It was a good thing I had Arif Martin [*sic*] for producer, 'cause he'd keep asking and asking me until he got something outta me about whether I like liked the back-up or not. I was real pleased with the way the first album came out. After two days, the guys I was working with came back . . . we quit about ten one night and they all went out to eat together, came back and ended up reading my lyrics all night. The next day they decided to go back and do some of the tunes over. They developed a real interest in me which meant a lot. I've seen those studio musicians crank out those sessions two hours a day in Nashville. That's why we didn't go to Nashville to do the first album, we went to Memphis. Down in Nashville, they've got this particular sound that can be bought from the finest musicians around, but there's no real feeling. I didn't want to get caught up in that.

Did you consider "Take the Star Out of the Window" a follow-up to "Sam Stone"?

No. As a matter of fact, I was a little bit afraid to put it on the album . . . because I thought it might be taken like that.

Is it one of the five new tunes?

Yeah. I wrote a whole bunch of tunes right after I recorded the first album . . . July of '71, it was quite a while ago. I was so glad to get those tunes on the first album down on record. Some of those songs I'd been singing over three years. . . . "Sam Stone" I wrote in 1969. Once you get tunes on a record you feel like you're done with them, like you can go on. Otherwise, if they're still unrecorded, they bother you.

Did Dylan really record "Donald and Lydia"?

He's not recording by himself at all. He's goofing off. Or at least that's what he tells me. Every time I go to the east coast, I run into him. He's all over the place. He's got some new stuff on his own, but he hasn't recorded it yet. He went into the studio to record "Donald and Lydia" and a couple other new ones of his. I don't know whether it was the musicians or not, but he didn't like the way they sounded. So he didn't do anything with them . . . he's not gonna go in and record until he feels that he's ready to.

People seem to be so amazed that you can write the way you do and be so young.

A guy asked me about that yesterday. He said, "You're only 26? You write like you're so much older." I mean, I don't know. I just assume everyone my age knows just as much as I do and probably more. I suppose if I was older before, I'd know the answer. That's what I told him. (laughter)

I write the way I do for several reasons. One, the songs are for myself. I didn't hear songs like this. So I figured if nobody else was gonna write them, I might as well, so I could hear them. The second is because I tend to put things very basically . . . and if I could write songs in the same manner, then I could get people to accept them, and enjoy them.

I'm not going to be playing clubs anymore. It'll be nice, because clubs really get to you. After playing the same place fourteen shows for a week . . . it really drives you up the wall. When I really get this concert tour rolling, I'll be able to bring people I really like along on tour with me for my audience to listen to. It ought to be a lot of fun.

JOHN PRINE

Bruce Pollock | 1975 | *In Their Own Words: Twenty Successful Song Writers Tell How They Write Their Songs*

When Bruce Pollock was compiling the twenty songwriters he felt were key for his *In Their Own Words*, he cast a net that included Pete Townshend, Felice and Boudleaux Bryant, Melvin Van Peebles, Frank Zappa, Melanie, Doc Pomus, Randy Newman and, yes, John Prine. At the time of the interviews, Prine was between the bumpy folk and ragged rock of *Sweet Revenge* and the Steve Cropper-produced *Common Sense*, which obscured the most innocent aspects of his origins *and* his impending move to Elektra/Asylum. He explored his at times scattered writing process—including the way he let songs mature—and unpacked some of his characters, his influences, and the way he evolved as a young writer.

Pollock, who's won awards for fiction and music journalism, was seeking to weigh the processes and goals of songwriters of note in the post-rock age. His exploration is more clinical, hardly offering the effusive exchange some of Prine's other critics brought to the process. Largely a shy artist, Pollock notes in the introduction to Prine's chapter that "the taciturn ex-postman" could become chatty "sometime around the third drink."

Still married to his first wife and living in Chicago, Prine was a working artist with a great deal of acclaim and few of the traditional trappings of success. In spite of the "new Dylan" tags, he was yet to find a radio hit—and the tension of languishing with his integrity intact allowed a candor that was matched with a reasonable willingness to explore what Pollock seemed to be seeking. —Ed.

Although at first he may sound like an early incarnation of Bob Dylan, lyrically John Prine has a voice all his own. Fusing his country and western background with a rock beat and folk sensibilities, Prine has succeeded in producing over a relatively short career, a body of work that is as powerful as it is eloquent. Plus, he's got a sense of humour.

His songs, which focus on life's little people, have drawn the praise and respect of everyone from Kris Kristofferson to Bette Midler, including Dylan himself. 'Sam Stone', about a returning Vietnam soldier turned junkie, is a classic of the post-'60s period. Far from another protest song, it renders reality with imagery both shocking and profound.

The interview with John Prine took place at a restaurant in New York City. The usually shy and taciturn ex-postman warmed easily to the subject at hand, becoming quite verbose . . . sometime around the third drink. "A lot of stuff has come out of just writing a couple of pages and rambling on, going from one mood right into another. Then I put it away and if I wait long enough I pull it back out and the good lines stay there and the others just fall right off the page. You can't tell the good lines from the bad lines right at first sometimes—it's a matter of editing. I happen to type at the same speed I edit, so a lot of times I can knock out stuff while I'm typing it.

"Once I had about three-quarters of a page that I got three songs out of. A stream of consciousness thing that didn't make any sense at all as it was. That's why I made it into three different songs. A lot of times I'll find a good line that I just can't use in the thing I'm working on, and rather than try to beat it to death, I'll file it away and pick it up when it's fresh again. I've done that really often—gotten two songs out of one thing I've started on.

"I'm very sloppy about keeping papers straight. My wife tries to keep it all together, but I purposely leave it around because I like to surprise myself. I like to write stuff and forget about it and then find it again.

"Usually the best thing is a real, real strong line that's a strong image. Sometimes an entire song will pour right out after it, if it's real strong. In most of the ballad stuff I do I try to use a chorus like a needle and thread, to pull the song together. A lot of times I've written just with the idea of experimenting. 'Donald and Lydia'—I had no idea what I was going to write about, but I knew how I was going to set the song up. I was going to set it up character by character.

"In general I'd say it's not subjects I'm trying to pinpoint, it's different moods. I'm trying to find a situation that would fit the mood. I'm more interested in the framework. A lot of times I'll pick the form before I write the song, because otherwise you run out on too many tangents. If you happen to run out on a good tangent, fine . . . then you can start all over again with that.

I asked him if he constantly revises his songs or if he gets them done rather easily and moves to the next.

"A song's not finished until I consider that I'd do it for anybody. But when I finish it, right there and then it's certified. I've heard other writers give suggestions years later about changing a line or something, but once I finish a song—this is even before I record it—I figure it's like a book on a shelf. It's already done and I can't do anything about it.

"I do have a lot of stuff that's half finished. I've got a song that I've been working on for a year and a half. The first part of it came out in like three seconds—the first verse and chorus. I can't get any further than that and keep up with the original theme of it, so I have to keep going back to it until I get it right. I really hate to stop when I start with an original idea, because it's really hard to pick up on it again. It's possible, but it's real difficult.

"'Mexican Home,' on the third album, took me two and a half years. I had to end up changing the melody in order to finish it. The old melody had been finished first and I couldn't fit the second half of the song into it, so I changed the entire melody and wrote new words for it. Of course, now I have the original I melody for some new words, and it's a good one.

"When you hear somebody else do the song, that's when you get a chance to criticize lines that you wrote. Whenever I hear my own records, I know it's my voice. I'll end up listening to the arrangement. But when I hear it done by somebody else . . . sometimes it brings up lines I thought before were just a link between two other lines, and all of a sudden that line stands out, depending on how someone interprets the song.

John provided his own assessment of his songwriting talents.

"I think I'm a better lyricist than melody writer, so I'm trying to balance out the two, because what I'm doing is writing songs, I'm not writing stories and I shouldn't always let the story carry the thing. That's my main criticism of my own writing. I'm consciously trying to stay away from ballads.

"Remember when the comedians used to get up and recite Elvis and they'd try to make it sound stupid? It would always fall flat because of course the lyrics didn't mean anything without the music. Those were some of the greatest lyrics, very simple and basic, and they went exactly with the tune. I would like to be able to write that kind of lyric too."

We discussed early radio experiences.

"The people who made the biggest impression on me as lyricists were Hank Williams, Dylan, Roger Miller—because he managed to write humorous songs that weren't novelty songs, and I hadn't heard anything like that. Then I didn't hear anything until Kristofferson came along. I can remember my first contact with his stuff was an article where they had some of his lyrics. And these lyrics carried their own melody. He writes like he's got a meter built inside of him. I asked him once if he worried that much about meter (his stuff is just so perfect) and he said, 'I just throw in "oh Lord" if it doesn't balance out.

"Jimmy Webb has written some real nice stuff. A lot of people in Nashville have excellent ears. They're Tin Pan Alley writers, but they're good at it. The Beatles wrote songs that flowed like Chuck Berry stuff and Buddy Holly stuff—which I'm sure they were very aware of when they wrote them. Their stuff caught so many different people on so many different levels—that's what was no nice about it."

I asked what pains John Prine had to go through in order to rise to the ranks of the professional.

"Well, when you're an amateur and you're writing songs everybody is going to have some sort of criticism. They've never criticized a song in their life, and you say 'Hey, I wrote this,' they'll say 'Well, that one part there needs changing.' So I tried to write songs that nobody could possibly criticize. But after doing that, and after recording and everything . . . I still have people come to me and tell me they loved a song for the wrong reasons. They really didn't understand it at all. I thought the songs were basically self-explanatory, but they weren't. So I just went ahead and let people like them for the wrong reasons. But I figured, I don't really have to knock myself out to explain things. I can be a little more abstract."

Prine started writing songs at the age of fourteen.

"It was after I got out of the army that I started writing anything serious. Of all the people I admired I never found anybody that I thought was saying exactly what I wanted to say, and that's why I wrote. But my first reaction was that I thought there must be something wrong with my songs, because they were a lot different from the stuff I'd heard. I thought if they're that much different, then why hasn't someone done them before. I'd sing them at first for friends, and they were encouraging, but I always felt like I was imposing on them. I never thought of selling songs until about a year before I went on the stage."

Finally we touched on how the singer/songwriting lifestyle, the public aspect, affected his writing.

"I would stop performing if I thought that it was really hurting my writing. I try and stay away from doing a whole lot of touring.

"Another thing—this is a result of being a recording artist. Around the time a record is finished I refuse to write for like a couple of months, even if I feel like it. Mainly because a lot of people haven't heard the new stuff, and I'll be going around doing it . . . and it's impossible for me to have a song finished and not go out and perform it. It's impossible for me to keep it locked up for six months or more."

BRUISED ORANGE: PRINE GETS HIS SECOND WIND

Robert Hilburn | 1978 | *Los Angeles Times*

Robert Hilburn was well on his way to being the West Coast's preeminent rock critic when his rave review of Elton John's Troubadour show sent the flamboyant showman and melodically powerful songwriter into the stratosphere. Newly minted as a critic who changes careers, Hilburn was always looking for greatness he could single out.

John Prine, fresh from his critically acclaimed—if radio-snubbed—debut, was a perfect subject for the man who would become the *Los Angeles Times* lead pop-music critic. A vocal advocate of Prine's writing and more Kentucky-style, country-leaning rock, Hilburn championed the folkie who'd swerved into both raucous jabbing stomps (*Sweet Revenge*) and finger-picked Appalachian extractions (*Diamonds in the Rough*), which stood in direct opposition to L.A.'s Laurel Canyon singer/songwriter ethos.

Coming into the Steve Goodman–produced *Bruised Orange*, Prine was feeling the toll of the star-making machinery failing to pay off. Having departed Atlantic and moving to Elektra/Asylum, the introspective everyman was in the final throes of burnout, torpor, and his own concern over his lack of desire.

Noting that Prine's first four albums had most likely failed to sell in total as many copies as the soundtrack for *Urban Cowboy* (1980) did in a single week, Hilburn felt the pain. Given their long-standing relationship, Prine was candid with Hilburn about his state of mind—and the impact of a summer spent in Nashville with legendary Sun Records veteran "Cowboy Jack" Clement.

Though the pair did not discuss the album Clement and Prine never completed, nor did they address the fumes of Prine's first marriage that was fraying at the seams, Hilburn recognized and dug into the conceptual undertow in *Orange*'s songs. Sagely, he also drilled into the parallel between Prine's circumstances and those of the B-movie star with the failing motion picture in "Sabu Visits the Twin Cities Alone." —Ed.

Bruce Springsteen's first album in three years is going to dominate the pop press' attention over the next couple of weeks, but another important record-maker makes another long-awaited return this month—John Prine, whose first album since 1975 has just been released by Asylum.

Titled *Bruised Orange*, the 10-song collection reaffirms Prine's position as one of America's finest folk-oriented songwriters of the '70s. Only Bob Dylan, Joni Mitchell and Jackson Browne are in his class.

Unlike Springsteen, whose *Born to Run* success three years ago propelled him onto the covers of both Time and Newsweek, Prine is something of a trade secret.

His tunes have been recorded by such respected pop figures as Bette Midler, Johnny Cash, Joan Baez, John Denver and Bonnie Raitt. Still, the combined sales of his first four Atlantic albums probably was less than last week's tally for "Saturday Night Fever."

Bruised Orange may finally bring him a wider audience. Produced by Steve Goodman, the LP has a brighter instrumental texture than Prine's previous efforts and it features—on balance—the most accessible batch of tunes since his heralded 1971 debut album.

The new collection bristles with energy and spirit that is due in large part to a rekindling of Prine's musical interests. One of the reasons for the three-year delay between albums was a change of record companies, but there was also a darker reason.

For nearly a year, Prine stopped writing. He didn't know at the time if he simply couldn't write any more or just didn't want to write. The only thing he knew for sure was that the songs stopped coming.

"The first time I saw John Prine was at Earl's (club) in Chicago," Jack Newfeld, a respected New York political writer, once noted in his Village Voice column.

"It was like watching Willie Mays catch a fly ball for the first time at the Polo Grounds or like the first time I heard Bob Dylan at Folk City."

Newfield's remarks were typical of the excitement Prine's debut album sparked among those who'd heard it. Normally the most one can expect from a first release is one of two promising songs—something to suggest an artist has potential. With Prine, it was different. He arrived as a fully developed talent.

The 13 songs in his first album were brilliantly crafted and hauntingly evocative. They combined traces of the humor and social compassion of Woody Guthrie, the emotional purity of Hank Williams and the arresting lyric bite of Dylan.

However familiar the individual themes, Prine's treatments were fresh and convincing. There was sensitivity and purpose in his work that usually made other writers' songs about similar subjects seem shallow and plodding.

"Hello in There"—a staple in Midler's repertoire for years now—remains a classic look at youth-oriented society's neglect of old people. "Far from Me" is a marvelously designed look at the delicate undercurrents in a fading romance; "Donald and Lydia" is a stirring exploration of two people's loneliness.

So why didn't Prine's music catch on? Some listeners thought his voice was too ragged. Others complained his music was too country for mass pop tastes. Still others suggested Prine's songs were too "down."

For those and other reasons, Prine's music got little or no AM airplay. Without that exposure, he had to rely on touring to build an audience. Within a couple of years, he had worked his way up to 3,000-seat auditoriums, where he'd often headline over singers who had Top 40 hits.

Yet his own albums—which contain some of the most compelling songs of the '70s—continued selling at a disappointing rate. By the end of '75, Prine was both frustrated and weary. The road and other pressures had drained him.

"I wasn't getting any enjoyment out of the music any more," the 31-year-old Chicago-based songwriter said during a recent L.A. visit. "I was confusing it all with having to go to work or something. I'd come home from a tour and I wouldn't even want to see the guitar, much less write a song.

"I was dangerously close to the point of going out on tour again just because I had to keep up an income. I was afraid I was going to become one of those people who just float around the record business. You know the kind—the people who sit around all day trying to figure out what the public will buy or what's going to be the next trend. They're interested in making records, but they're not interested in making music. I knew it was time for me to sit down and check things out again."

For Prine, the desire to write and make music was regained last summer in Nashville. Away from the competitiveness and business orientation of the L.A. and New York record scenes, he found a relaxed, joyous spirit among the musicians in Nashville.

Jack Clement, a producer and writer who has worked with Johnny Cash and Waylon Jennings, was especially helpful. That's why Prine salutes Clement on the *Bruised Orange* album cover: "Thanks for the Summer of '77."

"Clement was having fun with music. So was everyone around him," Prine says. "He had a band come to his house every morning at 10 and start playing in his living room. One day he had an eight-piece group playing 'Brazil.' There was always so much going on that you wanted to join in. . . ."

Several of Prine's tunes on *Bruised Orange* seem to have grown out of frustration and confusion over the pre-Nashville period. "Sabu Visits the Twin Cities Alone" is a wry, yet poignant look at an artist having to go on the road to hawk his own work.

In the song, Prine uses the imaginary tale of Sabu—an actor billed in the 1940s as "the Elephant boy"—going on a promotional tour. He spotlights the actor's unglamorous chaotic plight: *Sabu was sad/The whole tour stunk/The airlines lost/The elephant's trunk.*

Then he contrasts the actor's journey with a young fan's excitement in spotting the actor:

"Hey, look Ma —
It's the elephant boy
Bundled all up in his corduroy
Headed down south towards Illinois
From the jungles of East St. Paul."

Prine wrote the song during a tour. "I had done a particularly mediocre show in St. Paul one night and when I got back to the hotel there was a Sabu movie on TV," he said sitting in his manager's office.

"I didn't connect with it right away, but it seemed kinda funny. Here's this kid riding though the jungle, always by himself, looking confused and with never any particular place to go.

"I had started to feel the same way. When I started writing the song, I figured there might be some other connection. He was a movie star with an agent. Some of his movies must have had trouble at the box office so they probably sent him out in the middle of winter to a shopping center and dressed him in a suit. . . ."

———

As in past Prine collections, there are both light entertainments in *Bruised Orange* and deeper, more deliberate commentaries. Several tunes deal with various shades of romantic involvement. "If You Don't Want My Love" is a bittersweet, highly commercial love song co-written with Phil Spector. "There She Goes" is a rollicking look at marital incompatibility.

The album's most consistent theme, however, is the who-can-explain-it inexactness of life that is examined in such tunes as "Crooked Piece of Time" and "That's the Way the World Goes 'Round."

"Chain of Sorrows," which brings a touch of Memphis R&B to Prine's normally folk country style is perhaps the album's most striking song. It's a gently philosophical reminder against letting disappointments sour you.

You can gaze out the window
Get mad and get madder
Throw your hands in the air
Say, "What does it matter?"
But it don't do no good
So help me I know

Supported by a blistering saxophone solo, the track features one of Prine's most full-bodied arrangements since "The Late John Garfield Blues" on his second album. It also demonstrates Prine's growing confidence and control as a vocalist.

Even though *Bruised Orange* looks like Prine's best shot yet at the charts, it may still have trouble getting airplay. When AM programmers look to Kansas' "Dust in the Wind" and Barry Manilow's "Can't Smile Without You" as the ultimate in honest, embracing sentiment, Prine's songs may be viewed with suspicion. But he's ready to take his case to the stage again. Prine has just put a new band together for a tour that includes June 7–8 stops at the Roxy.

PART III

The Toll of Being Acclaimed

JOHN PRINE IS SO FINE

Jay Saporita | January 21, 1975 | *Aquarian Weekly*

Originally formed in 1969 to cover "hippie culture and healthy lifestyles," the *Aquarian Weekly* was really about the music happening in the tristate region of New Jersey, New York City, and eastern Pennsylvania. There for the nascent rise of the CBGB punk scene—and a period of years in the mid-'80s and early '90s as *East Coast Rocker*—the *Aquarian* captured the visceral sense of how rock music made people feel.

Nowhere was that on greater display than Jay Saporita's full-immersion night on Prine's bus in 1975 between shows at The Bitter End. With the electricity of New Journalism's rhythms and details, he captures the textures of road life; a bus hang that includes Ramblin' Jack Elliott on the lam from Bob Dylan's Rolling Thunder Revue, Shel Silverstein, *and* Beat poet Allen Ginsberg; the economics of touring, owning a bus, and paying for a life; and the chill of plunging into the December night and crossing the street for a second show that evening.

For Prine, about to tour Australia, New Zealand, and Japan with the Eagles, it is a balancing act of what can be afforded, how to manage acclaim and create something that keeps him engaged. Swerving between narrative accounting and conversation, Saporita strung a wire between how the touring life manifests and what a no-nonsense thinker believes about it all.

They spoke about producers (notably Steve Cropper), labels (Atlantic), and game changers (Goodman, Kristofferson, Paul Anka), but also the existential stuff (building a tour bus, cars, songs, and religion). Like a catch-up after too many years, there's a truth and liveliness to the exchange that's as brisk as midnight air on Bleecker Street after that second show. Without oversentimentalizing the blue-collar life of song, this profile is a perfect time stamp of rock 'n' roll life before cell phones, the Internet, or flying private. —Ed.

Winter in the City. Towering and formidable, row after row of buildings encapsulate the cold, leaving a thick frozen blanket over the streets. Whirls of a cruel wind pierce through layers of clothing. Ears and noses numb, toes ache. Exposed skin turns red and chafes.

A bitter December night and a long line of people are patiently waiting for the doors of the Other End to open. Bent away from a frigid breeze blowing down Bleeker Street, they huddle to the wall hidden under an array of hats, hoods, scarves and huge coats. A fog of breath fills the air every time someone speaks. It's late, close to 10 pm, and inside John Prine is just finishing the first show, comfortable in the ambiance of an encore. A second show is scheduled for 11:30 and in less than an hour the shivering mass of ticketholders will be seated, thawing with a stiff drink in hand.

Across the street, a behemoth bus is settled against the curb. Its engine purrs a soft and constant hum. Its bulk blocks the streetlights throwing a wide shadow across Bleeker. The destination window reads "PRIVATE" and dark curtains are hung in the other windows. The usual according-door is tucked away, replaced by a curtain of heavy material that is pushed aside to enter. The bus is Prine's quarters, his "hotel-on-wheels." A wagon built with special pride to include all the necessary comforts, providing an alternative to jet travel and sterile, forever identical hotel rooms.

A steady flow of heat bathes the interior. The driver's seat has been left intact, but for a console-type push button telephone on the dashboard. The remainder of the bus has been refurbished, refined and wholly resurrected. The floors are plushly carpeted, the walls paneled and decorated. The standard seats have been gutted, replaced by a compact and portable living facility. The front section consists of two small couches, a lounging chair, and a color t.v. Further on is a kitchen with a sink, a range and wood-finished cabinets.

There are eight bunks beyond that, and a bathroom. Each bunk is equipped with an 8-track stereo and headphones. Towards the rear, behind a closed door that insures privacy, is the master bedroom, complete with a double bed and bathroom with shower. Above the headboard of the bed, built into plywood shelving, is an 8-track deck and another television.

The bus swells with guests when the first show ends. A thin, balding man sprawls on the coach, eyes riveted to the television. A young woman, dabbed with make-up and possessing the prominent cheekbones of a model, sips a bottle of beer. In the kitchen, a bottle of wine is being gulped down. Ramblin' Jack Elliot, fresh from Dylan's Rolling Thunder Revue, tugs at the curling brim of his hat, pushing it down to the bridge of his nose. He plops himself between two svelte blonde women, an arm around each.

Shel Silverstein, the ribald songwriter, runs a hand over the satin skin of his denuded head, Allen Ginsberg stops by, his massive beard recently cut away to reveal a still youthful face. He hunches in, wearing sneakers and worn, fitted clothing, exchanging soft greetings with everyone.

Prine, multitude Heinekens churning inside him, climbs on the bus, ambling to the bedroom. His hair is puffed loosely, hanging haphazardly, cascading carelessly over his forehead. A cigarette burns to a butt in his right hand. He's wearing a hooded sweatshirt, zippered against the freezing temperatures outside, and jeans. Slimmer than three years ago, his slight frame is just beginning to bloat at the belly from multiple bouts of beer. Wild, furious flashes of energy flush through him, the rewards of an excellent first show.

He sits on the bed, inhales deeply on a fresh cigarette, and using both hands pushes his hair back from his forehead. The door is closed, the blast of the party fading to a murmur. Outside, all but the last in line have gone in and been seated. Inside, enveloped in warmth, we begin.

THE AQUARIAN: SO . . . WHERE'D YOU GET THIS BUS?

PRINE: We built it. We bought the shell. The plumbing, sink and stuff we had a cabinet maker do. We had a bus last year with my band on tour. We rented it. So like we just avoided all the mistakes we learned when we built this one. Don stays with the bus when we rent it out. He just got back from New Orleans for ten weeks and we're going to put it up for another 15 weeks and it will be paid for.

A: IS THIS THE END OF THE CURRENT TOUR?

P: Yeah, I'm just finishing up for the year. I'm taking a couple of weeks off, then I'm going to Australia. Australia, New Zealand and Japan. Going on tour with the Eagles.

A: JOHN PRINE AND THE EAGLES?

P: Yeah . . . it will be a ball, man. Joe Walsh is with them now. We never got a chance to play together in the States 'cause they play 50,000 seaters and it's crazy and everything, but over there we're going to be playing like 3,000–5,000 seaters so we're going to go out and do some acoustic stuff. I'll do my show. They'll play with me with my electric stuff and then do their regular show. Then we'll jump around and see everything in Australia. It's supposed to be summer in Australia now, man!

A: I NOTICED A RECORDING TRUCK OUTSIDE THE CLUB.

P: We're recording a bunch of stuff live. Then I'm going into the studio when I get back and do the whole trip. What I'm planning on doing right now is re-recording some of the earlier stuff . . . like "Pretty Good." I'm trying to make a single out of "Pretty Good," and then mix it with the live stuff. Put that stuff together and have it out in April. Then in September there'll be an album of new stuff.

A: LAST TIME OUT WAS WITH A BAND. YOU'RE BACK ALONE AGAIN. WHAT HAPPENED?

P: Ran out of money. I'm trying to put a new band together for the fall when I go out with the new stuff.

A: YOU LIKE WORKING WITH A BAND?

P: Yeah . . . I love it. I was doing an hour by myself anyway, but I mean that was going to take care of the overhead of the band, the sound system, the lights . . . but *Common Sense* sold better than the rest of them but not enough. I make my income from personal appearances and so I paid for everything with the band.

A: IT WAS COMING OUT OF YOUR POCKET?

P: For sure. I don't ask the record company for nothing I've got to owe them. I like to stay even. So, we ran out of money.

A: YOU'RE BASICALLY A FOLKIE. STARTED WITH AN ACOUSTIC GUITAR BACKING YOURSELF, YET YOUR ALBUMS ARE FUILL OF MUSIC AND YOU ENJOY WORKING WITH A BAND. WHEN

YOU WRITE THE SONGS, DO YOU HAVE THE OTHER PARTS, THE ADDITIONAL MUSIC IN MIND?

P: Some I write with the other parts in mind. Some I know will be just me and my guitar. I don't know . . . I just like music. For about a year and a half—two years I was doing concerts and it was all "an evening with . . ." Two and a half hours I was doing by myself and I'd turn around and there'd be just a curtain and a microphone . . . you know? And there I am two and a half hours and I wanted to be able to turn around at one part of the show and see . . . you know . . . see somebody and say something like "go like this" to a lead guitarist or something. Just to hear somebody else play.

Like me and the Nitty Gritty Dirt Band were playing together Halloween Night in Louisville. And after they're done I came back out and they're playing behind me. We were doing Chuck Berry stuff and that. I had a whole lot . . . I hadn't sang for a couple of nights and my throat wasn't bad and I had breath to mess around with and was fuckin' with the phrasing a lot. I really liked that. Just hearing somebody else play.

When I was putting my band together, I didn't know exactly what I wanted. I had to wait a while until I heard exactly what I wanted to hear. I didn't know how to tell anybody what to do or anything. When I had the audition, I just had the guys sit back with somebody and jam together and listen to them jam and I wouldn't introduce myself. I wouldn't want the guy to come in thinking he was gonna play my songs. If he can jam with those guys and like it—then we can teach him the songs.

A: THE WHOLE THING OF PLAYING WITH A BAND . . . THERE'S A CHUCK BERRY TRACK ON *COMMON SENSE* CALLED "YOU NEVER CAN TELL." HOW'D THAT COME ABOUT?

P: I was just going around humming it a lot and I couldn't get the single. I kept hearing it on the radio, about every two or three weeks some station would play it. Rick Vito, the guy who does all my guitar work, it turns out he'd been playing it all along. So we were talking about it one night, like up all night singing it and we walked into the studio ten the next morning, and we told Cropper like . . .

"We worked on this Chuck Berry song and we want to cut it." That's why the thing moves too quick 'cause we said, "We got to cut it . . . got to cut it . . . you know, like, immediately!" That song's so neat . . . the way Berry does it . . . slow . . . his words are incredible! Whew! Steve Goodman gave me for my birthday a 1942 Victory Model jukebox. It's all wood because of the war . . . you couldn't get any metal. It's all wood and just plays 78s, right? And there's a 78 of Chuck Berry doing "30 Days." The speaker sounds like a big car radio . . . it's all fuzzy and the sound comes buzzing out. Johnny Ace is on it. It's great. I put the jukebox next to my pinball machine and put the lights out and watch them both . . . it's incredible.

A: STEVE CROPPER, THE FAMOUS "MIDNIGHT HOUR" MAN . . .

P: Right . . . the reason I did *Common Sense* . . . about the time I started the band . . . that was the kind of stuff I was writing at the time. Cropper's name popped up and I said, "Wow. I wanna work with Steve Cropper; he's great." He put some horns on my record that I swear had just come off an Otis Redding track. Like these sounds comin' through the fog—woooo. It was nice working with him. I don't know if I'll do the next one with him, probably with someone else 'cause it's not the same kind of stuff, but he's great.

A: EVER BEEN INTO CARS?

P: Cars? Into cars? Yeah . . . I got a 51 Ford . . . for my Christmas present I picked it up. Just pulled all the chrome off it. It's gonna be all redone and when I get back just put the chrome back on. You know, dual exhausts.

A: WHAT WAS THE FIRST CAR YOU EVER OWNED?

P: That I ever owned? A '62 Grand Prix. And I couldn't keep the payments up so I got a '55 Buick. Hmm. Ha.

Prine, a few years back, was working a mail route through Chicago as a steady job and playing the clubs—the hoots at night. Learning the craft, sharpening the words until they stung like a needle and left sore, bothersome reminders. Making friends, some extra money, but, most important, being heard. Still, it was a grind, trying to go further knowing you're good but stagnated by the situation. For Prine, the grind came to a halt in an unexpected rush of two weeks. Fourteen days from a hungover, after-hours performance for Kris Kristofferson, John Prine was in Chicago with a record contract. A jolting flash and the mailman had become a recording artist:

A: JOHN, THE RUMOR GOES THAT KRISTOFFERSON HEARD YOU PLAY AND WEEKS LATER YOU WERE ON YOUR WAY TO A RECORDING CONTRACT. WHAT'S THE WHOLE THING BEHIND THAT?

P: That's about it. Kristofferson heard me in Chicago. Goodman brought him over to hear me. Goodman was opening a bill for Kris, right? Goodman said I want you to hear a buddy of mine so he brought him over to hear me. A couple of weeks later I got a plane ticket to New York. Paul Anka . . .

A: PAUL ANKA?

P: Yeah, he was my first manager. He gave us, Steve came with me, plane tickets to New York. So we went. He said he'd pay us for a demo and take it around. Something happened. Well, we'll talk business later. So, we come here and Kris happens to be playing down [in] the Village the night we get in. Kris puts me up for a guest set. He and Carly Simon were playing. So we came around, saying like: well? you know. He put us up for a guest set and the next day I got a record contract. I was in the studio two days later.

A: THE CONTRACT WAS FROM ATLANTIC.

P: Right . . .

A: ATLANTIC.

P: Right . . . Wexler was done and he hadn't been in the Village in ten years. Bobby Neuwirth and Kristofferson's piano player kept him there. They didn't tell him what he was down there for. I found this out later. They kept telling him stories and stuff . . . like he'd stand up and they'd order him a drink or something and sit him down. They made him stay until I did my guest set.

A: SO RIGHT BEFORE THAT YOU'RE PLAYING SMALL CLUBS IN CHICAGO TRYING TO MAKE IT . . .

P: Yeah, I was a mailman. I was doing the clubs in Chicago.

A: IS THAT HOW YOU MET GOODMAN?

P: Yeah. We were both writing and playing the clubs so we were bound to run into each other. I met him at a club and we just became really tight. We were both musicians just playing around. I was playing somewhere and so was Goodman. I didn't even know he was playing with Kris. He calls me up at four in the morning at this club and the chairs are up on the table and I'm sitting around waiting for my check. I'm asleep . . . I'm just laying around; he calls up and says: "Hello, John? I'm bringing Kris Kristofferson over with some people. Get ready to do a show." So they came over and sat there . . . Kris felt horrible. You know, he said, 'all the chairs are up on the table and stuff . . . this poor kid's gonna get up and play?' I sang for an hour and a half. It was crazy man. 'Cause I was knocked out by Kristofferson just being there.

A: DID STAGEFRIGHT SET IN?

P: I didn't think about it. I just played. I always liked my stuff so I did anything I wrote. I mean . . . I would never go up to someone and say, "hey, can I sing for you?" or something. I just figured if someone's gonna hear it, they'll hear it sooner or later.

A: WHAT WAS KRISTOFFERSON'S REACTION?

P: I had to sing some songs twice. He wanted me to do three or four things again.

A: WHERE'D ALL THIS TAKE PLACE?

P: In a club called Old Town. I'm gonna do a couple of nights there at the end of the year. To start off the new year. I'm gonna go in there . . . it seats like a hundred-twenty people. The sound system isn't the best but a lot of stuff is going on at the place. Goodman and I are both going back. He's doing two nights and I'm doing two nights. I remember, right after I got back, right after signing with Atlantic, I still hadn't done anything yet, still hadn't played outside Chicago. I hadn't been in the studio yet

. . . nothing. I just signed this contract with New York . . . it was like NEW YORK, like a picture.

So I'm going home with a record contract in my hand, a banjo on my knee or whatever and the first night I get back, Loudon Wainwright's opening at the Quiet Night. So I go down to see him, at this time he's on Atlantic, so I wanted to ask him 'cause there weren't many people like him with the company. I wanted to ask him how they were doing. I went over to introduce myself but I didn't want to bother him. So, you know, I said my name's John. I was talking with my head bowed down, talking into my beard, and I said I just signed with Atlantic. I was wondering how it was, you know? He just took a look at me like—what is this? What the hell are you talking about, kid? So we meet two months later and he says to me I've never forgotten that time you came up to me . . . I couldn't understand a word you said! Loudon's crazy, man.

A: WAS IT AROUND THEN THAT YOU MET BONNIE RAITT?

P: Me and Bonnie had been playing together. I was at the Bitter End and her album had just come out. She was opening with Fred McDowell at The Gaslight. We used to work together a lot in '72 and '73 when Bonnie and Freebo were working alone. As we both got bands it got harder and harder to get together because the expenses of two bands and a double show. So we're getting a chance to work together a little bit now 'cause I'm alone again. We love to play together . . . and we been together since the beginning. She's great. She's fun. Man, she's a walking heart.

A: JOHN, IN YOUR EARLIER ALBUMS, THERE ARE HINTS OF A CHRISTIAN OR CHURCHGOING BACKGROUND. A FEW OF YOUR SONGS DEAL WITH DEATH—HUMOROUSLY LIKE "PLEASE DON'T BURY ME" AND POIGNANTLY IN A PIECE LIKE "HE WAS IN HEAVEN BEFORE HE DIED." WHAT DOES DEATH MEAN TO JOHN PRINE? WHAT HAPPENS WHEN YOU DIE?

P: Anybody you ever came in contact with, that's how much you live on. Whenever you lose someone else, if you're real good friends with them, you're a part of them. If you're still living—then they are too. That's how I figure it. My family moved to Chicago from the South. They used to go to church in the South, my mother and father, but church was more a social thing. When they got up North, people weren't as friendly, so they didn't go.

Going to church in the South was like . . . everybody sees each other. They all eat and sweat and sing and it's terrific. Up North everyone was real solemn and shit so my parents didn't care; they didn't go. It wasn't so much to them, they just wanted something to do on Sunday morning. So, we were raised to go to church. I mean, talk about religion . . . I was just going to say religion's a very spiritual thing. Shit, that's a politician's answer for you.

A: CAN WE QUOTE YOU?

P: Yeah, you see it's difficult for me to even listen to someone talk about it, let alone talk about it myself. People talk about any organized religion . . . I can hardly relate. They want to take a little bit off you when you're doing it. So many things. People are doing quaaludes one day, the next they're into religion, the next day it's something else. You see them three weeks later and say how's that going and they say what? what? What are you talking about? Where's some reds? You know what I mean? All these people changing like that.

A: "COME BACK TO US BARBARA LEWIS HARE KRISHNA BEAU-REGARD."

P: Right.

There's an empty pack of cigarettes on the table, crushed into a ball. More than a few drained bottles dot the bedroom. A fifth of bourbon has been slowly sipped until just a murky brown spittle splashes at the bottom of the bottle. Through a part in the curtain, the street is empty and lifeless; it seems much colder now. A knock on the door and a bitter walk across the street to the dressing room. The Other End is filled with an anticipatory audience.

The dressing room is small. A narrow cubicle, decorated with huge advertisement posters from The Bitter End, the club's maiden name. There's a rectangular mirror, encased by lightbulbs, and set above a small dressing table and a row of clothes hangers naked on a long steel pole.

On the dressing table is a silver bucket, containing four bottle of Heineken's. They are opened and buried to their neck in ice. Two of these will accompany Prine to the stage. Next to Prine's guitar is a pitch pipe.

Prine changes into a woven Mexican shirt. A deep gray, red at the shoulders. He kneads his fingers through his hair, tending to it in the mirror for a moment.

As he tunes his guitar, twisting the pegs slightly to adjust the strings, he falls silent, concentrating on the proper pitch. He starts to play, at first just randomly picking out notes then into a song. Full force now, his voice strong and loud. He stays on the same song, again and again running through bits of it, interrupting himself for a taste of beer or a cigarette. Intensely now, head back and eyes closed, the flow of the guitar, the meter of the words pulsing through him.

P: I don't think about the audience before I go on 'cause that gets you real nervous. I get the rhythm going without playing so that the first time I hit it the guitar's almost behind me. You know, like I'm waiting and waiting and waiting . . . just for the right second and all of a sudden—boom! That's it, you know? You go into it like that. Whatever I have to do . . . maybe I might just have to climb a ladder in order to get like that . . . you know? But I just got to get ready like that so . . . that I . . . can . . . just . . . POP.

Working his way through the audience to the stage, his guitar held in front of him, his head bobbing, staring vacantly. Building the steam, climbing that ladder, pushing it so hard that by the time he's onstage, he's about to burst. He dives into the first song, "Forbidden Jimmy," with a powerful thrust. Almost screaming the words, spitting out sprays of energy, bobbing back and forth towards the mike. Standing on his toes, and weaving from side to side.

He bounces lightly on the balls of his feet in a strange staggering dance. Between songs he fiddles with a cigarette, leaning back and comfortable, launching into long rambling prose pieces concerning the songs. Working alone, no curtain but a brick wall at his back, he plays long and hard. His older pieces are as strong as ever, straining emotions in the silence. He does two new songs (both he's still working on) and, though humorous, they sparkle with masterful twists of language.

More beers. Countless cigarettes. Two hours later, another encore, and Prine wearies his way back to the dressing room. He changes into his sweatshirt, leaving the Mexican shirt over the back of a chair. Drains the last Heineken, still cold in the ice bucket, and secures his guitar into the case. An excellent show behind him, he eases out of the bar. Tonight, he deserves a nightcap.

TEN YEARS OF FOLKS: 20 YEARS OF THE EARL

Dave Hoekstra | November 1981 | *Illinois Entertainer*

To celebrate the Earl of Old Town's twentieth anniversary, the *Illinois Entertainer* sent Dave Hoekstra to interview John Prine and Steve Goodman ten years after their breakout success as part of the Chicago entertainment monthly's November 1981 cover package. As a place for working people to find work, Chicago developed a strong local music scene; a place where—between the college and post-Summer of Love crowds—enough clubs existed, and a healthy folk, blues, and singer/songwriter—later alt/country—community emerged.

Prine and Goodman, a decade into the music business, looked back on 1971, how their careers came together and the Chicago clubs that fostered their music before anyone knew their names. Humor undercuts Prine's assessment of what has proven, for him, to be the most difficult piece of "the record business." His union president father's advice was the one thing from 1970 and '71 that echoed loudest from the memories of a magic time in the pair's life.

Hoekstra would become the longtime music critic at the *Chicago Sun-Times*. He would also author books, produce documentaries, and receive the 2013 Studs Terkel Community Media Award. But here, as a young writer, he demonstrated an ability to get people to recall details and bring readers into the memories.

Equally vital, the *Illinois Entertainer*—like *Aquarian*—is one of the rare entertainment weeklies still in existence. *IE* is thriving, continuing to cover the music and events people in the Chicagoland want to know about. —Ed.

Just as the Earl of Old Town begins its 20th year of business, the folks down the street at Lum's have to spoil the last vestige of neighborhood funkiness by closing down and promising to reopen as something called "Weinerwalds," no doubt some type of Me Generation restaurant, which serves up quiche and sushi to people in alligator shirts.

Further south on Wells Street, the owners of the Royal London Wax Museum have finally thrown in the towel and are shipping their surrogate Ernie Banks and Hugh Hefner to the East Coast.

Just what is going on here?

In 1971, young musicians from the Earl, or green comedians from Second City could combine the Wax Museum and Lum's for a perfectly enchanting night on the town when they weren't hustling for a gig.

In 1971, Ernie Banks was more than a wax figure in a museum. He was finishing up his final year as an active player as the Cubs finished in third place.

In 1971, we were listening to "Brown Sugar" and "Have You Ever Seen the Rain?" while Jim Morrison died in France. Our political thoughts focused on Richard Nixon and the Viet Nam War. All of this had an impact on the artists who worked the Chicago folk clubs, particularly the Earl of Old Town, the Quiet Knight on Belmont (now Tuts) and the defunct Fifth Peg on Armitage Avenue.

The intense political climate and electric musical atmosphere either gave folk musicians topics for material, or subjects for songs of escape.

For artists like Steve Goodman, John Prine, Bonnie Koloc, Bill Quateman, Jim Post and Megan McDonough, the summer and fall of '71 proved to be a turning point in either their professional careers or personal lives.

Chicago journalist Ben Hecht once said, "Time is a circus always packing up and moving away." This summer we chased down Prine, Goodman and friends and asked them to look back at the circus ten years ago.

These are their memories.

The trailer area behind the ChicagoFest main stage had suddenly been transformed into a high school homecoming after Steve Goodman and John Prine's performance in August. The area filled with old friends and relatives offering congratulations to the performers and band members. We retreat to the quieter trailer, where it doesn't take long for Goodman and Prine to look back. After all, this has been a night for memories.

"I've been thinking a lot about August of 1971, in fact I remember August first almost right to the day," says the 33-year old John Prine dressed in a sleeveless tee-shirt and black Levi's.

"I recorded my first album in late June or early July and came home from Memphis with the tapes," he says. "I played them for my father (Bill) around the first of August. I didn't even have a tape player, I had to borrow an old Weber from my father-in-law who was a janitor at Proviso West.

"Anyway, as I played the tapes, my Dad listened to them from the other room with the door half open. I asked him why he was in the other room, and he said he wanted to pretend he was listening on a jukebox," Prine says with a smile.

"When we were done with the tapes, my Dad said, 'that's all right,' Prine recalls. "He liked Hank Williams and Roy Acuff songs, and I guess my stuff reminded him of that. And, I wrote 'Paradise' for my father." Bill Prine died two weeks later, on August 16, 1971.

"He gave me some good advice. He said to watch out for those fuckin' lawyers," Prine says. There is a slight pause.

"And he was right. If there's one thing I had problems with over the years, it's been the record company executives and all of the attorneys without any musical sense whatsoever. There are some exceptions, like Jerry Wexler, but there aren't many," Prine says. As soon as Prine returned to Maywood in the late summer of 1971, Steve Goodman was planning a trip to Nashville to record his first album on Buddah records.

Goodman, now 33, says with a chuckle, "We didn't know what we were doing. It was right after John had recorded his first album. It was an exploding time for people. Of course (Bonnie) Koloc already had been a star, selling out Mister Kelly's, but then both our albums came out (Goodman's and Prine's) and we learned we just had to take things day by day.

"I still live that way," Goodman says, in reference to his recent move to the West Coast.

Most people know the story of Kris Kristofferson and Paul Anka wandering over to the Quiet Knight to catch Prine's set. Goodman wanted them to see the former postman sing his story songs, and the visit wound up with trips to New York for both Goodman and Prine.

Prine recalls, "I still was kind of confused. I didn't know what I wanted to do, outside of getting a job where I didn't have to get up early in the morning. Steve began working the circuits in late '68, and already had been to New York for six months.

"Anyway, Anka comes to see us and calls backstage," Prine explains. "We figured it was a chance to let the girls meet him. It turns out Anka has got a couple of plane tickers to New York and some leads with record companies.

"Well, I was still hesitant. I didn't know if I wanted to commit myself. Then Steve says, 'Have you ever been to New York?' and I said, 'No,' and he says, 'Let's go!'" Goodman and Prine break into laughter before Prine continues with the story.

"So we get to the airport on Sunday and pick up a *Village Voice,*" Prine says. "We see that Kris Kristofferson will be warming up Carly Simon at the Bitter End, so we rush down there to say hello to our newfound friend."

Kristofferson saw Prine and Goodman and asked them to come onstage. In the audience was Atlantic Records mogul Jerry Wexler, who, according to Prine, was in the Village for his first time since 1956.

"He had come to say hello to Carly. Kris, who was running around with Carly like Warren Beatty, Donnie Fritts (Kristofferson's piano player) and Bobby Newark [sic] kept Wexler there all night with stories and jokes. The idea was to keep him there long enough until Steve and I go onstage."

Eventually Prine and Goodman took the stage. Prine performed "Paradise," "Hello in There" and "Sam Stone." Goodman did "City of New Orleans" and "Would You Like To Learn To Dance?" Wexler wanted to sign Prine the next day.

Goodman says, "We thought since someone bought us the plane tickets we were supposed to sign. We were just being honest people."

Prine interrupts, "We should've signed right there."

Instead Prine waited for a few days before coming to terms with Atlantic, and Goodman stayed in New York for two weeks before connecting with Neil Bogart of Buddah Records.

Goodman laughs. "I only had six songs at the time. John had 31."

Another little known bit of history happened at the Bitter End after Prine signed with Atlantic. Kristofferson was still at the New York club when Bob Dylan drove up on his motorcycle . . . after his bike accident. Prine was in the audience and Kristofferson told him Dylan wanted to hear some of Prine's material.

"I gave Dylan one of the first pressings of the record," Prine recalls. "Two weeks later, I was playing my first gig ever outside of Chicago. I was playing with David Bromberg, Steve Burgh and Goodman, but I needed a harmonica player.

"I asked if there was anyone around. Now this is only my second night, and Dylan comes up. He had brought a harmonica and learned the words to all the choruses of my songs. I introduced Dylan and about two people were clapping. No one believed it. They thought Dylan was either dead or on Mt. Fuji," Prine chuckles.

"And all this happened in 1971," he adds.

Goodman says the trips outside the Midwest served as a confidence builder for both artists.

"We knew we were okay, but until we got out in '71, we really didn't know . . ." he says.

"But, you can still live pretty good in this town on light bread," Goodman says. "You can still find an apartment at semi-reasonable rates. You can skate a little and that's why we never thought of leaving until we did. This place has nothing to do with the music business, but it has a lot to do with music.

"And Earl Poinke and Richard Harding (owner of the Quiet Knight) kept it together. Those two guys did as much for the music scene here as any of the musicians," Goodman says.

Goodman thinks he turned the corner professionally when Arlo Guthrie recorded "The City of New Orleans" in July of 1972.

"It was the first time I felt there was room for me in the circle in terms of doing this until I couldn't do it anymore," Goodman explains.

At the same time, Prine says he was uncomfortable with his early Seventies label as a "protest singer."

"I never liked that. I didn't think my songs were like that anyway. I know and appreciated the craft from someone like Phil Ochs," Prine explains.

"I never tried to tell my audience anything except my own opinion," he continues. "Most people were already believing what you were saying. They were just there to pick up girls and get high anyway. They're doing the same thing now, but they don't need a social injustice to do it.

"It all seemed a bit phony to me. I meet a lot of people who were real good and cared a lot about what they were doing. I cared about what I was doing, but I was just a guy at the bar singing. "Isn't that just the shittiest thing you ever heard?" where the other things were like (Prine breaks into the tune of 'Old McDonald's Farm') 'Why don't we tear down the White House today? ei-ei-oh?'"

And the trailer shakes with laughter . . . at old times.

FREELANCE INTERVIEW WITH JOHN PRINE

Dave Wallace Jr. | December 1980 | *Hot Rod*

Since reporting on a San Fernando Raceway drag meet in 1964, photojournalist and editor Dave Wallace Jr. has interviewed countless motorsports personalities—plus one singer-songwriter. Dave's byline has graced national publications ranging from the *New York Times* to this December 1980 special edition of *Hot Rod* magazine —Ed.

In our special issue [this] December [. . .] the subject is a '51 Ford owner whose background, except for one or two things, reads like a HOT ROD advertising salesman's computer print-out sheet describing the "average" subscriber.

Male, about 30 years old, once married, Illinois-raised, owner of four vehicles—only half of which are actually running at any given time—he works hard, makes just enough bread to get by, spends more than he should on his cars. His girlfriend drives a 327-powered, 4 speed '56 Chevy. His idea of dining out is a drive-in restaurant, plain cheeseburger and fries. Distracted by women, music and cars—not necessarily in that order—he spent an extra year in high school, graduating just in time to get drafted. He went to Germany as an Army mechanic, returned to a job with the Chicago Post Office, spent his Sundays at the drags. Shucks, as far as he's concerned, John Prine is just another gearhead from Maywood, Illinois, like the guy in his song "Automobile."

Prine's HOT ROD habit first came to the magazine's attention in 1979, during a jam-packed performance at North Hollywood's famous Palomino Club. "I *supported* HOT ROD Magazine for about eight years," he told the audience. "I used to buy two copies every month 'cause the first one always got greasy."

One Friday night about a year later, photographer Ron Hussey and I found ourselves just across a cheeseburger from this celebrity reader. *Storm Windows*, his eighth LP (Elektra/Asylum 6E-222) since he quit the Post Office in 1970, had just been released to rave reviews, and The John Prine Band was busy rocking L.A.'s Greek Theatre only 24 hours earlier, but tonight John Prine was talking hot rods. "When I was a kid, I had a buddy named Williard Lewis. He had a '55 Chevy, and one day we put his mother's best sheets out in the backyard, took the engine apart, laid it all out like HOT ROD does, and took pictures. We left it like that for two and a half months; we couldn't figure out how to put it back together again. It rained on it, the sheets got real muddy, and everything rusted, but we got these great shots of the motor."

He doesn't think much of most late-model cars, and in his own way, Prine is trying to help bring back the good old days in Detroit. "I've always had a private theory about music and cars, that the reason the older cars developed so much power was because of the music being played at the time. And the reason cars looked so good in other years was because the music was good—that's what gave the cars their lines, y'know? So I'm trying to make music to make the guys that design 'em start putting things on 'em again."

Like the rest of us, John's automotive passion is limited only by time and money—both of which are lately in short supply. A cracked block had recently sidelined his rare '51 Custom Club Coupe (his every day wheels since 1975), he'd just installed Abarth headers on his black '59 Porsche and replaced the clutch he fried doing his stereo sound effects for his *Pink Cadillac* album, and his equipment van needed insurance and a carburetor. All three awaited his personal attention following a nationwide 1980 concert tour—not to mention a tired old Cadillac in storage. "Yeah, I lent this guy 300 bucks to buy an electric guitar a couple of years back, and he never could come up with the money. But one day he drove up in this powder-blue '67 Caddy convertible, so I told him I'd just throw in another deuce and keep the car instead. Last time I seen it, there was two squirrels living in the back seat. It needs a new motor, but I ain't got the bread to do that with right now. Aw, man, when I get the bread I'm gonna have *20* cars!"

The cruising John sometimes sings about all began with a black-on-black '62 Grand Prix prepared for the northern Chicago street scene, which centered in the Sixties around a busy drive-in called Skip's Fiesta. One Sunday in '64, he took a shot at legal competition at Osewgo Dragway, resulting in possibly the shortest drag racing career on record. "I had this '60 Impala, 348, 4-barrel, 3-speed on the floor. I was working at the Post Office and going to the strip every Sunday, and I finally decided to run my 348. Now, I haven't got any speedometer, no tach; on the street I'd been shifting by ear. So my first run time in trials, a GTO pulls up next to me with headers wide-open, and I couldn't hear my engine. I wound that sucker out in the first and dropped the rear end! Four guys have to push me off the side, and all day long I'm watching the races and there's my car, sitting in the ditch by the starting line. I don't even know what the finish line looks like!"

As long as incurable car nuts like this guy and Bruce Springsteen, among others, keep making the music of our time, the hot rod's continued influence on American culture is assured. If his music keeps selling record albums, John Prine will have that '51 Ford back together in no time at all. And not far away will be one greasy copy of HOT ROD.

JOHN PRINE: HOW DO YOU LABEL HIM?

Robert Hilburn | 1982 | *Los Angeles Times*

By 1982, Prine had had it. The exploratory years of Asylum had seen the return-to-form *Bruised Orange* produced by his best friend Steve Goodman, the raw rock/rockabilly rave *Pink Cadillac* helmed by Knox and Jerry Phillips (with a little help from their father, Sun Records founder Sam Phillips), and the smoother roots/songwriter outing *Storm Windows* produced by Muscle Shoals vet Barry Beckett. But Prine was still without a deal. He was also out of a marriage—and largely out of Chicago, save for his parents and brothers.

While some artists might've been at wit's end, Prine seemed almost ebullient when the *Los Angeles Times*' Robert Hilburn arrived in Nashville for "the recent Country Music Assn. convention." Still Prine's staunchest defender, Hilburn penned a piece that takes the industry to task for allowing the songwriter's career to falter; impaling the business, Hilburn wrote, "When the record industry finds it impossible to effectively market his music, it is not just *his* problem. The whole industry needs to reflect on the situation."

Prine seemed far less concerned. Joking, naughty, offering "a subversive chuckle," their encounter at the sprawling Opryland Hotel finds Prine freer than he's felt in years, in a profile ostensibly to advance upcoming West Coast tour dates in Huntington Beach and San Diego.

Whether from seeing Steve Goodman making his own Red Pajamas Records work, in the face of a leukemia battle that made major labels leery of signing the hard-working folkie, or because of Prine's sheer exhaustion with record company marketing and promotion departments that didn't know what to do with his music, this freewheeling interview finds Prine planting the seeds of what would become one of America's first artist-with-options independent labels: Oh Boy Records.

Though he joked about a Christmas single for Oh Boy, the man that Hilburn says "contributed to a body of work as distinguished as any since Dylan's mid-'60s period" also noted his own musical restlessness. Knowing Hilburn's profile will be read by every West Coast record executive who claims to love songwriters, Prine spoke with a tone that gently chucked an industry that cared more about repeating what sells than feeding artists' souls.

"How Do You Label Him?" offers the sarcasm and candor that Prine employed with journalists he forged a meaningful trust with over time. It was a sacred bond. Not just a fan—though Hilburn was certainly that—here's a writer who saw the bigger picture Prine existed in and, like Prine, sought to understand how to make it work. —Ed.

NASHVILLE—John Prine looked as dishevelled as a man who spent all night on a park bench as he rummaged through his pockets to find a misplaced business card. He carries his tapes and notebooks in the large, open canvas bags you see in airport souvenir shops. Prine, an ex-mailman from Chicago, lives here now, but he spends a lot of time on the road because most of his income is from concerts. He swears he's going to open an office here next year and hire a secretary so he can get organized.

But first Prine, one of the most acclaimed non-sellers in pop music, wants to tackle a record industry that simply hasn't been able to adequately accommodate his talent. Failing to break through commercially after eight albums for two labels, Prine is in the embarrassing position of being without a record company now.

Prine, however, laughs off that stigma.

"It's funny how people act when they hear you haven't got a label," he said. "It's like there has been a death in the family or something. 'Oh, you're label-less, sorry . . .' Hell, I was label-less for the first 24 years of my life. I'm talking to some labels now, but I want to make sure. I want to make the right move.

"At one time, I thought the important thing was being on a label—whatever label. I went to Atlantic and Asylum with the highest expectations, but neither worked out. I'm not saying it was their fault. Maybe I moved in a different direction from what they expected. But I want to make sure that the next label I sign with is a service to me. All too often, artists end up servants to the company."

"The record business nearly screwed me up," said Prine, 35, as he sat in a room at the Oprland Hotel, here during the recent Country Music Assn. convention. "But I'm not going to let it get the best of me. I'm going to totally reverse my thinking—just like I did in the Army.

"I made it real tough on myself the first six months I was in the Army because I hated the discipline. Then I realized you could make it a lot easier by adopting the right attitude. When you had to salute, you just pretended you were saying, 'The hell with you.' You'd be amazed the difference it made."

It has taken Prine far longer than six months to deal with the wackiness of the record business, but he thinks he has finally learned how to "salute" that organization, too. Prine's main concern is finding the right label for his albums. But he's also planning to start his own "Oh Boy" Records for special singles and other projects. With "Oh Boy," he vows to wheel and deal with the biggest labels.

With a subversive chuckle, he outlined part of his strategy. "The next time they have one of these conventions here, I'm going to open up my booth. I'll buy some procaine, which is what people often use to cut cocaine with. It's legal and the disc jockeys that stop by the booth probably won't know the difference. It looks just like cocaine. I'll pour it out on a table and people'll go wild. I'll also hire a stripper to dance around and I'll hand out cigars. Meanwhile, I'll play my record and we'll see who causes the biggest sensation around here."

Lots of good writers have trouble selling records, so what's the big deal? Prine, who'll be at the Golden Bear in Huntington Beach tonight and at the Bacchanal Club in San Diego on Saturday, isn't just a *good* songwriter. He's possibly the best folk-country songwriter to emerge in America in the 1970s and when the record industry finds it impossible to effectively market his music, it is not just *his* problem. The whole industry needs to reflect on the situation.

Few pop artists have attracted as much critical acclaim with a debut as Prine. The Village Voice's Jack Newfield compared hearing Prine's music in 1971 to seeing Willie Mays catch a fly ball for the first time. Lots of people compared the young writer to Bob Dylan. Both drew on folk and country influences and touched deeply with their words.

The special quality in Prine's writing is his ability to comment so eloquently on those who are frequently described as "ordinary people," those who are neither hero nor anti-hero.

"Hello in There," a Prine song popularized by Bette Midler, speaks of the way we tend to sidestep old people, perhaps not wanting to face our own future. The song mixes a poetic grace with the conscience of a public service announcement: *"Ya know that old trees grow stronger/And rivers just grow wilder every day/ Old people just grow lonesome/Waiting for someone to say/Hello in there, hello . . ."*

In other songs, Prine exhibits humor, heart and insight as he dealt with such feelings as disillusionment, integrity, despair, loneliness, neglect. Prine cultists quote his lyrics the way baseball trivia fans swap prized information.

Despite its excellence, Prine's debut album was ignored by radio stations, thus losing all chance for commercial success. Pop stations called Prine's style too country, while country stations argued it was too pop. Both shuddered at the ragged vocals.

Rather than tone down his music to fit more easily into a pop or country style, Prine continued to pursue his creative instincts. His second and third LPs weren't as consistent as the first, but the highlights contributed to a body of work as distinguished as any since Dylan's mid-'60s period.

Prine added to his commercial difficulties in 1975's "Common Sense" by introducing hard-rock elements which confused his early folk followers. He left Atlantic Records after that album did poorly and dropped out of the record business for two years.

After regaining his enthusiasm for songwriting in Nashville, Prine signed with Asylum Records in 1978 and recorded *Bruised Orange*. The LP mixed a bright instrumental texture with his most accessible batch of songs since his debut album and it proved to be a good seller: nearly 100,000 copies.

But Prine returned to a searing brand of rock in *Pink Cadillac* and sales dropped sharply. The lost momentum wasn't regained by last year's softer *Storm Windows* and Asylum refused to pick up Prine's option. Rather than try immediately for another contract, Prine decided to make an album and shop it around. He hopes to have the LP finished early next year. He's also working on a play involving many of the characters from his songs. It could be ready by next summer.

"I want the freedom to be able to move in whatever direction I want and know that the company I'm working with will be behind me. If you don't have a hit single right away, labels tend to give up on your album and start asking, 'When are you going to give us the next album?'

"Well, it may have taken a year to make that album and I'm not ready to give up on it. But there's nothing you can do. That can be real disheartening. I'm going to make sure the next company knows exactly what they're getting before we sign the contract."

Meanwhile, Prine enjoys being part of the music community here.

"There's a lot of energy and writers to work with here," he said. "Nashville is also real compact. Everyone has an office on Music Row. You can go door to door and visit all the publishers and record companies."

Added a joking Prine, "I was even thinking about becoming a mailman again so that I could pitch my songs every morning. I'd go from office to office, saying, 'Here's your electric bill and here's one of my new songs.' I could be the local character: 'John Prine, the singing mailman.' I'd probably make the 10 o'clock news."

Though Prine wants to place his own album with a major label early next year, he's serious about starting Oh Boy Records. He'd use it for both his own special projects and for other Nashville artists. He hopes to have a limited edition of "I Saw Mommy Kissing Santa Claus" out soon.

And, he's planning to give it a novel push.

"A friend of mine bought about 650 Christmas trees, so we're going to open a lot on the corner," Prine said. "We'll pipe 'I Saw Mommy' on a loudspeaker and offer everyone who buys a tree a free record or everybody who buys a record a free tree. That might make the news, too."

Beneath the humor, Prine is serious about making the record business work for him—a determination growing out of 10 years of frustration.

"All the attention on the first album was great in one way, but it was also tough," he said. "I felt like people expected me to do more—be more—than just what I wanted to do, which was keep writing songs. I started to feel guilty when things didn't happen faster, as if I were letting someone down."

He also acknowledged that his changes of style may have hurt his commercial momentum, but he still defends the shifts.

"When I got to the point one type of song became too easy, I wanted to try something else," he continued. "After 'Billy the Bum,' for instance, I knew I didn't want to write any more story songs, evn though people kept asking, 'Hey, John, why don't you write any more of those story songs?'

"There was no challenge left in that. That's the same reason I didn't want to write any more songs about old people or any more songs about drug addicts. I wrote them once. It might have made more sense to do it, but I wanted to keep my music alive. That was always my biggest goal and I've feel I've done that. When it came to sales, I figured I'd just have to wait until it was my time. I'm a patient man."

PART IV

"I *AM* a Record Company" b/w Welcome to Nashville City Limits

JOHN PRINE ON *BOBBY BARE AND FRIENDS*

Bobby Bare | March 28, 1985 | The Nashville Network (TNN)

Bobby Bare was an outlier outlaw from almost the beginning. A songwriter's writer, like Tom T. Hall, he knew what good is—and he'd made enough of a mark that *Rolling Stone*'s Chet Flippo had covered him in the counterculture tabloid.

A future Country Music Hall of Famer, Bare embraced writers Billy Joe Shaver ("Georgia on a Fast Train," "Old Five and Dimers Like Me"), Shel Silverstein ("Marie LaVeau," "Daddy What If"), Tom T. Hall ("(Margie's at) The Lincoln Park Inn"), and Mel Tillis ("Detroit City"), as well as penning "500 Miles Away from Home," "Jesus Christ, What a Man," and "Motel Time Again."

Affable, rugged, and a good talker, Bare was soon staked in a cable talk show. Loose, built around the notion of how pickers and songwriters hang out when nobody is around, Bare's recipe of being in a recording studio as often as a television studio helped.

Given Bare's Chicago connections, it was inevitable he and Prine would end up together.

Prine had been making his presence felt in greater and greater ways since falling in with Jack Clement in the summer of 1977. No stranger to Memphis or Muscle Shoals, Prine found Music City a place where the creative community came together much the same way it did around the clubs and neighborhoods of Chicago.

One of Prine's good friends was British expat Roger Cook, who wrote both the Hollies' "Long Cool Woman in a Black Dress" and the ubiquitous "I'd Like to Teach the World to Sing (in Perfect Harmony)." Sharing a dry sense of humor and love of adventure, the pair teamed for Don Williams's number-one country hit "Love Is on a Roll."

Like Tom Sawyer looking for a fence to paint, Prine did a walk-on cameo when Cook and Clement appeared on *Bobby Bare and Friends* in April 1989. With Prine dressed in a rugby shirt and a hat resembling Williams's signature cowboy hat, the trio's easy-going camaraderie was on display.

Whether that led to Prine's invitation to appear again in episode seventeen of season three isn't clear. What *is* clear is Bare's deep respect for Prine's craft and emotional clarity. Bare not only untangled Prine's roots—including his days playing opposite the Second City theater, where John Belushi and Bill Murray would come listen between shows—but also dove into how songs are born and can escape unwritten, celebrated some of the chestnuts in Prine's catalogue, and got his two guests discussing the crazy glue that bonds friendships on the road.

With Oh Boy in its nascent stages, Bare would be the last to think seceding from the major-label shuffle was a bad idea. While some Nashvillians spoke of Prine's gifts with utter reverence but rolled their eyes at his eschewing the major label system, Prine exulting in simply hanging with his peers defines this appearance, more than any of the label gossip. –Ed.

Bobby Bare: My friends, tonight are probably two of the most legendary cult folk heroes alive today. I'm talking about the great John Prine and Ramblin' Jack Elliott. They're individuals. They live their life and they sing their songs the way *they* feel it.

John Prine may not have had one of those big commercial success records, but he's been heralded by music critics the world over as a brilliant talent who crafts songs as detailed as a finely stitched garment, a man whose songs use the social commentary and humor of a Woody Guthrie and the emotional purity of a Hank Williams. . . .

I've asked John Prine to kick us off with a song that's one of my favorite John Prine songs, that's gonna give us a little insight into his philosophy on life: "Spanish Pipedreams."

Take it John. [*Prine Plays.*]

Don't go away, cause we're gonna meet John Prine in just a minute. [*Back to music, song ends cold.*]

Bare: John. Prine. *The* John Prine. John Prine . . .

John Prine: [*Tight shot of a big smile*] I gotta cousin in Bowling Green. His name's John Prine, too.

Bare: Oh, maybe we got the wrong one!

Prine: [*Laughing*] You might have . . .

Bare: Nah, we got the right one. When you wrote "Spanish Pipedream," where did that come from? Why didn't you call it "American Pipedreams"?

Prine: Ah, well, it was . . . It's about blowing up your TV, you know? Going out and living in the sticks. It's like a romantic idea, and I always thought Spanish stuff was kind of romantic. So I called it "Spanish," but I should've just called it "Blow Up Your TV" cause that's the words everybody . . .

Bare: Yeah, that's what everyone calls it anyway: "Blow Up Your TV."

Prine: I know. I was telling the guys in the band, I'm just gonna stop naming songs, and wait til somebody goes, "Hey, sing that song about blowing up your TV," or something. Then name it then. And if they don't ask for it, I won't cut it. [*Laughs.*]

Bare: You're probably the biggest cult figure in America. How's that feel?

Prine: That word always bothered me.

Bare: Always bothers me, too.

Prine: I feel like I was in [*cigarette smoke escapes from his mouth*] Jonestown, or something. That's what a cult is to me: where people dance around in voodoo stuff and shake things. Course I've played in places like that, too, but I know what they mean.

I've had people explain it to me over and over and over again, like it's "a cult." Does that mean you're supposed to have a devout but small following? [*Laughs.*] Y'know?

Bare: Well, you have a fanatic following . . .

Prine: Oh, they're great. Boy, they're great. They stick with me throughout the years. It's really nice.

Bare: I'm one of 'em. [*Prine nods.*] I'm . . . one . . . of 'em.

Your songs always have lyrics that have a message in 'em that have tremendous impact. I've never really heard a John Prine song that I didn't say, "*Wow* . . ." So many of 'em: "Sam Stone."

Prine: Yeah, I wrote that one as a mailman. I was a mailman for six years up in Chicago, delivering the mail. After you learn the route and get to know most of the dogs, there really isn't much to think about out there; you're just sticking these letters in the slot. So it was kind of like spending eight hours a day in the library without any books. I'd just be making up songs on the route.

I wrote that one. I remember writing that one on the mail route. I couldn't wait to get home that day to get the guitar out and see if it actually worked on a guitar.

Bare: Sing it, sing part of it.

[*Prine sings and plays; Bare looks on appreciatively, almost lost in the details of the first verse.*]

Prine: It's kind of a lullabye, too.

Bare: Did you actually know a "Sam Stone"?

Prine: A mess of 'em, pretty much. Me and about six of my buddies all got drafted about the same time. January of '66. That was about the time they went from about 20,000 troops in Viet Nam to 500,000, you know? And they said, "It was still a conflict." We were just over there protecting things . . . half a million troops? They sent a bunch of us to Viet Nam; they sent me to Germany, and one of the other guys went to Germany, some of them they kept in the States. But when we all got out a couple years later, everybody had changed quite a bit.

It was the end of '67, beginning of '68. I couldn't quite piece it together, what was so different about it. Whether it was just being away, growing up or something. A lot of the guys had been in Nam . . . had a buddy from Germany, when he got out, I called the house and he was in the veterans' hospital, having shock treatments. You know, he just went bananas.

I knew when I saw all his shoes pointing in the same way under his bed, that he wasn't really out of the Army. Had his hangers all hanging the right way, and I said, "Oh, *oh*, he's in trouble . . . If somebody blew 'Reveille' right now, he'd run right out the window."

A couple of the other guys just had drug problems and stuff. But I believe everybody had a brother or a husband or a son that didn't come back at all. A lot of the ones who came home, it seemed like they didn't come back. It seems like they're still not home.

And there weren't no parades, or nothing. I'm 38 now. But all of us kinda grew up on Audie Murphy movies. After I saw "To Hell and Back," I passed an Oldsmobile car lot on the way home, and I jumped up on the hood, and I shot everybody out on the street.

But when our war came along, they want to be ashamed of it. We ain't got no parades or nothing, so it was kind of weird. I wrote that song to kind of explain it to myself. You know, what the feeling was.

Bare: Well, you did a good job on it. We're gonna take a little break. When we come back, we're gonna hear you sing a little bit about Muhlenberg County.

Prine: Well, alright.

Bare: So, don't go away.

[*Prine starts "Paradise" alone at a mic. The band is there and shown as the song rolls out. The fiddle turns up the bluegrass Appalachian aspect of the song.*]

Bare: [*Seated on a couch, studio lounge*] "Paradise"! Muhlenberg County. I *love* that song, John! Come here. [*Prine sets down.*] You're from there . . .

Prine: My mother and father come from there. My brothers and I were all raised up near Chicago. Maywood, Illinois. But we used to return to Muhlenberg County a lot when I was a kid. Cause it's a neat place, a Walt Disney kinda place. Like "Song of the South."

Bare: How'd you get started in Chicago? I know you played a lot around the Earl of Old Town. I used to hang out there myself.

Prine: [*Fishing something out of his coat pocket*] I've been writing since I was about fourteen, but I never thought about doing it for a living. As far as I got with that was standing in front of the mirror, trying to curl my lip and look in the mirror and see how I should hold a guitar. You know? I learned how to smoke that way [*puts a cigarette in his mouth*], too.

Bare: Did you learn how to light 'em?

Prine: Yeah, yeah. [*Searching in pockets*] I used to have matches in those days. Here's some. [*Bare laughs as Prine reaches for a pack of matches beside the couch.*]

But I was playing around with writing for six, seven years. [*Strikes match.*] One day, I found myself down at a place called the Fifth Peg down on Armitage Avenue. It was across the street from the Old Town School of Folk Music. [*Lights cigarette.*] I was watching an amateur thing, and people were getting up; they were pretty bad, you know? [*Laughs.*]. I'd had a couple of beers too many, and I said so. Loudly.

Some guy at another table said, "Well, why don't you get up?"

And I said, "Well, of course."

I got up and sang, "Muhlenberg County," "Hello in There" and "Sam Stone." They asked if I wanted a job as a singer. So I had to run home and write six more songs just to fill up forty minutes. At that time, I wrote another six songs, that ended up on my first record, in about two weeks.

Bare: When did you first meet Steve Goodman?

Prine: I met Steve after I started playing at the Fifth Peg. Steve come over to check me out. Everybody was coming over to check me out.

Bare: It's just a small area up there in Old Town where the clubs were.

Prine: Yeah, and a lot of 'em hung out at the Earl of Old Town. Goodman would play over there all the time. Right across the street was Second City; John Belushi was over there at the time.

He used to come around, to the Earl of Old Town when they had breaks at Second City. Belushi would come across the street. When we had breaks, we'd go watch Second City.

Bare: Did you get to know Belushi pretty well?

Prine: Belushi used to do Marlon Brando singing my songs. That was a thing. He'd jump up onstage at the Earl, doing "Angel." [*Prine starts extending his arms, embodying Belushi as Brando, saying*] Make me an annnngel, that flies . . . from Montgomery."

He was . . . I always really liked John a whole, whole lot. He got me on "Saturday Night Live" later on. Much later when somebody cancelled out, they called me last minute. He got me on there.

But I met Goodman at the Earl of Old Town. I'd heard his song on the radio, "City of New Orleans" 'cause he didn't have a record out, but there was one station that would play tapes, tapes of new songs. I figured I *knew* what Steve Goodman looked like from listening to his voice. You know how you kind of get a picture?

I thought he was this tall, skinny guy with a college haircut and a long drawnout face with maybe a little goatee or something. And this little guy comes in with these big fat cheeks. He comes up to me; shakes my hand and introduces himself as "Steve Goodman."

I think from that minute on, we were just buddies. We did it *all* together. We conquered the musical world in New York. We got record contracts within the first twenty-four hours we hit New York. It was all like a Lana Turner kind of story.

Bare: We *all* loved Steve Goodman. I used to go up to Chicago and play the Quiet Knight, and Steve Goodman . . . I think my last show would end up about midnight and Steve would be at the Earl. So I'd finish my show and go with Steve to the Earl, drink beer and pick until our nose bled. Good people.

Prine: He had a five o'clock license.

Bare: I used it, too. [*Big smile.*] You wound up recording on Steve's record label, Red Pajamas.

Prine: Nah, Steve had his own label. He did his own records on Red Pajamas. And he started selling them. I had been thinking about starting a label, but Steve went ahead and did it. He actually sold records! Started selling 'em at the gigs, like people would buy 'em.

Or if there were record reviewers, the writers would put the PO Box—and people would send in for them. It was starting to work out real good. Steve made three albums on Red Pajamas.

There's gonna be another album coming out on Red Pajamas. There was a tribute in Chicago to Steve Goodman with Arlo Guthrie and Bonnie

Raitt, Jethro Burns and a whole bunch of good people who all one way or another had crossed paths with Stevie. It come out real good. They recorded the whole thing. It's coming out on his label, Red Pajamas.

Bare: Then you finally put your thing together with Oh Boy Records. How'd that get started?

Prine: Well, I was kind of kidding around, telling my wife, who was my girlfriend then, I'd kind of like to have my own record company, and call it "Oh Boy."

She said, "Why?"

I said, "Because when things are going real good, I could just go, 'Oh *boy*. Oh-boy-oh-boy,, whatta year we've had. . . .," [*Rears back, smiling.*] And when things aren't so good, you can go [*drops voice*] 'Oh, boy . . .'" I just kinda wanted to do it, so I made a red vinyl Christmas single of me singing "I Saw Mommy Kissing Santa Claus," and me and Rachel, my wife, singing my version of "Silver Bells," which sounds more like Jerry Lee [Lewis]. Just a different version of it. We put it on red vinyl, so if somebody didn't like my singing, they could sit and look at the Christmas tree [*holds the record up like a viewing prism*] through the red vinyl. [*Laughing harder.*] And that's how we kicked off the record company . . .

Bare: I'll tell you what: any time a John Prine record comes out, that's an event. All of the major record companies, they have no idea what to do with a creative person like you. But you have a new album that's out now. And I've got a copy of it right here. It's called *Aimless Love*.

Prine: Yeah, *Aimless Love*.

Bare: [*Surveying the front cover*] You look neat there, John.

Prine: I know. You know my hair's never looked like that! It got like that all of a sudden, and [McGuire] snapped that. Then it got messy again.

Bare: You're kiddin' me.

Prine: Nope. [*Both laugh.*]

Bare: Tell you what: you can't get this record, not anywhere at all. Except from John Prine.

Prine: There is no middleman, no swarthy little character in Cleveland, who gets the money from the people who want the music—and then he takes most of it and twirls his moustache [*twists the corner of his moustache and shakes his hand as if throwing dice*], then sends me twelve cents.

I'm giving the records right to the people. They give me the money. If I can save enough money, I'll make another record. Or I might buy a little red boat, and send 'em pictures of me in my boat and say, "Thanks."

Bare: I'll tell you what. I'll make it easy! If anybody wants this record, write to me at the Nashville Network—and I'll make sure you get the record. And I'll keep part of it, for touring.

Prine: I'll be checking your mailbox.

Bare: Have you ever toured with Rambling Jack Elliott? I know you have.

Prine: Yeah, I sure have. When I was learning how to play guitar, fourteen and fifteen, my older brother Dave taught me how to play guitar. He'd given me a couple Ramblin' Jack records—and I just really dug the way he sang. Then, matter of fact, I can remember him mentioning . . . "Blowin' in the Wind" was out by Peter, Paul, and Mary . . . My brother said, "You know that song 'Blowing in the Wind'? The guy who wrote that sounds a lot like Ramblin' Jack, so you oughta go pick up his album." That's how I got my first Bob Dylan album; figured anyone who sounds like Ramblin' Jack, I wanna hear 'em.

Bare: Tell you what: anyone named Ramblin' Jack! They only made one of him. Then threw the whole mold away.

Prine: People aren't sure why they call him Ramblin' Jack. He is well-travelled, but that's not the reason they call him that.

Bare: Well, why do they call him that?

Prine: I don't believe I've ever heard him finish a story.

Bare: [*Laughing*] He just rambles on.

Prine: Yeah. When he gets to the end, it sounds beautiful, and I remember everything. But I don't quite know why.

Bare: John, when you were out on tour, did you write any songs?

Prine: Nah, I can't . . . I don't write too much on the road. I might get some ideas, or sometimes if someone wants to sit up all night and write up a song. Steve Goodman and I have done that several times. Wrote real late at night out on the road. But I have come off the road with a lot of airport stationary full of ideas and other things. Sometimes, I lose 'em, but I like to read 'em years later. I get a kick out of 'em.

Bare: Where do you write best at?

Prine: I don't know. I'd move there if I knew where. [*Laughs awkwardly, shakes head.*]

Seems like the morning is the best time to write. Just get up and grab your guitar, play. It seems like everything is fresh, like they've been up there [*touches his temple*] cooking all night. Something, the first thing that comes off the top of your head in the morning, might be a song.

Bare: How would you describe your style of writing?

Prine: Well, I think I write the way that I do because of a vitamin deficiency. I don't eat any vegetables. I just eat meat and potatoes. I think I'm trying to make up for in my writing what I lack in vitamins. Cause some of the songs are pretty weird.

Some of the songs, I don't tell people about right away 'cause I don't know what they're gonna think about them.

I've heard other songwriters say sometimes a song just comes to you, and if you don't write it down, it's just gonna go on down the street—and somebody else is going to write that same song. They travel around like that.

Some of these songs, I don't know whether to let 'em go, keep on going down the street or not. I wrote this one song, called "Sabu Visits the Twin Cities Alone." I stayed in my room for about three days 'cause I thought the song police were going to come after me, or something. But it turned out to be a pretty good song anyways.

JOHN PRINE STARTS FROM "ZERO" AGAIN

Dave Hoekstra | July 20, 1986 | *Chicago Sun-Times*

They say you can't go home again, so when Dave Hoekstra talked to John Prine for his new gig at the *Chicago Sun-Times,* he went to Nashville to check out the songwriter's new life. Having just released *German Afternoons*, his second album on his own label, Prine had a genuine tenderness towards his former hometown.

With seven major label albums, the freedom of his own record company suited him. And while the numbers were humble, the profits were all his. By keeping things country and acoustic, the overhead was reasonable—and his influences were on full display.

Given Hoekstra's hometown bona fides, the conversation went in myriad directions. Exploring a long-rumored screenplay based on characters from his debut, Prine brought a sense of whimsy to the prospects; he also shared an idea for a second screenplay that opened up a side of Prine forged hanging out with Second City comics John Belushi and Bill Murray.

Sharing lessons he learned from Steve Goodman, Prine was generous with accrued wisdom. He was quick to acknowledge his friend's gift as not just a producer but also a man who serves songs instead of records.

Nothing was as animated as Prine on his cars. Tooling around Nashville in a red Corvette, the pair talked about what really mattered: automotive priorities. For John Prine, yet to win a Grammy, cars offered similar freedom and exhilaration to those promised by major acclaim in the music industry.

For the readers back home, the story offered a few polaroids of Prine's state of mind as the dust of leaving Chicago, the majors, and everything he knew settled. —Ed.

83

NASHVILLE: Blue has turned to gold in the rearview mirror of John Prine's new Corvette.

"Maybe because it's been 15 years now, but the questions I got asked all the time about how me and Steve Goodman got started—it seems in the last couple of years they've become a bit more special than they seemed to be," Prine says after a thoughtful pause toward the end of an interview under the poolside veranda of the Sheraton Music City Hotel. "Now it seems like another time—back a ways—and real special. It's funny. You work real hard and then getting out (of Chicago) wasn't like getting out of a little town, it was just calling for a different music scene.

"All the things that went down the first four or five years seem real special to me now," Prine says. "It's almost like they're painted a special color when I think back at them. It's more than a pleasant memory—it's just real nice. Sometimes things have to change and move along before you can put them in some kind of proper perspective. Once something is done, you can't change it, so I'm glad it's a real pleasant memory rather than not."

The 38-year-old Prine is reminiscing while sharing a dozen chicken wings with me and Angie Varias, his drummer for the *Pink Cadillac* and *Storm Windows* albums. Kicking back in blue jeans, a black untucked T-shirt and bare feet, John Prine is content. Laced with soothing Nashville bluegrass persuasions, his just-released *German Afternoons* album is a heralded return to the traditional country-influenced tones of Prine's first three records. And by looking back, he's looking ahead toward an "Our Town"-salted screenplay derived from "John Prine," his 1971 landmark debut album.

"I'm thinking about writing a screenplay, and writing it is the hardest part," Prine says with a laugh. "There's enough people interested that if I were to write something, they could get everything in motion. It's something I could do because I'm off until Labor Day. I've been asked about this (screenplay) since 1976, which would mainly be about the characters of the songs from my first album. The whole idea surrounding it is they all wind up at Thanksgiving dinner together. I'd take one simple figure like Sam Stone, who ODs within the first two minutes and he walks up a ladder and sits on a plank and become the narrator.

"We got close to getting something down in '76, but the songs got in my way," Prine says. "I was still too close to the songs and it felt real weird. It got to the point where I was going to call (song characters) Donald and Lydia on the phone and talk to them. They were real nice, they served their purpose, and that was it. The further I get away from it, I can look at it a bit better. I thought, 'If nothing else, I'd sit down and try to write a couple of pages on each character,' go into a bit more description and then maybe I won't identify them so much with the songs."

Such a screenplay would not only incorporate Sam Stone and Donald and Lydia, but other Prine creations, such as the ill-fated James Lewis (from "Six O'Clock News"), the Angel from Montgomery, Loretta and Rudy from "Hello in There" and Prine's own western Kentucky roots in "Paradise." (Prine's grandfather on his mother's side was John Luther Hamm, a Kentucky guitar-as-banjo picker in the style of Merle Travis.)

"Then I've got a second idea for a screenplay called 'The Perfect Joke,'" Prine says. "It's about four guys in a cell—you know the old wives' tale that the best dirty jokes come from convicts. They've got nothing better to do so they write jokes—it's almost like 'The Dick Van Dyke Show.' These guys pace up and down in the cell and they try and write the perfect joke.

"On visiting day, one guy tells his wife the joke, his wife tells her boyfriend and by the time one of the guys gets out, he gets in a cab and the cab driver tells the guy the joke, but he screws it all up. The guy kills the cab driver and goes back to jail."

After the independently released *German Afternoons* and *Aimless Love*, Prine has exhausted his ideas for songs.

"I'm on zero for writing right now," he says. "All the stuff I've back-logged and the things I've written the last two years is all on records, except for three rock 'n' roll songs (that may appear on an upcoming EP). I've got nothin' half-done. It's a perfect place to be. I like to be at zero."

German Afternoons is a deeply poetic effort moving from the delightfully offbeat "Linda Goes to Mars" (derived from a tune Granddaddy Hamm sang called "Where Has Nancy Gone?") about a spaced-out spouse to the beautiful "I Just Want to Dance with You" balanced with a gentle Tex-Mex samba.

"*German Afternoons* has been out two weeks and we shipped 10,000 the first day," he says. "It's up to 17,000 already. The independent thing (his Oh Boy! Records) is working out pretty darn good. I couldn't imagine dealing with any majors—unless on my own I made a real pop-sounding record.

"I think the majors stifle a lot more artists than just me," Prine continues. "Although I can't say that much bad about them because they gave me a free swing to do anything I wanted to do. And I did.

"But just say I was still with a major right now," Prine postulates. "I could see 'em, watching someone come up every couple of years. They'd see Ricky Skaggs selling records (contemporary bluegrass), so they'd say, 'Let's go that way.' Then they see Dwight Yoakam come on with something ('cowpunk') that nobody could get past the door with, and now they're talking kids into doing that type of music.

"They put you on somebody's coattails, and that ain't what I do. As long as I can keep above water with what I do, I don't have to worry about what year it is or who is doing what. And I'm doing all of this without radio."

Prine has always carried an independent creative streak. After 1978's intelligent, blue-collared *Bruised Orange*, considered the finest record of his career, Prine's sequel was a lovingly sloppy rockabilly-tinged *Pink Cadillac*, somewhat produced by Sun Records legend Sam Philips and his sons, Knox and Jerry, in Memphis, Tenn.

"Musicwise, I was already wanting to do an album like *Pink Cadillac* while we were doing *Bruised Orange*," Prine says. "But (producer Steve) Goodman saw the songs for *Bruised Orange* were what they were and should be recorded thusly. That's why we had a bunch of arguments cutting *Bruised Orange*. I was into another place musically, but he was just trying to service the songs, which was a real important lesson to me. That's what I do all the time now.

"I'll take a song and if I'm confused about it when I get to recording, I'll refer back to a tape of when I first wrote it," Prine says. "It's real easy to get away from a song, so you have to service it. Otherwise, nobody will ever hear how it was in the original state. Ever since Goodman showed me that, I've been trying to follow along and record the song for what it is.

A proper example is one of the staples of Prine's recent tour, a new song called "Let's Talk Dirty in Hawaiian."

"I wrote that two weeks after we finished *German Afternoons*, so I couldn't put it on the record, but it's been stealing the whole show. I made up Hawaiian words so they sound like dirty words in Hawaiian. Like, 'Lay your coconut on my tiki' or 'What the heck a mooka-mooka dear.' It's like a Hawaiian Shriner's song, and people are going nuts over this stuff. So I'm going to put it on a single and include it with *German Afternoons*. I'll put it on green vinyl with palm trees on it."

Prine has been receiving hearty inside endorsements from Bob Dylan, who said *Aimless Love* was one of his favorite records in a long time. "Yeah, I heard from Tom Petty's bass player that Dylan was listening to the record all through his Australian tour."

How does Prine feel about all the Dylan comparisons at the outset of his career?

"I thought it got to be a little too much—it finally got in the way, especially for people who had never listened to me, and who were trying to make up their mind," Prine says. "Other than, that I got tired of reading it."

Not as tiring is the matter of Prine's little red Corvette.

"I finally sold the '59 Porsche that I used on the cover of 'Sweet Revenge,' which was the only album cover I ever took in Chicago," Prine says. "It was shot down by the gun club on Lake Shore Drive. I only used it two months of the year—it was in the shop more than I had it. This kid down the block kept making me offers on it.

"I bought a used '73 ski-boat last summer and we've used it a lot, so I thought I'd sell the Porsche and get a little bit bigger boat. So I did it. But I've still got my four-door Cadillac that doesn't go fast enough. I go down to the Cadillac dealer to ask about a front-wheel drive to make it go faster, and just then the owner of the dealership pulls out of the garage with this '86 red 'Vette with a smoked glass top.

"I didn't even recognize it was a 'Vette, but it was his car and they said any car he had was for sale," Prine says. "It had like 300 miles on it. They give me the keys, I take it for a half-hour, I come back and say, 'I don't care what you gotta do, but figure out a way you can present this to my accountant. If I tell anybody, they're going to have a stroke.' And man, those cars are fun. It's fun to go get that quart of milk that you forgot—especially if you got a radar detector.

"And I've still got my red '51 Fordomatic—I'm not going to get rid of that or my old '76 BMW," Prine says. With a laugh, he adds, "Now we've got four cars and none to pull a boat with. I may have to buy a pickup truck to pull the boat."

Prine pauses, and says, "Aw, it's not like the old days when, after a car would run down on me, I'd just talk to (Chicago folkie) Fred Holstein."

Aw, but the old days are smiling in the rearview mirror.

JOHN PRINE TURNS MEAT AND POTATOES INTO MUSIC

Bob Millard | 1985 | *Country Song Roundup*

Country Song Roundup was the oldest country music fan magazine extant when Bob Millard went to Prine's house to talk about starting a label, life in Nashville, doing it his way—and how a grown man from Chicago cooks this supper. It was the only time the songwriter spoke to the magazine, confirmed for his book by then editor Rick Bolsom, who stewarded the magazine until its ultimate shuttering when its parent company went out of business.

Bob Millard, the *Variety* correspondent in Nashville, was a big deal. He would ultimately write or contribute to *The Judds*, *Amy Grant: The Life of a Pop Star*, *Music City, USA: The Country Music Lover's Travel Guide to Nashville and Tennessee*, *Country Music: 70 Years of America's Favorite Music*, and *What's What in Country Music*. Having spent time as the pop music critic at the *Dallas Times Herald* and contributor to the more intellectual *Country Music*, he was positioned to understand the realities of a major-label artist striking out on his own, Prine's place in the music scene emerging after the outlaw country of visionaries like Waylon Jennings, Willie Nelson, Kris Kristofferson, and Johnny Cash, and how Prine's friends helped define that place.

Cozy, relaxed, honest—you can almost smell the gravy. With Millard's practiced critic's pen, he manages to draw in the true country music fans who'd just started hearing Prine's songs through Don Williams's number-one "Love Is on a Roll" and what many believed a traditional bluegrass standard, "Paradise," recorded by the Nitty Gritty Dirt Band *and* Johnny Cash, who also cut "Sam Stone" and "Unwed Fathers" during this time.

"Unwed Fathers"—cowritten with the legendary Bobby Braddock, who'd penned "He Stopped Loving Her Today," considered by many the greatest country song ever written, as well as "Golden Ring," "(We're Not) The Jet Set," "Would You Catch a Falling Star," and "D-I-V-O-R-C-E"—also connected. First recorded by Tammy Wynette; then Gail Davies, one of Nashville's few women producers; then Johnny Cash, the track—matched with Don Williams's number one—established Prine's place in actual country music. *Country Song Roundup* further ratified his place in a genre that meant so much to his parents. —Ed.

Five years since his last LP, singer/songwriter John Prine has a new album out, his ninth, called *Aimless Love*. It's on his own brand new label, Oh Boy! Records, and it is probably his most country-sounding offering to date. Prine has been writing and touring throughout his albumless '80s, so *Aimless Love* is something of a "greatest unrecorded hits" collection, since the songs will be familiar to those who've seen him perform during this past half-decade. The album offers Prine's version of "Unwed Fathers" and "Only Love," which have garnered between them cuts by Tammy Wynette, Gail Davies, Johnny Cash with Willie Nelson and Don Williams. Also included are "Maureen, Maureen," "Bottomless Lake," "Oldest Baby in the World," "Be My Friend Tonight" and other classics of Prine-iac irony, good humor, and skewed but fondly sympathetic observation of the condition of the average Joe.

"Seems like everybody leads off their stories that John Prine has been reduced to putting out records on his own custom label because the biggies dropped him," said Prine somewhat peeved. "It's not like that. The majors can really help you if you got a hit single to promote, but that's not what this is. We're doin' it this way, and we're learning as we go. We like to say that we aren't making mistakes; We're just learning something new all the time."

CSR caught up with Prine in his kitchen, whose walls and refrigerator door are covered with newspaper clippings, Christmas cards, post cards, scribbled phone numbers, and color snapshots of cats, friends, and John with his cats and friends. In addition to the ordinary clutter, Prine's kitchen is graced by a coveted ASCAP Award for "Love Is on a Roll," which he co-wrote with Roger Cook.

"I got (the ASCAP Award) hung in my kitchen, facing my refrigerator," Prine explained, with a characteristic trace of amusement in his voice. "It's hanging there to remind me that it brought home the bacon that year. It was a slim year for bookings, and that money came in handy."

Despite Prine's semi-image as a drinker, we sipped ginger ale and colas from ice-filled plastic glasses as we talked and he cooked a pot roast and potatoes dinner. If he likes a reporter, Prine can be very warm and open. Otherwise, he's still fairly open, but you don't get dinner.

Short, dark-haired and mustachioed, Prine has dark, sparkling eyes. Laugh lines with crow's feet mark his face with the signs of one who, despite the tragedies of his father's death at the beginning of his career and the recent passing of longtime close friend, songwriter Steve Goodman, maintains an upbeat view of the world. He is one of the best-loved country-rock-folk cult heroes of the past 15 years, having been likened to "Bob Dylan with a sense of humor," though he doesn't really like the comparison. Though Dylan is a friend and admirer, Prine likens his own voice to more traditional country artists.

"I always figure that if Bill Monroe didn't know how to play quite so good and would sing a little off-key, we might sound a little more like each other," he explained.

Even those who've missed the pleasure of hearing him on concert or on his own records for Atlantic and Asylum have undoubtedly heard many John Prine tunes on both country and pop radio and didn't know it. His songs have been recorded by a bevy of top artists including Johnny Cash, Tammy Wynette, Gail Davies, David Allen Coe, Don Williams, Jim & Jesse, John Denver, Lynn Anderson, Jackie DeShannon, John Cougar, Bette Midler, Bonnie Raitt. Cash, DeShannon, Denver, Anderson and Jim & Jesse cut *Paradise,* his tribute to strip-mined Muhlenberg County, Kentucky. Lynn Anderson's version was a country hit, but Jim & Jesse's bluegrass arrangement has spawned dozens of small-label bluegrass cuts of the song that made a villain of the Peabody Coal train.

Bonnie Raitt made a hit of the poetic "Angel from Montgomery." Gail Davies cut "Unwed Fathers" on her last RCA album; Tammy Wynette charted that same song as a single last year; and now Johnny Cash and Willie Nelson have cut it as a duet. Coe titled album *Hello in There* after one of Prine's tunes, and he had an early hit with the Steve Goodman/ John Prine lampoon "You Never Even Call Me by My Name."

Prine moved to Nashville from the Chicago area in 1980, drawn here by a creative connection with "Cowboy" Jack Clement and a growing attraction to a beautiful young blonde bass player named Rachel Peer (now his wife) who hung around Clement's studio. Prine's Nashville move was preceded in the early '70s by recording his third album *Sweet Revenge* at the now-defunct Quadrafonic Studios here, under the direction of producer Arif Mardin, whose credits include a wide range of artists including Willie Nelson and the BeeGees. Prine and Mardin used players like Grady Martin and Reggie Young from Chips Moman's American Studio in Memphis. His second album, *Diamonds in the Rough*, was cut in New York, but featured all acoustic bluegrass instrumentation, recorded live in the studio with no overdubs.

Prine was already well-known in Music City circles for such country-covered songs as "Paradise," "Hello in There," and "Illegal Smile" which was the theme song for a short-lived TV series called "The Texas Wheelers," before he eased into Nashville residency in 1980. He found his commercial country songwriting connections simply by hanging out around John Prine and Rachel Peer. Rachel toured for years with Don Everly and the Dead Cowboys Band. First to make the Music City-Prine connection was Roger Cook.

"It started out, like most things with me start out, it started out with friends first," Prine explained, petting a white house cat and watching the stove where potatoes boiled. "They turned out to be songwriters. I mean, I'd heard Roger Cook's songs, but I didn't know which ones were his songs. And he didn't know dink about me. He really didn't, except he'd heard some people say some real nice things about my writing. We became friends before we ever listened to each other's work. You'd just find yourselves together around midnight, playing dominos and he takes a uke wherever he goes. He'd whip out the ukulele and we'd write a song a together, 'cause that's what songwriters do. I learned how to co-write writin' with Roger Cook. He's such a pro, and he approaches it as a craft. It kind of made me write more within a foundation, while it made Roger go outside of what he could ordinarily do. We'd end up with a really pretty song and usually pretty commercial, too."

Ever the happy-go-lucky adventurer, Prine just sort of fell into these commercial country songwriting connections the same way he more or less lucked into the record business in the first place. Born in 1946 in the working class Chicago suburb of Maywood, Illinois, John Prine quit his job as a Chicago mailman and started playing in Chicago nightclubs in 1970. He was discovered almost instantly by Kris Kristofferson and Paul Anka after film critic Roger Ebert ("At the Movies" star with partner Gene Siskell) accidentally heard Prine play.

"Roger (Ebert) wrote me up in the *Chicago Sun-Times* in his movie review column after I'd been playing for only a couple months," said Prine. "He had never heard of me—nobody had, really—and he just came into Earl's Old Town club (sic) to get a beer 'cause the movie he was supposed to be reviewing was so bad he walked out on it.

"He wrote in the paper the next day 'Such-and-such movie was so bad, I walked out, then I went down the street to get a beer and heard a guy who sings little movies in his songs. The place was packed after that."

Prine's scratchy Chicago nasal whine often colored by the softening sound of laughter that's just about to erupt combined with songs about everyday people in tragic situations that make up more of your life than the cheatin' or rhapsodic episodes of most popular or country songs carried him quickly to New York for a record deal with Atlantic. Songs like "Sam Stone" and "Your Flag Decal Won't Get You Into Heaven Anymore" told about the Viet Nam War era with more pathos and gentle good humor than any other songs of that time. They won him great notoriety and the unfortunate comparison with Bob Dylan.

His song "Paradise" became an anthem for the environmentalists in the mid-'70s at the same time it touched the nostalgia nerve of a whole generation of hillbillies transplanted from the rural South to the factories of the North during the Depression. But it was his satiric lampoon of the "Dear Abby" advice column that almost carried Prine out of the folk-country ghetto to the top of the pop and country charts in the mid-'70s. The song was in the news earlier this year when Dear Abby herself was duped into publishing a verse of the humorous tune and actually answered its complaint.

"I was on tour with Randy Newman when we cut that for a possible live album up at a college in upstate New York," Prine recalls. "We wound up using the live version because all the studio cuts we did sounded flat. I had just written the song, and that was the first time I'd ever performed it. The record company wanted to put it out as a single. They thought it would go all the way, and it probably would have, but I wouldn't let 'em."

That moment of decision was probably the point at which Prine's cult-level success was capped, because he hasn't yet had a similar chance to again get his own voice such wide radio exposure. Why did he turn away from the almost sure shot at mainstream popularity?

"I didn't want to get famous like that and have people think all I did was novelty songs," he said, mashing his potatoes while I stirred his beef gravy. "I used to tour a lot with Randy Newman when 'Short People' was a hit. It hurt him about as much as it helped him. The audience really changed. About half the audience that came at that time weren't the kind of people who'd ever come to a John Prine or Randy Newman concert before. They were rude. Fights would break out down in front of the stage. I'd just stop playing and do a blow by blow. 'He's up, he's down,' cause everyone was watchin' 'em anyway, so why pretend it wasn't goin' on? I just didn't want to get known as the guy who did the novelty hit. You get stuck with that and you never shake it off."

Prine's own performing style is decidedly folkie, largely because he learned to play from his folk-influenced older brother Dave. His sensibilities as a writer are so naturally country and of the ordinary man, partly because his father Bill Prine was an unrepentant honky tonk regular who turned a broken radio each Saturday night to the faraway sounds of his own rural Kentucky childhood—the Grand Ole Opry.

"My father had a radio for years that he used to put in the window facing south to catch WSM and the Grand Ole Opry," said the friendly dark-haired singer, picking beef bits out of his teeth as we finished dinner. "This was taped from falling off the stools over the years. My father would put it up in the window and point it to the southeast. He'd hold it side ways and then point it and aim it at Nashville; and me and him would sit there and listen to the Opry together. He'd turn it till you could hear Marty Robbins or Hank Snow."

In the middle '70s, Prine started visiting Nashville on a fairly regular basis, performing in local clubs, then hanging out with his new friends among the Nashville underground.

"Lee Clayton (who wrote 'Ladies Love Outlaws') showed me the town," Prine recalled. "He took me to the Ryman, backstage at the Ryman. I'll never forget that. Backstage was about two people wide, and all those people had to hang out right behind the curtain. Then when Dolly Parton came by, you had to get right up against the wall and let Dolly by. Standing there and peeking out and seeing that crowd that was the real thrill, besides standing there next to Ernest Tubb and Roy Acuff. Lookin' out, peeking out from behind those curtains and seein' that crowd with their fans. It was real hot July, and the fans were all goin' back and forth like they had a string goin' through all their wrists: all the fans were going along at the same direction."

Prine paid homage to tradition and his father's Old Kentucky roots by cutting "Nine Pound Hammer," which was written by Opry star and Muhlenberg County native Merle Travis. It was his discovery as a youngster of Roger Miller rather than the Opry stars that really set free his creative imagination. Already writing songs by age 14, Prine took heart when he heard songs like "Dang Me," "England Swings," "King of the Road" and other oddities from Roger Miller's unique catalogue. Like many young writers, Prine was writing tunes to impress girls in his adolescence and was ecstatic to find his early songs compared with those of a successful tunesmith.

"I played 'em for a girl at my high school, and she said they sounded like Roger Miller," he said. "I said, 'Who's Roger Miller?' So she played me 'King of the Road.' I said, 'there's hope! There's a lunatic out there that's got records on the radio. I told Roger this many years later, when Kristofferson introduced me to him, I said, 'You were a ray of hope for me.'"

Nashville has become home for the Chicago native with Kentucky roots. He's found a place for himself in the country music community, just as his songs did before he arrived. Not least among the reasons Prine loves Nashville is that they understand his kind of food here. The meal he generously shared with this journalist is more than simple nourishment to Prine. He calls it his diet for creative success.

"I'm a meat and potatoes man," he said, chuckling. "That's all I eat—meat and potatoes, potatoes and meat. If it don't run, I don't eat it. Bobby Bare asked me the other day when we were taping for his show on Nashville Network, what I attributed my songwriting ideas to. I looked him in the eye and said: 'It comes from a vitamin deficiency.' If I ever ate a vegetable, I'd probably turn real normal and have to go back to work for the Post Office. I told him it's meat and potatoes and lots of sugar in my iced tea."

Prine roared with laughter as we cleaned the table and rinsed the gravy off the plates before stacking them on the counter. How could anyone that talented who conveys an infectious love of life so obviously not be a huge star? Well, he is a huge star to tens of thousands of college circuit concert goers annually. He's even bigger in maybe hundreds of thousands of other fans when you consider that if his first album keeps selling at the same rate it has for the last 14 years, it will earn a gold record in early 1987—without ever having been on the charts.

PORK ROAST FOR A GERMAN AFTERNOON

Ronni Lundy | 1991 | *Shuck Beans, Stack Cakes, and Honest Fried Chicken: The Heart and Soul of Southern Country Kitchens*

Ronni Lundy, *Louisville Courier Journal*'s music editor throughout Nashville's much-buzzed-about "credibility scare" of the late '80s, had a vision. Born in Corbin, Kentucky, the bright-eyed journalist carried a local and regional authority that allowed her to connect with country music's brightest stars by speaking to their heart—and gut.

Famous for her connection with the notoriously prickly Dwight Yoakam during his ascension and for trading recipes with Naomi Judd as the Kentucky-based mother-daughter duo the Judds were becoming one of the biggest acts in American music, Lundy could write authentically for national publications from *Esquire* to *Gourmet*, *Bon Appetit* to *Sunset*.

With Lundy's understanding of the dialect, the palette, and the cooking styles, it wasn't long before Atlantic Monthly Press approached her about doing a cookbook. The woman who would win 2017's James Beard Book of the Year Award for *Victuals* made her cookbook debut in 1990 with *Shuck Beans, Stack Cakes, and Honest Fried Chicken: The Heart and Soul of Southern Country Kitchens*.

Deemed one of the six essential books on Southern cooking by *Gourmet*, *Shuck Beans* showcased Lundy's love of regional food and merged it with country music's biggest stars' memories. It took people, especially from the Mountain South, home.

For John Prine, who played Don and Phil Everly's annual benefit in Central City in Kentucky's Muhlenberg County, home would always have a waft of his grandparents' place in Paradise. When Lundy reached out about participation, Prine wholeheartedly signed on. Not only did he provide his coveted pork roast recipe, a favorite of late-night pickers and songwriters around Nashville, he spoke so glowingly of his mother's hash that Lundy felt the need to include it, too.

"Food really takes people back home," Lundy says. "And John was so sweet, he had his mother's notes for how to make it, which he sent along." —Ed.

John Prine's First Trip to the Opry

Singer/songwriter John Prine's family is from Muhlenburg [*sic*] County, Kentucky, and although Prine was born and raised in Chicago, he says at heart he's always been a Kentuckian.

"It's like I'm from there, but just wasn't actually born there. When my mother was carrying me—about eight months along—they came down to Kentucky and the Smokies and the Grand Ole Opry, so I was nearly born down South. Hell, I'd already been to the Opry in 1946, before I was even born."

Prine grew up hearing his father talk about that Opry trip. They hadn't bought tickets in advance, and when they get to the door, it was sold out. But his Dad pointed out his very pregnant wife and how they'd driven all the way from Chicago.

"My Dad said: 'We've got to see the Opry. Why every Saturday night I sit at my kitchen table and point my radio to the south just to hear it.'"

His father thought he got better reception if the radio was facing Nashville, Prine said.

And sure enough, the ticket-taker, swayed by such dedication, relented and let the Prines in.

"The way we were raised in Chicago was as if when my Dad's ship came in we were all going to back to Kentucky. He escaped Kentucky because he didn't want to work in the mines. But he never lost that longing to go back there and he always thought it was his home."

Pork Roast for A German Afternoon

John Prine says he likes all kinds of food, but the country food his Kentucky-born mother and grandmother made is his favorite. When he cooks that's the premise he starts with. But like his grandpa, Prine's also an improviser and inventor of sorts. One of his best culinary dishes is a simple country pork roast with a twist.

Prine rubs the roast with lots and lots of pepper and a little salt, puts it in a paper roasting bag, adds sweet German wine, and lets it roast slowly to make good juice. He cooks pork chops the same way.

I'm not a fan of bag baking. I guess I'm afraid the paper will drink up the juices while I'm not looking. But I discovered that Prine's technique is perfect for the clay pot—and I bet you'll think so, too.

The name of this dish, by the way, comes from Prine's wonderful, bluegrass-flavored 1986 album *German Afternoons.*

"I had this guy explain to me once that a German afternoon is like you go into town with some errands to run and stuff to do, but then you run into an old buddy you haven't seen. And you drop into a bar for just a minute and start to talk. And next thing you know it's already evening and you've just spent a German afternoon."

This roast is the right incentive for such a German afternoon. Call a friend over, pop it in the oven, and enjoy the rest of the wine while the roast fills your house with its sweet heady fragrance.

4-pound pork loin roast

2 teaspoons freshly ground pepper (tellicherry recommended)

1 teaspoon salt

1 cup Riesling

1 tablespoon flour

Soak clay pot top and bottom in water for 15 minutes. Trim excess fat from the pork roast. Mix salt and pepper together. ("Any good black pepper, freshly ground will do, but the tellicherry has a fragrance that goes especially well with the wine.") Rub salt and pepper into the roast all around. Pour the wine into the bottom of the clay pot, then place the roast in the wine bone side down. Insert a meat thermometer into the thickest part of the roast, being careful not to touch the bone. Put cover on and place the pot into stone-cold oven. Turn heat to 425 degrees. Roast for 1 1/2 hours or until the thermometer registers 185 degrees. Remove roast to serving plate; degrease the juices. Put a tablespoon of the grease in a small, heavy saucepan on medium heat and add the flour, stirring to make a smooth paste. Pour the degreased juices into this, stirring to smooth and let thicken. Serve the gravy on the side. Tomato Pie is delicious with this. *This makes enough to feed 6 for dinner, but it's better served to 4 or fewer with some left over for pork roast sandwiches the next day.*

Pot Without a Handle

"I cook my pot roast in a cast-iron thing called a waterless cooker," Verna Prine says.

"When I was growing up, they'd always say, 'You can cook a pot roast as long as you've got a pot to cook it in and a window to throw it out of.'

"That pot has a lid fits real tight. It had a handle at one time, but it just wore off. My God, I guess it was one of the first things I got when my husband and I got married. And I have to use pot holders now to move it around and cover and uncover it. I'm about the only one in the family can use it. And my boys sometimes say, 'Ma, you just keep that thing because you're the only one can work it.'

"But I keep it because nothing tastes so good as a pot roast cooked in old cast iron. In fact, I have several pieces of cast iron for my cooking and to me there's just nothing like it."

Verna Prine's Hash

The country cook's ability to make magnificence from meager stores is nowhere displayed so well as in a hash. Carved from the skimpy leavings of the previous day's roast, dressed up only with onion and maybe a few diced potatoes, then poured over a plain toast or a biscuit, this humble hash can, nevertheless, have a most addictive flavor.

John Prine's mother, Verna, learned to make hash from her mother-in-law Idell Prine. "I had four boys to feed and a husband and hash was one real good way to do it."

So good that her husband sometimes brought home a six-pound blade roast and said, "I don't want nobody else touching this for anything else. I want it to be hash."

So good that Prine says when he goes to visit his mother in Chicago these days, she sends him back to Nashville ". . . with Tupperware on the airplanes—big Tupperware things of hash. She asks me what I want for birthdays and Christmas: I say, 'Ten pounds of hash.'

"And I say, 'I couldn't think of a better present, Ma, 'cause every time I eat it, I think of you.'"

4-pound blade roast with bone
Salt
Pepper
1 onion, sliced
1 onion, chopped very, very finely

Be sure to get the blade with the bone when you're buying your meat, Verna Prine says, because that's what gives both the roast and the hash its flavor. In fact, she puts the bone in the pan with the hash while it cooks to give it more flavor, and you will too if you know what's good. Trim fat from the outside of the roast and render it in a heavy cast-iron pot (one with a snug-fitting cover) over medium heat. Remove fat, leaving hot grease, and brown the roast on both sides in it. Salt and pepper both sides liberally after they are browned. Sprinkle sliced onion over top of meat, cover with lid and roast in 300 degree oven for 2 hours. If roast doesn't yield enough juice, add ½ cup water before roasting. When roast is done, take it out of the pot and let it cool at least enough to handle. It's really best, though, if refrigerated overnight. Refrigerate drippings separately, so the grease will rise to the top and can be easily skimmed off.

When you're ready to make the hash, cut meat into thin, small pieces—about the size of a thumbnail—and put in a heavy skillet with a lid. Add the degreased juices, and enough water—if necessary—to just cover the meat. Chop an onion very finely and add to the meat.

"I don't know if it makes any difference in the flavor, but I had to chop my onions real fine because my kids—when they were little—if they found a piece of onion in something, they wouldn't eat it," Verna Prine said.

Lay the big bone from the blade roast in the middle of the hash, and then cover and simmer for about an hour. Taste and season with more salt and pepper, bearing in mind that the Prines are all "great ones for pepper."

Remove the bone from the pot before serving. Verna said she sometimes served her hash on hot biscuits, but most of the time, she just served it on a plate like a thick stew with mashed potatoes on the side.

"I had one boy, not Johnny, who used to like to eat his hash on his mashed potatoes and then catsup on top of that," she said. But I wouldn't recommend it, since the flavor is too good for such doctoring.

This will feed a mom, a dad and four hungry boys.

Hash as Muse

Some people cook to eat, but sometimes John Prine cooks to write.

"In order to write songs, I need to get my mind somewhere else. I can't have my total concentration on my writing. So I write when I'm driving, when I'm cooking. I very rarely write behind the guitar. Cooking's one of the best times for me to write.

"So, I was in the kitchen a while back working on making some hash like my Mom does. And it was the week the Berlin Wall came down, you know. And they had these TV shows with people dancing on the wall and stuff. So I wrote me a song right then called 'Dancing on the Berlin Wall.' And it starts out:

'I want your East German kisses on my West German face

Let's hang old Gorby's picture up above the fireplace

Tell all the friends and neighbors and bring Grandma in her shawl.

Tonight we're going dancing on the wall.'

"Anyway this song just came out pretty fast and I liked it. And I think—yeah, I'm pretty sure that batch of hash came out pretty good, too."

BIOGRAPHY FOR RELEASE OF
GERMAN AFTERNOONS

Holly Gleason | 1986 | Oh Boy Records

When Prine was ready to release *German Afternoons*, the gamble seemed more reasonable than when Oh Boy put out its first album, *Aimless Love*, truly by mail order. Between the success of Steve Goodman's *Artistic Hair*, *Affordable Art*, and *Santa Ana Winds* on Red Pajamas—started by their managers Dan Einstein and Al Bunetta during his best friend's final years battling leukemia—and the response to Oh Boy's debut, Prine believed they could figure out how to be a meaningful label.

Without truly knowing how it would all come together, Oh Boy continued building relationships with distributors, chains, and individual stores who would agree to COD (cash on delivery) in what was a ninety-day net business. In the world before GoFundMe, the Internet, and streaming made music accessible, his fans continued sending in checks, saying, "Send me the record when it's ready."

If people scoffed, Prine was too busy touring and enjoying life in Nashville. Much of his world was uncharted when Oh Boy's powers-that-be put a barely twenty-something on a plane to meet Prine for a bio interview in Vienna, Virginia, at the iconic Wolf Trap. With Prine seeking to define his place in contemporary music and create a sense that his label wasn't folly, the two-hour discussion was more than "then we cut this. . . ." Prine was thoughtful, seeking to show people where his values were and what this label really meant.

"Show people *who* he is," was the mandate, "and help them get this wasn't a last resort or the only option but a decision to put the power of what happens to his music in *his* hands. And try to capture his personality, because he's more than the guy who wrote 'Sam Stone,' but people don't always want to see that."

Vulnerable. Awestruck. Funny. Serious. Aware. True.

It's a lot to put into 1500 words, but that—and trying to mention the record—was the job.

"We're less worried about the record," I was told. "People are going to buy it 'cause it's John. We want people to understand." —Ed.

"My brother Dave taught me a chord and the first time I down a chord and I didn't muffle it, well, I just sat there with my ear on the wood even after the sound died from the vibrations. From there, it was me sitting there alone in a room singing to a wall."

And what about his very first audience?

"Well, the wall seemed to like it . . ." Prine says now with a twinkle in his eye and his characteristic understatement. That wall has an awful lot in common with the countless people Prine has touched with his songs over the last decade and a half. He's certainly come a long way since he made his first appearance at the Westlake Hospital in Maywood, Illinois, the son of union boss William Mason Prine and his wife Verna Valentine Hamm.

Being third in a family of four children meant that Prine "got away with everything," which included the latitude of giving his imagination free reign. Coupled with a childhood that was rich with classic American values and traditions—many which would later be incorporated into his songs—like the summertime visits with his relatives in Paradise, Kentucky.

While building this foundation, Prine was also evolving from just another kid into the one of the young men hanging out on the street corners of Maywood. It may seem an unlikely nurturing ground for someone who would become both a non-judgmental social commentator and a champion of the common man.

"The good thing about it was it was a real assorted group of guys. One town'd be Italian and another'd be Polish or whatever. But my town was just a mixture: there were people from Appalachia, Blacks, Puerto Ricans; you got exposed to all different types of people. And you learned that deep down, they all had something good about 'em—even the worst ones."

It would take a stint in the service and a job with the Post Office before Prine would make his public debut at an "open mic" night at a local bar fueled by a few beers and the knowledge that he could do it better than everyone else he'd seen that evening. "There were all these amateurs that were getting up," Prine recalls, "and they were terrible. So I started making some comments about it, and the next thing I knew somebody said, 'well, if you think you can do it better . . .' And I said 'I could' and I got up on stage and played 'Sam Stone,' 'Hello In There' and 'Paradise' and people seemed to like it." Including the club owner who promptly offered Prine a job. After asking how long he'd have to play for, he went home and wrote what became his self-titled debut album. It wasn't long before a little guy from Chicago named Steve Goodman met Prine and would become his best friend as well as being responsible for bringing Kris Kristofferson to The Earl of Old Town to see Prine, a move which would result in Prine's gaining a national label deal.

From there, Prine went from being a local singer/songwriter to being an artist on a national label, lavished with praise from critics around the country. Throughout Prine's label migrations, which would eventually cover eight albums and two companies, he continued refining his voice and attracting fans who identified closely with his emotional sharpshooting. "It's a great feeling when you put something in a song and other people say that's exactly how they feel. That's the most gratifying thing about songwriting for me: it's always been a real outlet for me—being able to put those feelings down."

Among the songs Prine penned at this time were such classics as "Please Don't Bury Me," "Fish and Whistle," and "Souvenirs," and there were also more humorous offerings which proved that Prine could find the irony in it all: "Dear Abby," "Sabu Visits The Twin Cities Alone," "Illegal Smile," even "Christmas in Prison."

But John Prine's special visions and personal integrity—something which attracted Better Midler to cover "Hello In There," Bonnie Raitt to adopt "Angel from Montgomery" as her own and numerous country artists such as Gail Davies, Tammy Wynette and Johnny Cash to release their versions of "Unwed Fathers"—wasn't best served by the big labels' way of doing business. He had his following, enough people to keep all of his releases in print (as *John Prine* draws dangerously close to gold), but there had to be something else to making records.

So John Prine called it quits with the big companies and took some time to re-think what he was doing. Out of that soul searching, John Prine, the singer/songwriter/and even guitar player, decided to put on another hat—record company executive. He formed Oh Boy Records after moving to Nashville and decided to start making records his way. As he noted shortly after the release of *Aimless Love*, his first independent album. "I got to the point when I was on labels, I couldn't wait to get finished and out on the road. Then I didn't care if I made another record for three, four years . . . This, for me, was a positive move. We weren't at the end of our rope. But we'd talk to labels and it just didn't seem to make any sense because I just didn't fit in with what they do. They're used to putting out one kind of music and I can't just crank out songs for the radio."

Continuing in that philosophy is *German Afternoons*, another collection to which Prine applied the less-is-more principle. The music of Prine's second Oh Boy release smacks of Appalachia, with acoustic instruments buoying his growly vocals. As always, the lyrical scope is direct and the stories simple yet moving.

So now Prine has it both ways: a loyal following and being able to make *his* music *his* way—doing whatever he believes is best for the songs. It must be working, critics from *Rolling Stone* to *The New York Times* to *People Magazine* continue to sing his praises, believing he's doing the best work of his career. Perhaps that's because he's contented, living in Nashville, and writing songs with friends like Bobby Braddock and Roger Cook. There is one thing, though, that still bothers him. "I'm looking for a '59 Bonneville convertible in good shape and I can't seem to find one. At this point, I might even consider a hard top."

TODAY SHOW FEATURE—GERMAN AFTERNOONS

Mike Leonard | August 1, 1986 | *The Today Show* (National Broadcasting Company)

With *Aimless Love* showing that a musician without a major record company behind him could sell enough records to not just sustain but actually *grow* his career, John Prine was the David who slew Goliath. Years before established artists who could still get major label deals would take their recording careers in their own hands, Prine blazed the trail forward—and never looked back.

There was no template; Prine, Bunetta, and young manager Einstein made it up as they went along. So deep was the hunger for Prine's music that, long before there was a distribution pathway for Oh Boy or any DIY label to work with, fans sent in checks for fifteen and twenty dollars for records that weren't yet recorded.

Prine had always been a man of the people; now the people showed up for Prine. That passion was on full display when Emmy-winning television journalist Mike Leonard journeyed to Wolf Trap for a segment for *The Today Show*.

It was 1986. Music on network morning shows was rare, reserved for the biggest stars only. But a package? About a folkie? On a teeny self-financed label?

Though *Rolling Stone* deemed *Aimless Love* "a treat," with writer Don Shewey assessing that "John Prine, the elegant pop songwriter, is still in top form," he was a long way from the majors. But that appealed to the Chicago-based Leonard, who had the latitude to tell *any* distinctly American story on America's number-one morning show.

Beyond the sold-out concert, Leonard went to Nashville, first to Prine's kitchen, with producer Jim Rooney and then-wife Rachel Peer Prine, and then to the Cowboy Arms Hotel and Recording Spa. There, legendary Sun Studio engineer and songwriter Jack Clement weighed in on Prine's gift as the Carter Sisters worked upstairs.

"It was such a family operation," Leonard marvels. "Whether you were in Nashville, which was such a small town, or dealing with the Oh Boy people, you realized: these were all people who were invested and engaged because they cared. They cared about John. They cared about the songs. They cared about the people who loved John and the songs . . . and the love was mutual." —Ed.

[As the original formatting of Leonard's shooting script has been retained, here's a quick reader's guide: The voice-over is the text that appears in paragraphs with their initial lines indented. Words in captions are something akin to stage directions—"sot" means "sound on tape," a shorthand cue for prerecorded audio to play. In some places, I've added dialogue tags for clarity. —Ed.]

It's funny (laugh) how the simple things appeal to us. The everyday ups and downs of life . . . as best told across a kitchen table.

(sot Prine)
"It's just a comfortable place. It's close to the fridge too."
(ns music and fade under)

And close to the guitars and harmonies that wrap those simple thoughts into songs. The songs of John Prine. John Prine, not exactly a household name.

(sot Prine)
"(shake head no) I don't think I'm going out of my way to avoid it but it certainly isn't what I've ever really wanted."
(ns music up and fade)

What John Prine has wanted is what he's getting. Here in a sold out concert at Wolf Trap near Washington, DC . . . (music up) . . . or here with his wife and a friend at his kitchen table in Nashville. It's his ability to simply connect with people.

(sot Prine)
"And they go, 'Yah, I feel like that.' And so I play it in three chords so if they want to learn a John Prine song they can learn it in a hurry. That's

how most of my songs get around . . . is people starting out playing hear me and they go, 'if that guy can do it anybody can.'"

Actually, it's not that easy. The business of popular music caters, more and more these days, to the big hitters. The major record labels therefore have a bit of a problem with the John Prines of the world . . . so says his manager, Al Bunetta.

(sot Bunetta)
"If you didn't fit into any demographic group, pop, country, r&b, nobody really knew how to market . . . market this."

Yet the fans are there, the hard core loyal group that have supported him through his 15 year career. What Prine needs is a record company executive who can appreciate that. He found one . . . himself. Meet Mr. John Prine the executive . . . the president of his own label, Oh Boy Records.

(sot [Prine])
"I didn't start my record company to be against what big record companies are doing. I just didn't think they were offering a chance for artists that were selling records, the volume I do. Like somebody's got to somewhere because people want the music.
(ns and music fade)

They want the silly songs.

(ns and music fade)

They want the sad songs.

(ns and music fade under)

And if they want his latest album, *German Afternoons*, they can get it in some record stores or by mail order. Like any new company, the handful of employees at Oh Boy are trying to do it right, so they ask their customers to write.

(sot Dan Einstein)

"We encourage our audience to send in comment forms enclosed in every mail order record. A feed back form and we read them and we take their advice very seriously."

Meanwhile backstage, the record company executive frets . . . (ns up) as the singer, songwriter practices, nervously.

(sot [Prine])

"Once I get out there I'm fine. It's always easier for me to talk to a whole lot of people than one on one."

(ns music and fade)

And it's the way he talks . . . and sings that sets him apart. Even in Nashville, where music is always in the air. Upstairs in this recording studio where the Carter family works on an album and downstairs, in an office where John Prine works on his friends.

(sot ["Cowboy" Jack Clement])

"Well, he's not like most of the songwriters around here. He's got a different slant on things."

(sot Prine)

"I don't think my stuff has any time on it. I could've done this stuff 40 years ago or I could do it 40 years from now and there wouldn't be that much of a difference. I'm not writing about fads. I'm writing about the people and what happens to them. The funny things that happen and some of the tragedies."

(ns and music up)

Simply put . . . by a man gifted in that comfortable kitchen table kind of way."

(music up and fade)

For *Today*, Mike Leonard, NBC News, Nashville.

NOT EXACTLY MISSING IN ACTION

Gil Asakawa | February 1992 | *Pulse!*

Prine and Goodman had both been Colorado favorites since playing Boulder's Tulagi in 1972. The deep humanity and strong awareness of social issues that permeated Prine's music without ever turning into explicit protest connected him mightily with the hippies, outdoorsy types, ski bums, and military people scattered around the state.

For Gil Asakawa, the music editor of *Westwood* who would eventually help establish NPR's eTown, Prine defined the level of excellence a singer-songwriter could deliver. Asakawa remembers being ushered into Prine's dressing room at a University of Colorado show early in his career—and Prine being as lovely to his uninvited guests as if they were from *Creem*, *Crawdaddy*, or the *Rocky Mountain News*.

"But that's what made him special," Asakawa says. "He was just kind . . . and interesting."

Coming into his own during the early days of South by Southwest, then an indie roots music event running four days in Austin, Asakawa had become friendly with Prine's managers. Having expressed interest in what Prine was doing during a fallow period, he was thrilled when an advance cassette of *The Missing Years* arrived.

With long lead times, those advances gave writers an advantage—and Asakawa took it. Reaching out to Tower Records' *Pulse!* magazine, with its slogan, "We listen to a lot of records; we write about the ones we like," he locked down a profile assignment that would break as *The Missing Years* released.

Prine, committed to this album enough to work with an indie publicist for the first time, understood the game was changing. The organic press he always generated greased the way for larger stories placed by a former Elektra Records press domo who'd also gone independent, George Dassinger.

To score a major feature in America's premier music retailer's magazine was a massive win. Not only did the Denver-based Asakawa contextualize the more potent production and guests, he also considered Oh Boy's place in the stratosphere and Prine's undoing of a seven-figure deal from a major label. —Ed.

"Hey, you have to go away first to come back." That's how John Prine responds to people asking if the title of his latest recording, *The Missing Years*, signals a career comeback for the durable singer/songwriter. After all, he's never taken time off from his constant touring schedule, though he hasn't released a new album since 1986's *German Afternoons*. (The stop-gap *John Prine Live* was released in 1988.) The longest break of his recording career came between 1980 and '84.

Ironically, Prine has been thinking in the back of his mind that his new album would be his last before taking an extended break; instead of being a comeback, *The Missing Years* would have signaled a farewell.

Not to worry. Thanks to the creative and commercial success of *The Missing Years*, Prine feels rejuvenated, and intends to continue his career as vigorously as ever. "I'm crazy about it," he explains about the record, the fourth to be released on his own Oh Boy label. "I've found my producer. Not that I was disappointed before, but Howie (Epstein, of Tom Petty's Heartbreakers) got me to sound more like I do live." The recording is the first in Prine's discography that reflects the same loose energy he radiates onstage, without losing the quality of the studio. "On some of my records, I feel I was uncomfortable, and I can hear it when I listen to them," he says. "You know, it's like a photo where you're uncomfortable and think you look weird, but people keep saying, 'Oh, but your hair looks great.'"

On the new disc, Prine looks, or more importantly, sounds, marvelous. *The Missing Years* is as stereo- and radio-friendly as anything he's released since 1978's classic *Bruised Orange*, which was produced by Prine's late friend and mentor Steve Goodman.

Partly, it's because Prine has written his usual assortment of wonderfully timeless observations on humanity's foibles, and partly because a motley crew of friends and admirers—from Bruce Springsteen, the

Divinyls' Christina Amphlett, Bonnie Raitt, Phil Everly, and Petty on vocals, to instrumentalists such as David Lindley, Albert Lee, various Heartbreakers and members of the Desert Rose band—have lent their talents with low-key cameos.

And perhaps most importantly, Prine and Epstein both agreed to pull out the stops and spent the money to get the sound just right, especially for radio's notoriously close-minded programmers. "We were hocking our insurance policies to pay for this. We really felt that it would sell, and it has. It's at 70,000 already, and we're getting played on rock radio for the first time in 10 years. Hell, I'll take anything. They can play me on Rush Limbaugh's talk show if it'll help."

He may not need the help. Because of the rise in his commercial success, he puts any thoughts of retirement on the back burner. "I wasn't threatening my manager or anything like that. I feel like I've been successful, you know. But I was losing interest," Prine says. "I wanted to do something else for a while, to make me want to play again. If this record hadn't done well, I probably would have quit. Now I can't stop."

That's a relief to anyone who's followed the drawling, Chicago-born songwriter's work since his self-titled 1971 debut. The album featured two of Prine's best-known songs (thanks to renditions by dozens of other artists, including Raitt and Bette Midler), "Angel from Montgomery" and "Hello in There," along with classic songs "Sam Stone" and "Donald and Lydia," the kind of carefully observed narratives that Nanci Griffith might gladly give away her innocent persona for. Prine quickly became a critics' favorite and a darling of the '70s singer/songwriter set, even earning the dreaded "new Dylan" tag.

Prine's talent, however, has never rested in wordy stream-of-consciousness and myth-mongering. Throughout his prolific and varied career (his records have wandered through folk, rockabilly, rattletrap rock & roll and country styles with equal ease and familiarity), his artistic palette has been variations of three-chord strum-and-mumble verses and choruses with little pretension to high art. Instead, Prine has always projected an image of the workaday Joe who happens to notice things and people around him more than his pals. Prine's best songs, whether it's the early, funny "Dear Abby" or the heart-wrenching "Unwed Fathers" from 1984's *Aimless Love*, are tinged with bittersweet bemusement. The combination, painted over Prine's rough canvas of a voice, makes for more human portraits than most artists manage in a lifetime of creative struggle. The sure sign of his adept way with a song? Not a single John Prine record has gone out of print, though he moved from Atlantic (his early work) to Asylum (several of his late-'70s albums) to his own Oh Boy label.

Now, he's perfectly happy being his own label magnate. To illustrate, Prine tells a story of his last brush with the majors: "A few years ago, I was all set to sign to a major label—I mean, we'd signed the papers and everything. I went to a party where there was a room full of label people and a VP said, 'Welcome aboard.' And I thought to myself, 'I don't want to be on a fucking boat with this guy. I don't want or need their advice on my music. They don't have a clue.'

"The '80s, because of the major labels, were like a musical purge," he continues. "It was like Stalin or something, just ridiculous, when people like Bonnie Raitt and Van Morrison were both dropped from Warners at the same time. Instead of going on some small label, though, I started my own, and during the years when there didn't appear to be any market for this kind of music, we did all right. We knew it was more fun to have our own company, and on that level, each small sale was personally gratifying."

Prine's catalog is available primarily through Oh Boy's network of mail-order and hip retailers. The Asylum albums are now available on Oh Boy CDs, and Prine hopes he'll eventually get the rights to his first Atlantic albums on CD on Oh Boy.

And fans can expect more new materials in the years to come, including more sets produced by Howie Epstein. Returning to the topic of his satisfaction with *The Missing Years*, Prine points out that Epstein wasn't afraid to prod him to make the best album he could. It's chock-full of evocative descriptions of emotional entanglements, told as only Prine can see them. "Picture Show" veers off from the young James Dean into the soullessness of Hollywood tourism; "Take A Look At My Heart," co-written with John Mellencamp, is a guy-to-guy warning to his ex-wife's new beau; "It's A Big Old Goofy World" is Prine's stock-in-trade, a wiseacre's assessment of life even as he struggles to write a song about it all. "Jesus, the Missing Years," is the song that gives the album its title. It follows Jesus through some wild '60s-era travels, including stints hanging out with the Beatles, Rolling Stones and George Jones.

One of the best, if cryptically silly, songs is "The Sins of Mephisto," which nonessentially conjures a slew of baby-boomer icons from hula hoops to Lucy and Ricky Ricardo. "This song goes to the heart of the record," says Prine. "I had 12 songs done, and I was proud of 'em. But then Howie sits down and says, 'We need another song.' I said, 'Are you crazy? I don't have another song in me—you can do an autopsy and you won't find anything.'

"So, I locked myself away for a week, until I came from as far left as I could. Actually, I thought 'Memphisto' was a real word. I thought it was the city in Egypt that Memphis was named after. But it turns out that city was called Memphis. I decided I was confusing it was Mephistopheles, the devil. So, I thought, 'OK, it kinda makes sense—Memphis, the blues and the devil and all."

He kept the title and the song, because it inexplicably worked, even down to the goofball line, "*Exactly-odo, Quasimodo.*" "It's a phrase I've used for several years," he says, "and I was determined to work it into a song."

PART V

Coming into His Own

SPECIAL DELIVERY: EX-MAILMAN JOHN PRINE PROVES HE CAN STILL CARRY A MESSAGE

Cynthia Sanz | April 1992 | *People*

John Prine had fallen into a rhythm he rather liked. Tour as needed, make records that he wanted . . . when he wanted. He liked fishing. He liked hanging out. He liked being left alone. And it worked for him.

Prine had a body of work so bountiful, he couldn't sing all the songs people wanted to hear as it was. Since he wasn't beholden to a record company's bottom line, there was no threat of being dropped or suspended because the machine needed feeding.

It wasn't that he was uninspired after the Grammy-nominated *German Afternoons*. Waylaid by a divorce, content to hang out talking about old cars, making pork roasts for his friends, and traveling for work and pleasure, he'd settled into a groove.

The Missing Years, when it happened, reckoned with Prine's protracted divorce from Rachel Peer, finding love, and the equanimity that comes with wanting only good things for people. Humor, irony, the strange rhymes and whimsical metaphors. Prine's roots were showing on a cover of Lefty Frizzell's "I Want to Be with You Always." The uncoupling book-ends "All the Best" and "Everything Is Cool" share space with the fraught "Great Rain," the surging "Take a Look," and the half-spoken, myriad-conversation-starting "Jesus, the Missing Years," where the smile on his face is audible.

Having spent almost a decade creating a meaningful distribution network and forging alliances with major record chains Tower Records, Peaches Records and Tapes, and Musicland, the world was primed for *The Missing Years*. While it didn't create the same flashfire that Bonnie Raitt's Nick of Time Grammy-sweep did, Prine won his first Grammy, toured—and sang "Angel from Montgomery" most nights—with Raitt, and found his fame rising.

People had always been the province of movie stars, TV people, and other pop-cultural denizens. Musicians never tested well, so if you weren't quirky, controversial, or a pop sensation, don't bother.

Prine thought the whole thing was a little silly, but he knew people read *People* at the beauty shop. He loved that. So the notoriously fame-thwarting artist agreed to let a reporter and photographer Slick Lawson into his home on Lindawood Drive as well as his rehearsal space to capture "the person."

Cindy Sanz, who ultimately wrote the story, found the subject disarming. If not a fan of Prine's music before writing the profile, she recognized the quirks (a Christmas tree all year round), the poetry to the laundry list lyrics, *and* the pathos of a man finding true success after coming in hot with his debut, exiting the major-label game on his terms, then creating a career that suited him.

In eight hundred words, she distilled—for anyone buying the magazine at the grocery store or reading in their doctor's office—a twenty-year career hitting an apex with humanity and insight. To be part of the cultural conversation, especially in the early '90s, meant being "big enough" for *People*.

Says Sanz, "I'd never heard John Prine on the radio in San Antonio, but reading the file that came in from Nashville and seeing the pictures, you could tell this man was not only accomplished, he was someone who'd worked hard to never lose who he was. It was a fun story to write." —Ed.

On the title track of his latest album, *The Missing Years*, John Prine conjures up an explanation of what might have happened to Jesus during a gap in his biblical biography. The man from Nazareth saw *Rebel Without a Cause*, invented Santa Claus, discovered the Beatles, recorded with the Stones, and once, recounts the singer with characteristic wryness, he even opened up for George Jones.

Fact is, Prine, 45, has some missing years of his own that could use some explaining. Hailed as "the new Dylan" when he emerged from the folk clubs of Chicago in the early '70s, he hadn't released a studio album in five years until now, and *John Prine Live*, in 1988, was the last most people had heard of him. What was Prine up to? Not much, he admits. "My music is very unplanned out," he says. "Sometimes I just haven't got any idea how to write a song. It's like I never did it before. It's not like a job that you find in the want ads." Happily, Prine has been making up for lost time. *The Missing Years* released last September, won a Grammy as Best Contemporary Folk Album earlier this year. One of its songs, "Picture Show," has even been getting radio airplay and, backed by Prine's first-ever video, landed in heavy rotation on Country Music Television.

This year with about 150 performance dates on his schedule, he will spend as much time on the road as in the three-bedroom Nashville home he shares with two cats, a minature Doberman and an artificial Christmas tree that he keeps up year-round. "A couple of years ago, I was going through my divorce and was real depressed," he says. "I thought the lights and decorations were so nice, I just decided to let it stay up."

When not onstage himself, Prine hits the local honky tonks to hear his friends perform, or fishes . . . or just stays home alone. "A great imagination is a great challenge," he says. "It's not like I'm a total loner, but I don't care to have three or four buddies come by the house and, like, let's go do something. I can just sit by myself and have this vivid imagination."

One thing Prine never imagined, though, was becoming famous. The third of four sons born to a tool-and-die maker William Prine and his wife, Verna, in Maywood, Ill., Prine began songwriting when he took a job as a mailman after finishing high school.

"There's not a lot to do out there once you know that're on the right street," he says. He made his performing debut by accident one night, when after a few beers, he mumbled some criticism of the talent during an open-mike night at a Chicago club and someone dared him to take the stage himself. He did, and before the night was over, the club owner offered him a job.

Soon after, Prine's pal and fellow folkie, Steve Goodman, brought Kris Kristofferson and Paul Anka to see him perform. The pair, pleased by what they heard, helped the mailman turned singer land a record contract, and in 1971 Prine released his first album to rave reviews. Over the years, his songs would find even wider audiences, thanks to recordings by performers like Bette Midler ("Hello in There"), Bonnie Raitt ("Angel from Montgomery") and Tammy Wynette ("Unwed Fathers").

But the hoopla and politics of the music business eventually wore thin. "I used to carry a bottle of Maalox in my guitar case," Prine says. "From being a mailman to traveling all around and having people writing about you—it kind of threw me for a loop." In 1984, after eight albums, Prine set up his own label (Oh Boy Records) and freed himself from the big companies' constant demand for new albums at regular intervals. "If my refrigerator broke down, I'd go out and sing and then I'd buy a refrigerator,'" he says. "I knew I could do this without a major record deal."

He is more relaxed about his private life. Twice divorced, he now dates a woman who lives in Ireland whom he sees about half a dozen times each year. "I'm not praying for marriage, but I got a feeling I will," he says. As for his resurging career, Prine seems pleased but cautious.

"People say, 'You don't want to be a star, do you?'" he says. "I'm not sure that's something I'd like to do, to be known everywhere I go. I'm not sure you can be your own person. And you kind of throw the whole neighborhood out of balance by not being yourself."

Photo captions:
1) "I thought people who were in the entertainment business were either from wealthy families or from France," says Prine. (guitar case, Cadillac)
2) "I don't like to throw anything away," says the singer (tending to the Christmas tree he has kept in his living room for the past six years).
3) "I think my songs come from a real special place," says Prine (rehearsing for an upcoming tour with Bill Bonk and Duane Jarvis). "I'm not sure where that is, but I'm grateful."
4) "I guess I was real reluctant to make music my whole life," says Prine (at home in his kitchen). "I thought that somehow that might not be a good thing."

TODAY SHOW FEATURE—
THE MISSING YEARS

Mike Leonard | 1991 | *The Today Show* (National Broadcasting Company)

Because Mike Leonard assigned his own stories, revisiting someone or somewhere he'd covered before was not out of the question. With his affinity for everyman and everytown kinds of subjects, though, it was rare to return—and rarer still that a previous subject experienced such a change in circumstances that another look from Leanord was genuinely needed.

But a lot happened between Leonard's 1986 piece for *German Afternoons* and Prine's seeming reemergence in 1991. Prine slipped into a rhythm of touring and drifting, and it seemed to many that he had lost the creative drive to make records.

John Prine Live, recorded over three nights at The Coach House in San Juan Capistrano, affirmed his position as a beguiling entertainer, one who knew how to charm, warm, and elicit laughter in all the right places. With a scant two songs from his Oh Boy releases (*Aimless Love*'s "Oldest Baby in the World," *German Afternoon*'s "Speed of the Sound of Loneliness"), the nineteen-song collection served as both a career retrospective and a way to deliver the songs in the more tender, even wistful way they'd settled into over the years.

Having seen Prine's dear friend Bonnie Raitt and Irish soulmaster Van Morrison dropped by Warner Brothers on the same day, there were those who wondered about the place of the 1970s tastemakers who'd not turned into Jackson Browne, Linda Ronstadt, and the Eagles. Content to play for the faithful, make kitchen-table records in Nashville, go fishing and play poker with buddies Keith Sykes, Roger Cook, and Dave Ferguson, and pal around with the Everly Brothers, Prine was good.

But when Raitt teamed with Don Was and recorded a series of stripped-down songs that put her soulful burgundy'n'candlelight voice and midlife reality forward, *Nick of Time* became a beachhead. Selling 500,000 records initially for Capitol Records, it would win three Grammys, including Album of the Year; in the tidal wave that followed, *Time* would hit number one on *Billboard*'s Top 200 Albums chart on its way to quintuple platinum status.

Maybe forty-five wasn't the end of the road. When Tom Petty and the Heartbreakers' bassist Howie Epstein suggested to managers Bunetta and Einstein that he'd *really* like to produce a John Prine record, they listened. Living with Carlene Carter, the cowpunk siren and daughter of June Carter Cash, Epstein was no stranger to roots music.

He was also no stranger to Prine's catalogue. After a meeting or two, the decision was made to go forward. *The Missing Years*, ironically titled for a song about the middle years of Jesus's life that no one seems to recall, was a fitting assessment of Prine's half decade.

Muscular and robust, there was a vitality to *The Missing Years* that shook the "yeah, yeah, he's great" complacency off the critics. Both Robert Christgau, the Dean of Rock Critics, in the *Village Voice* and Alanna Nash in *Entertainment Weekly* gave the album A grades, with Nash writing, "John Prine's best work has always been slightly cinematic and hallucinogenic, full of images that transport as well as provoke." His hometown *Chicago Tribune* assessed, "at the top of his form in a mix of evocative folk-country ballads and more rocking fare. . . . Goofily surreal and straightforwardedly sentimental by turns, this one's a don't-miss for long time Prine fans. . . ." and the *Los Angeles Times* recognized his romantic streak, "The rest of the time, Prine sings about love—how hard it is to grasp, how easy it is to neglect and lose, how wounding, how vital—in a way that seems truly lived, carefully thought out, and never stretches for melodramatic effect."

Leonard was sold. Having seen Oh Boy emerge as a genuine force, carried in the major record chains as well as doing a brisk mail-order business, he decided to check in as Prine hit the road as Raitt's special guest. Riding the tour bus, living the life, Leonard digs deeper into the weight of his legacy and the change in business. —Ed.

[*As the original formatting of Leonard's shooting script has been retained, here's a quick reader's guide: The voice-over is the text that appears in paragraphs with their initial lines indented. Words in captions are something akin to stage directions—"sot" means "sound on tape," a shorthand cue for prerecorded audio to play. In some places, I've added dialogue tags for clarity. —Ed.*]

(ins & pic singing)

"*. . . A young man from a small town with a very large imagination . . .*"
(crowd applause)

Riding along on a wave of applause, the middle aged man lugs his very large imagination through the small towns of the American midwest. Singer-songwriter John Prine is once again on tour . . . once again out with a new album to promote.

(sot Prine)

"Yeah it seems like it possibly might do better than any of the records I have ever done before."

For John Prine, it's been 5 years since the release of his last studio album. The title of this one . . .

(Prine to audience)

"It's called *The Missing Years*, where we tell everything."

(Prine sings [several bars of "The Sins of Memphisto"])

20 years and hundreds of songs ago John Prine, then a suburban Chicago mailman, stunned the record industry with the lyrical depth of his 1st album.

(Prine sings [lyrics from "Sam Stone"])

His words painted vivid pictures of those mighty battles fought by ordinary souls . . . a Viet Nam vet, strung out on drugs . . .

(Prine sings [another lyric from "Sam Stone"])

. . . an elderly couple struggling with the loneliness of aging.

(Prine sings [several lines from "Hello in There"])

That debut album received rave reviews.

(sot Prine & Leonard)
[Prine:] "Yeah, it got a whole lot."
[Leonard:] "And how did that affect you?"
[Prine:] "It gave me an ulcer (laugh). It did. It put me in the hospital about 6 times in 3 years with stomach disorders. It was like really a big change in my life. I wasn't planning on doing this for a living. You know, I didn't want to work in the post office forever but it was OK for then. I didn't think that people who grew up like I did got into show business."

Ultimately to share his songs and the stage with people like Bonnie Raitt, just one of many big time performers who have recorded his material.

(Prine and Raitt singing [chorus of "Angel from Montgomery"])

John Prine is now 45 years old. While greatly appreciated by his loyal fans . . . and widely praised by fellow musicians, he is still a bit of a mystery to the general public.

(ins & pic at restaurant)

Why he hasn't achieved more notoriety is puzzling given the accolades that flow from the music critics. They hail his writing . . .

(stand up)

. . . often using words like artist, poet, even songwriting genius, a description that Mr. Prine wouldn't choose for himself, not that he minds the praise, but genius . .

(sot Prine & Leonard)
[Prine:] "Uh, I don't think so."
[Leonard:] "Why?"

[Prine:] "Well, I mean, it's like, 'Your car is ready, by the way, what do you do for a living?' 'I'm a genius, thank you.' Genius. I got it right here on my card. Got genius plates on my car. Drivin' through a certain neighborhood, 'Hey, there goes the genius! Let's throw a brick at him.' I think that's the kind of thing I'd like to have said about me later, like after I'm in another place."

[Leonard:] "Why? Is it embarrassing?"

[Prine:] "A bit, yeah. You know I don't mind being called a poet because some stuff I write, I don't know where the heck else it comes from. You know it's new to me when it comes out . . . and it comes all rolling out in order and it's just right there."

[Leonard:] "Artist?"

[Prine:] "Yeah, artist . . . just the genius thing . . . it's cause the way I was in school. You know, like a genius to me would be like . . . I was the guy who threw a brick at the genius. You know, 'here comes that genius. Hey genius, figure this out!'"

(Prine sings [lyrics from "All the Best"]

The key to Prine's longevity can be found in the subject matter of his songs . . . the love, hope, sadness and comic absurdity that's present in everyday life. Longtime managers Al Bunetta and Dan Einstein hear the same comments from record stores all over the country.

(sot Einstein)

"It's not dated material. It's not something that's going to mold on the shelf."

Prine's 1st album, in fact, is still selling after 20 years on that shelf . . . positioned any day now to reach the 500,000 gold record level. Guns and Roses, on the other hand, sold 500,000 copies of their latest album just under two hours. That's mass merchandising . . . this is something more personal.

(sot Prine & Leonard)

[Prine:] "Right now I'm selling them door to door."

[Leonard:] "And how's that going?"

[Prine:] "Uh pretty good. 'Mrs. Johnson, you like this side or the other side? We'll give you a free brush with the record.'"

(Prine sings [lyrics from "It's a Big Old Goofy World"])

For *Today*, Mike Leonard, NBC News, Champaign, Illinois.

HOMETOWN HERO: JOHN PRINE COMES HOME TO GIVE BACK

Dave Hoekstra | **May 9, 2010** | *Chicago Sun-Times*

By 2010, Dave Hoekstra was an established voice at the *Chicago Sun-Times*. John Prine was a two-time Grammy winner and a man who'd created a label, then kept it afloat for three decades. Though he lived in Nashville and toured the world, he never lost his Kentucky or Chicago roots.

A long-standing relationship with photographer and director Jim Shea had expanded into conversations about filming a documentary. Prine had played a 2000 benefit for the Maywood Fine Arts Association after their dance studio had caught on fire; the homecoming show got Prine thinking perhaps a second show to benefit the center, where local students could explore the arts, would be a great way to anchor the as-yet-unreleased documentary.

Hoekstra understood the importance of both the charity and Prine's ties to the Maywood community. Rather than a standard show advance, he used his Sunday arts cover profile to revisit Prine's own early years in the neighborhood.

Calling from a Walmart parking lot in the middle of an Ozarks fishing trip, Prine was more than happy to revisit his youth. As much an homage to his father and where he grew up as anything, "Prine Time" demonstrates his love of family and where you come from. —Ed.

William Mason "Bill" Prine was a tool and die maker in the western suburbs from the 1930s to the 1970s. The rugged native of Paradise, Ky., had migrated north with his bride Verna to make a better life.

After his shift, Prine would adjourn to the front porch of his frame house on First Avenue in Maywood. He'd enjoy a quart of Old Style beer, with a second one for safe keeping in the freezer. He worked hard.

And then he would watch the world go by.

He felt the muscles of every passing dream.

"There was no interstate when we were growing up," his songwriter son John Prine recalled last week during a break from an Ozarks fishing trip. "First Avenue was a major route for semitrucks and traffic travelling north to south to avoid the city. I'd lay in bed at night and watch the headlights. Growing up on a four-lane highway, it was like a river. There was always something going on. We'd have all our talks with our dad on the porch." Bill Prine had a fatal heart attack on that porch in 1971. He was 56 years old. Prine gently references that hot August day in his 1973 ballad "Mexican Home."

Chicago's most acclaimed singer-songwriter returns to his hometown this week for two shows at Proviso East High School. The shows benefit the Maywood Fine Arts Association and are being filmed for a Prine documentary, which will also include the Sun-Times' Roger Ebert, who first wrote about Prine[,] and the timeless Earl Pionke, owner of the Earl of Old Town nightclub.

Prine is also the subject of two new recordings: "In Person and On Stage," a compilation of live recordings due May 25 on his Oh Boy label, and the tribute album "Broken Hearts & Dirty Windows," out June 22 on Oh Boy. (*johnprine.net*)

Musical Family

Prine was born in Maywood and attended Proviso East, as did all his brothers: Doug (a retired Chicago policeman), Dave (who taught John to play guitar in 1962) and Billy (a Nashville-based musician in his own right).

Prine's mother and father arrived in Maywood from Western Kentucky, where Verna's father ran a ferry boat on the Green River. The Prines rented the battleship-gray house on First Avenue for nearly 40 years. The house is still standing about a block away from the high school. Prine hopes to include the house in the documentary.

Proviso East opened in 1911 and has also produced luminaries such as Boston Celtics coach Doc Rivers, the late talk show host Mike Douglas and comedian Dennis Franz.

"I could see the school clock [tower] from my bedroom window," said Prine, who graduated from Proviso in January 1965. "I was late every day. I used to keep a pair of shoes by the side of the bed. My mother would holler because she didn't want to climb upstairs and drag me out of bed. I'd go, 'Yeah, I'm up.' Then I'd lean over, move my shoes along the floor like I was walking. And then roll over and go back to sleep."

Prine's father even attended Proviso East. The story begins in the frisky 1978 Prine ballad "Grandpa Was A Carpenter."

"That was my father's dad," Prine said. "He'd move his family to wherever he was doing jobs. My grandfather built the bank building on 4th at Madison in Maywood. My dad went to 12 different elementary schools because of his father's work. All up north because that's where the better jobs were."

Trout fishing in Arkansas

The Grammy-winning songwriter had called from the parking lot of a Wal-Mart Super Store in Arkansas. It was the only place in town with a strong signal. He had been catching rainbow trout with four friends.

"I've been coming to this same place since I was 14," he said.

The diversity of Maywood helped Prine find his way in life's rougher streams.

His father was a regular reader of the Sun-Times and Daily News. John heard his favorite songwriter, Chuck Berry, on neighborhood jukeboxes and would come home to absorb the Hank Williams Sr. and Spike Jones records from his father's collection.

"Maywood stuck out because it was integrated," Prine explained. "Later on, especially when I got in the Army, I was glad I grew up in that situation. I was with kids from Mexico, black kids. Some guys had never been away from home and were used to wherever they grew up. Maywood was a mixture of everything. Melrose Park was on one side and that was Italian American. Forest Park, back then, leaned toward German Americans and Polish Americans.

"You can tell by the restaurants.

"Oak Park? To Maywood it was where the rich people lived. In River Forest, everybody would point out [mobster] Tony Accardo's house. We'd ride by it on our bicycles."

Played benefit in 2000

Prine did the first benefit for the Maywood Fine Arts Association in 2000. More than 1,400 students learn piano, dance, hip-hop, tap dance, drama, drawing and other art disciplines at the school building, 25 N. Fifth Ave. The building's dance studio caught fire on March 12, and a recovery fund was established. "There's no charge for their programs," Prine said. "Those kids would never have this opportunity otherwise."

After the 2000 concert, Prine told his longtime manager Al Bunetta that the event should have been filmed. Prine reasoned, "I told stories from the stage about songs I wrote growing up. I told them if the song idea pertained to the Maywood area. It was stuff you normally wouldn't do in Pennsylvania or Florida. I saw people I hadn't seen in years. My whole gymnastics team was there. I had never been to a high school reunion, so I never knew the feeling of walking into a room and seeing faces 35 years later. It was a pleasant surprise.

"So, this time we're doing it again and filming it."

The documentary will include remembrances from all his brothers taped in Prine's Butcher Shoppe recording studio in Nashville. Prine will also lead a hometown tour similar to what he did in 1980 on WTTW-Channel 11's "Soundstage."

Prine's rich rhythms and witty wordplay echo the late country singer Roger Miller; whom Prine discovered through "Dang Me," the 1964 crossover hit that was popular while Prine was at Proviso East.

"I remember this gorgeous girl," Prine said. "She was so pretty the word was that she only went with college guys. My senior year I'm sitting behind her in art class. She had a voice like Marilyn Monroe, real soft. She turned around and said, 'Hi Jimmy.' I went out with her for four months and never corrected her. I didn't care what she called me. I let her call me Jimmy. She said to me one day, 'You remind me of that guy on the radio.' And I said, 'What guy is that?' She was talking about Roger Miller's goofy sense of humor. Because she was interested in me and I reminded her of him.

"I became a huge Roger Miller fan."

JOHN PRINE: THE BLUERAILROAD INTERVIEW

Paul Zollo | November 8, 2016 | *More Songwriters on Songwriting*

Paul Zollo, who served as editor of *SongTalk* for many years as well as managing editor at *Performing Songwriter*, teamed with Jim Shea for an as-yet-unreleased documentary. The author of *Songwriters on Songwriting*, Zollo has an empathetic approach to discussing songwriting process, influences, and how life informs art. The documentary is the reason he was there for this extended interview with Prine in 2016, and why his follow-up volume *More Songwriters on Songwriting* exists.

Culturally aware, this interview takes its time and provides Prine the unrushed rhythms needed to open up. Whether discussing minor chords, writing on a typewriter, or the power of imagery, the conversation is obviously instructive for any musicians or songwriters looking to strengthen their skills. But even music lovers will walk away with a richer appreciation of how much is inside the simplicity of these songs. —Ed.

"You can write about anything. Anything at all. As a matter of fact, the less familiar, the better."

He was then and remains a genuine songwriter's songwriter—in that he's written the kind of songs other songwriters aspire daily to write. Evidence is the vast array of covers of his songs by his peers, including Jackson Browne, Bonnie Raitt, Johnny Cash, Rickie Lee Jones, Willie Nelson, and so many others. Even Bob Dylan, since the first night Kristofferson brought Prine and Steve Goodman into their Greenwich Village fold, has been awed. "Prine's stuff is pure Proustian existentialism," said Dylan. "Beautiful songs . . . I remember when Kris first brought him on the scene. All that stuff about 'Sam Stone,' the soldier junkie daddy, and 'Donald and Lydia,' where people make love from ten miles away. Nobody but Prine could write like that." Kristofferson, despite unleashing Prine's genius on the world, admitted to being intimidated by him. "He's so good," Kris said, "we're gonna have to break his fingers."

When Prine and Goodman returned to Chicago after landing their deals, a celebration ensued for our local heroes, the entire town welcoming them with warmth and open arms. Unlike other big cities that reject locals who leave to make it big, Chicago has nothing but pride for those who come from our streets and take on the world. "We were like astronauts coming back from the moon," Prine said. "They might as well have thrown a parade for us."

Prine's lines are so evocative, so purely precise and finely etched, that they linger in our hearts and minds like dreams, separate from the songs. There's the rodeo poster from 'Angel from Montgomery', the hole in daddy's arm and the broken radio (from 'Sam Stone'), the old trees that just grow stronger (from 'Hello In There'). The kinds of lines you carry around in your pocket, knowing they're in there when you need them. His is a prodigious gift for capturing intangibles with language, such as the anomalous texture of Sunday nights he translated into 'The Late John Garfield Blues' or the ennui expressed so purely with the flies buzzing around the kitchen in 'Angel from Montgomery'. Whether writing about old folks so sorrowfully isolated that people call 'Hello in there' like talking to a kid in a well, or taking on the phenomenon of celebrity through the unlikely subject of Sabu the Elephant Boy, Prine has melded his staggering penchant for detail, his proclivity to be both hilarious and deeply serious (and often in the same song), with a visceral embrace of roots music. And doing so, he's made the kinds of songs nobody ever dreamed of before, or since.

As a kid his first musical love was country; endlessly spinning the Roy Acuff and Hank Williams 78s in his dad's collection, tuning into WJJD out of Chicago to hear Webb Pierce, Lefty Frizell and others "back-to-back, all night long." Roots music with stories to tell, the kind of songs he'd become famous for writing. And then a new kind of music arrived: "I was coming of age just as rock and roll was invented," he said like a kid on Christmas, along with his country heroes he added Elvis, Little Richard, Fats Domino, and the one he loved the most, Chuck Berry: "Because he told a story in less than three minutes," Prine explained. "And he had a syllable for every beat. . . . Some people stretch the words like a mask to fit the melody. Whereas guys who are *really* good lyricists, have a meter so the melody is almost already there."

He started playing guitar at 14—mostly old folk tunes taught to him by his brother Dave, who gave fiddle lessons. He quickly surmised he could take the same three folk chords and with a little rhythm play Chuck Berry, but his limitations then, as they have ever since, led him to his own songs. "I learned to write because I'd learn to play a Fats Domino song, say, and it wouldn't sound nearly as good as Fats Domino. So I'd just make up my own melody and write my own words. And anything I made up came out sounding like a folk song, because that was the kind of guitar I learned. If my brother would have been into Chuck Berry, then maybe I would have written all those songs as rock and roll shuffles."

When he was old enough, he got a job as a postman, which he loved, because he could write songs while walking the familiar blocks. "It was like a library with no books," he said. "When you've got your own mail route, day after day, it was an easy place to write."

For a string of consecutive Sundays he started coming to open mike nights at the Fifth Peg, a folk club on Armitage in Old Town. When he summoned the courage to perform, he played his handful of unheard classics—'Angel from Montgomery', 'Hello In There' and 'Donald & Lydia'—the audience was stunned speechless and forgot to clap. He figured he'd failed: "They just sat there. They didn't even applaud, they just *looked* at me. I thought, 'Uh oh. This is pretty bad.' I started shuffling my feet and looking around. Then they started applauding and it was a really great feeling. It was like I found out all of a sudden that I could communicate. That I could communicate really deep feelings and emotions. And to find that out all at once was amazing."

And the word spread like wildfire. When Kristofferson heard Prine and Goodman, he pulled some New York strings and landed them record deals. The rest is singer-songwriter history. It was 1971, the dream of the '60s was over and Goodman and Prine emerged with a new kind of song, eschewing the lyrical abstractions of the past to write instead story songs about real people. Songs with the concrete details and imagery of a novelist, but compounded, like Prine's hero Chuck Berry, into three-minute masterpieces.

We spoke on a sun-bright Tennessee morning, his voice a low, raspy whisper since his recent bout with cancer and subsequent throat surgery. But his stories were punctuated with frequent laughter—laughter at himself, and at the sad folly of a world he's written about so well for decades. Perhaps recognizing things he's put off forever, like doing this kind of interview, were worth doing now or never, he took a long time to generously delve into his personal history from the streets of Maywood to Germany to the Chicago folk scene to the nightclubs of New York and beyond. Though talking wasn't as easy as it once was, he enjoyed rummaging through the rooms of his own memory, which he found easier than recalling what happened last week. "I just gave a long interview yesterday to PBS," he said, "so I might get confused. Sometimes it's hard to separate yesterday from today."

Did you write your first song after you were in the army?

No, I wrote a couple early on. I learned to play the guitar when I was 14. I learned three chords and didn't bother to [laughs] learn much else. It got to where, if I wanted to learn a song and it had a minor chord in it, and I really wanted to learn that song, I'd learn it and the first thing I'd do is take the odd chord, as I called it, the one I had never played before—and put it in a new song of mine. Just to see where it would fit. See where you'd have to go emotionally for that to work. People would always tell me about minor chords—when you're writing a song, to put a minor chord in. For me, it's like doom. You know somebody's gonna be extremely sick or die if there's a character in the song. If it's a first-person narrative, you're gonna go off to war or something. [Laughs] Something bad is gonna happen when the minor chord hits.

That's funny, cause throughout all your songs, there's hardly one written in a minor key. They almost always start with a major chord.

I wrote in a minor key a couple of times over the years. Mainly just to experiment. Because I always felt if you start something in a minor key, then you're already down in the mine. [Laughs] You don't have to go to the mines, you're already there. [Laughter] Because you're in the minor chords.

Do you remember what your first three chords were?

Probably G, C, D. It may have been A, D, E because they're easier. I shied away from B7 for a long time because it took too many fingers. [Laughs]

'Hello In There' has that C maj 7 chord in it, has more chords than you ever use.

I remember specifically when I wrote it, I think I had learned 'Nobody Knows You When You're Down & Out'. It had about nine chords to it. I learned the song more or less as a lesson so I could sing and change chords quickly at the same time. And once I did that, I thought, "Gee, I'm gonna write a song with every chord in it I know." And that's "Hello In There." And I'm still surprised to this day the chords came out that well and sound as pretty as they do.

'Hello In There' is about old folks, yet you wrote it as a young man with a lot of insight into what it's like to be old. Do you remember where it came from?

I always felt, even when I was a child, really close to my grandparents. And later when I was a teenager, I just felt a kinship with older people. And I remember for a short time I had a best friend when I was about 11, he had a paper route and he'd give me a couple bucks to help him. And one of the streets had the Baptist Old People's Home on it. You'd have to park your bike and go inside with about twenty papers to the room where the people subscribed to the paper were. Some of the people, I guess, they didn't have many visitors. And to their other friends in the home you were like a nephew or a grandson. I picked up on that and it always stuck in my mind. I guess that's what it's like inside of any kind of institution.

Just the title, 'Hello In There', is so evocative. It implies the person is deep inside himself, hard to reach.

I do vaguely remember I tied it somehow to the first time I heard John Lennon sing 'Across the Universe'. He was already putting a lot of echo on his voice on different songs, you know, experimenting, I played that song over and over again and it sounded to me like somebody talking to a hollow log or a lead pipe. With that echo. I was thinking of reaching somebody, communicating with somebody, like "hello . . . hello in there. . . ." When I was writing the song, I thought these people have entire lives in there. They're not writers, but they all have stories to tell. Some are very, very down deeper than others. See, you gotta *dig*, you know? And that was all going through my mind when I wrote 'Hello In There'.

I didn't know what the song was gonna be about, actually, when I came up with 'Hello In There'. I knew it was gonna be about loneliness and isolation. I was still very much into using names [in songs]. I was a big fan of Bob Dylan early on, and his song "The Lonesome Death of Hattie Carroll" was a big model for me. I modeled "Donald & Lydia" after that song. As far as telling a story and having the chorus be the morale [sic] to the story. A wider morale [sic] than what the story's saying. Like where the chorus is all-consuming, a much bigger subject than what you're detailing. Yeah, that was much in the same way that any upbeat song I modelled after Chuck Berry, I modeled a ballad after specific songs, and that song of Bob Dylan's, 'The Lonesome Death of Hattie Carroll' to me was to be held up as a real model for songs, as was a lot of Hank Williams, Sr. songs.

It's surprising to hear the influence of Lennon and also Dylan to some extent, in that many of their songs were quite poetically abstract and surreal, whereas your songs tell clear stories with precise imagery.

Yeah. I don't know how I made that decision. It's what I was good at, but I might have thought it was a fault at first. I might have thought I used too many words to discuss a minor detail. But I soon found out the reason that was on my mind is because that's what I wanted to hear. I wanted to hear what was in somebody's purse. I wanted to hear that at the time of this emotional thing. I wanted to hear what paintings were hanging on the wall. I wanted to know whether it was a cheap refrigerator. [Laughs] I just did. It was kind of detective work.

You've always been one of the best at using pictures as symbols, like the old trees that just grow stronger in 'Hello In There', or the rodeo poster in 'Angel from Montgomery'.

[Pause] Yeah. I'm not sure where that came from. But I'm glad it did.

And 'Angel' came from?
    . . .the idea stuck with me. I went home I started 'Angel From Montgomery' with the words "I am an old woman named after my mother." I had this *really* vivid picture of this woman standing over the dishwater with soap in her hands, and just walking away from it all. So I kept that whole idea image in mind when I was writing the song and I just let it pour out of that character's heart.

That song was a lesson for so many songwriters about how to write in character. I remember hearing the song the first time with that opening, "I am an old woman," thinking what an extraordinary way to start a song, especially written by a man.

Again, I didn't realize all this at the time, but if you come up with a strong enough character, you can get a really vivid insight into the character that you've invented. You let the character write the song. You just dictate from then on. You stick to it, and whatever the character is saying, you have to figure out how to keep that in the song. You know? That's how I do it. I almost go into a trance. Once I've got an outline, a sketch in my mind, of who the person was, then I figure I'd better let them speak for themselves. Rather than me saying, "Hey, so here's a middle-aged woman. She feels she's much older." It wouldn't have been nearly as effective.

    I got asked lots of times how I felt I could get away with writing a woman's song first-person. And that never *occurred* to me, because I already considered myself a writer. And writers are any gender you want. You write from the character and how can you go wrong?

But there aren't a lot of songwriters, outside of Broadway, who write effectively in character. You do it, and Randy Newman does—
I love the way Randy does it. The character stuff, so determined that they believe what they're saying. I got to tour with Randy a lot early on. We did a lot of shows together, just him on piano and me on guitar.

You're similar not only that you're great at character songs, but also can be funny in songs, which isn't easy. You're both very serious and very funny.
Yeah. For me, I find humor in just about every situation. Even the most serious situations. And I find if you use it right, it allows the listener not to feel so uncomfortable. Or to even empathize with that character.

With 'Angel from Montgomery', do you remember where the title came from or why you placed it in Montgomery?
No, I can only guess like other people. I'm so far away from myself; I'm removed when I'm writing.

[A good friend] thinks I got it from the angel down on Michigan Boulevard [in Chicago]. There was evidently a gargoyle that came out from the Montgomery Wards building.

But I'm prone to think it's because I was a huge Hank Williams, Sr. fan and I knew he was from Montgomery. And I think that's where I thought the woman was from in this image that I had, this woman with the soapsuds on her hand. She lived in Montgomery, Alabama and she wanted to get out of there. She wanted to get out of her house and her marriage and everything. She just wanted an angel to come to take her away from all this. And her memory of this cowboy she had once—or whether she had him or not—it doesn't matter now.

Yeah, you're not only in her real life, but in her dreams, in what she's yearning for.
Yeah. Man, they did a book of the famous poster people here in Nashville, the ones who did those giant posters of Hank Williams and the Grand Ol

Opry and everything. They're still going today with the original presses. It's a great place to go. It's not far from the Ryman Auditorium. They put a book out of their famous posters. And the poster on the cover is a poster of a rodeo, a guy with a bunking bronco and it's got the words to the beginning of 'Angel from Montgomery' on it. And it's a really good-looking poster. I asked them to give me a copy of it. It looked very much like whatever I had in mind when I wrote it.

I remember as a kid listening to that song and learning so much about how you set the mood—instead of saying she's bored, you say, "There's flies in the kitchen/I can hear em there buzzin'/And I ain't done nothin' since I woke up today . . ."

I think the more the listener can contribute to the song, the better; the more they become part of the song, and they fill in the blanks. Rather than *tell* them everything, you save your details for things that exist. Like what color the ashtray is. How far away the doorway was. So when you're talking about intangible things, like emotions, the listener can fill in the blanks and you just draw the foundation. I still tend to believe that's the way to tackle it today.

Whenever I co-write with people—and it's very difficult to dodge co-writing in Nashville [laughs]—I tell people I'm just trying to write with myself right now, and it's very difficult to jump back and forth between the two. Because I enjoy co-writing when it's with the right person. I can go into a different head with a co-writer. Let them take the song on and I'm just helping them with their idea. But if I'm gonna write my idea, I want to stick with it myself. I usually won't be the one to initiate a co-write.

The old cliché for writers is "write what you know". Yet you seem to reach beyond your own personal experience often. A song like 'Sam Stone', about a man who comes back from Vietnam a junkie, is that someone you knew?

Well, I had just gotten out of the service myself. I got drafted with about six of my best friends, and some of them got sent to Viet Nam. Everyone I knew, they got back, they came back. I knew two kids I went to school with who didn't come back from Viet Nam. In fact, they didn't last a week there. But my own personal friends, they all came back. But there were big changes in their lives. And there are still to this day.

I remember when they first came back, whenever it seemed appropriate, I would question them about how it was there. I pretty much got the same story from everybody, that it was pretty much a wait and see situation over there. You could be in a place in Viet Nam where there seemingly wasn't much action, you weren't anywhere near the front. But it soon became evident that there was no front. There was always a front as far as if we made an invasion or they did and there was a battle going on, there was that. But the whole place was the front. You could be walking over to the officer's club for a drink some night and step on a mine. Or nothing would happen for six months, there wouldn't be a sound, and all of sudden you'd be walking around and they'd come over and bomb. And that kept you on edge, I guess, all the time.

I always thought one of the great mistakes they made in the service, I don't know if they even tried to correct it with the guys coming back from the Middle East, but if they spent half the time that they do getting you ready, and the intensity that they put you through in basic training for combat, if they spent half that time bringing you down and teaching you how to be a civilian, it would make a big difference. I would liken it to a person who has done prison time. They all speak of, especially if they've been in for a very long time, of how difficult it is to be back on the street. And how difficult it is be to accept freedom once you get used to living incarcerated. So all my friends that were over there were affected, like I said. I wasn't writing about anybody specific. I made up the character of Sam Stone, obviously, just cause he rhymed with 'home'.

But I remember a story in the papers about some soldiers coming home from Vietnam in San Francisco they landed. And some people at the airport—I don't know if they were protesters or hippies, or what—but they were spitting on them. Saying they shouldn't be over there killing babies and stuff. And I was totally repulsed by that. And here, mainly, I was against the way. And I was for all the hippies and didn't mind burning the flag and stuff, you know? [Laughs] I mean, to blame a soldier—maybe because I was one—I felt like, gee, you don't know what you're talking about. To blame the guys who are going over there. Because they didn't run to Canada and say they're not gonna fight for their country. But that just seemed really awkward and stupid to me.

So I wanted to explain through a fictional character what it might be like to come home. Not to be there, because I was never in Viet Nam. I was stationed in Germany. And I was drafted at a time when most people were being sent to Vietnam, and I thought I was going there for sure. But when the day came that they gave me orders to go overseas, I was thankful for it. Whereas other guys who got sent to Germany, as soon as they got there, they put in for Vietnam. They didn't want to be in Germany, they wanted to be in combat. And I'd just say [laughs], "You guys are *nuts.*" [Laughs] It's not John Wayne time.

I had my guitar over there, though I didn't do much writing. I was about three bunks down from a guy who sang beautiful Lefty Frizell songs. He could sing just like Lefty. And he and I became fast friends. I sang Hank Williams songs and he sang Lefty songs. I think 'Aw Heck' might have been the only song I wrote while I was over there.

Songs like 'Sam Stone' and 'Angel From Montgomery' are such mature, sophisticated songs for a beginning songwriter to write. Any idea how you were able to write at that level so early on?

No, I don't. I was very nervous about singing the songs in public for the first time. Because I thought that they would come across as too detailed, too amateurish. Because I hadn't heard anybody being that detailed. And I thought there must be a reason for that. I must not be doing it the right way, whatever the right way is. But I knew the songs were very effective to me. And they reached me. And I was very satisfied with the songs. But I didn't know how they would relate to other people because I didn't consider myself a normal person. [Laughter]

Did audiences take to them right away?

Right away. They were very effective. The first crowd just sat there. They didn't even applaud, they just *looked* at me. I thought, "Uh oh." [Laughs] I thought, "This is pretty bad." I started shuffling my feet and looking around. And then they started applauding and it was a really great feeling. It was like I found out all of a sudden that I could communicate. That I could communicate really deep feelings and emotions. And to find that out all at once was amazing. Whereas it would have been different if I would have written a novel or something and waited two years till somebody to write me back. And said, "I think we're gonna take a chance and publish it." That must be a whole different feeling. But mine was *immediate*. It was there before other people. Nobody knew me from Adam.

Do you remember the first song you wrote?

Yeah. I think I wrote two at the same time. I had a girlfriend whose father was a janitor. And the reason I'm telling you that is because he had access to a tape recorder, and nobody else I knew had one. They were really rare. A reel-to-reel. He got it from the language department. It was broken and he fixed it and had it at home. And I sat down and taped three songs for this girl and her sister. And the three songs were 'Frying Pan', 'Sour Grapes' and 'Twist & Shout'. And I know I didn't write 'Twist & Shout'. [Laughter] Those were the three, and I made her a present of them.

Years later, I ended up marrying that girl. She was my first wife. She found the tape. It was after I had made the first album, so I put two of those songs on *Diamonds In The Rough*. And those were the first songs I remember writing.

You said you wrote 'Sam Stone' and 'Hello In There' when you were working as a mailman—

Yeah. That was only six months before I first got up and sang, and six months after that I got a record contract.

When you started writing those songs, was your intention to become a professional musician?

I was surprised that the songs connected as well as they did when I first sang them for an audience. I think I was more surprised than the audience. I just got the nerve up behind a couple beers one night to stand up onstage—cause it was an open mic—and the competition, the bar, was very low.

Which club was it?

The Fifth Peg, which was across the street from the Old Town School when it used to be on West Armitage. . . . I was writing these songs totally myself not thinking that anybody was going to hear them. And I went from that to being a very nervous public performer. Who had no voice whatsoever. I would kind of speak the words. Very fast or very slow, depending on how the melody went. And I'd hold certain notes [laughs] to let people know I was going to the next idea. And that's about how limited it was. It was very painful for me to stand up in front of people and sing.

Meanwhile, I enjoyed singing. I would sit for hours just by myself and just bellow out and beat on the guitar. I loved the actual act of singing. But to listen to myself on tape or to sing for other people was really painful. And the first time people heard me [laughs], evidently they felt the same.

Steve Goodman was such an astounding performer—

He certainly was. I think Steve had arrived, except for timing. He really worked hard, and he was entertaining.

Did you learn much about performing from watching Steve play?

[Pause] Jeez, the way he handled an audience, you couldn't help but pick up things. I might not have thought about it like that at the time. I developed my own thing from my own mistakes. What I considered my mistakes. My own nervousness. I made it an asset. That's how I started talking between songs. I found out that people liked the stories I was telling—they were just totally out of pure nervousness—I was trying to kill time till I had to start singing [laughs] those painful notes again. I put the two together—the talking and the singing—and noticed that worked.

You just find out things from your own shortcomings. It's easy to say in hindsight, and I never would have said this at the time, but that's what I did—I gathered all my shortcomings and made them into the stronger points, you know, the points I could stretch cause they worked. You find out real fast when you stand just in front of twelve people what's working or not.

Do you generally have an idea in mind before you start writing a song?

Yes. Because otherwise I don't see any reason in sitting down [laughs] to do it. A lot of time I'll have the song written and I only write it down so I don't forget it. I could write behind a steel mill. But it's easier to get behind a guitar.

Is it easy for you to get to that place where songs start coming?

It's very elusive. Patience. You gotta learn patience. I know that I'm basically a very lazy person. At everything, including writing. As much as I enjoy writing, I would rather do anything in the world but sit down and write. But once I get into it, I'm into it. I mean, if you said, "Let's go get a hot dog first," I would always go for the hot dog. I wouldn't go, "No, let's finish this song." [Laughter] I'd say, "Sure!" [Laughter]

So you never force yourself to write—

No. [Laughs] No. Unfortunately a lot of your best first-person songs come from a person's relationship, from something awful happening to someone you love very much. So you wouldn't want to force those things. Not for the purpose of a good song. Some guys I've met, I wouldn't put anything past them. [Laughs] Some people, for a good song, might go through all kinds of changes to get to that.

Your songs seem to suggest you are having fun writing them, with the rhymes and the rhythms—

I almost need, not someone standing over me, I do need some prodding. I have to realize, jeez, okay, it's been long enough without a record. Because

I can afford just to go play my songs for big crowds. I play in some of the nicest places in this country. And they got nice dressing rooms. I've moved up to where the dressing rooms actually don't have rats running around in them. It'd be very easy to just keep doing that. But every once in a while, I've got to write and get myself into a fresh state of mind.

I don't write ten songs in two weeks and go into the studio. I just don't do that. I'll write three songs and love them, and I'll go sing them for a year and then write the next three. I just know how I am . . . there's nobody standing over me. I've got my own record company, my own publishing. I try and make a place for myself to write that I want to go to.

Having written such amazing songs right from the start, was there a sense after your first album that you had a lot to live up to?

Only after so many people told me that so many times. [Laughter] And then I got to remember that the gift I have, I only owe it to myself to honour that gift. Why try to write a better song about old people or a better song about a veteran coming home? Why try to update 'Sam Stone'? There's no reason to. So I try and stay true to wherever the writing comes from. And it comes from the deepest well of emotion. Whether it's something political, something humorous, something that might break your heart, if that's what's down in the well, that's what I'll come up with.

You said you write songs in your car. Do you mean that you write music, too, or just words when you're away from the guitar?

To me, the melody usually comes along hand in hand with the words. It's very rare that I'll get a little piece of music that I keep playing over and over, like something I'll do at a soundcheck that I can't get rid of. In order to get rid of it, I'll write a song to it. But usually they start with the idea or the image and I want to say one thing. Just one sentence. And I'll figure out who would say that and how can I build a song on that?

Do you collect titles and think of titles before writing?

No, but when I first started co-writing, at first I only wrote with really close friends who also happened to be songwriters. Just because I knew

I liked spending time with that person, so I didn't really care if I came out with a song or not. As long as we had a good time together.

One of the first people that I wrote with when I first moved to Nashville was somebody I didn't know, but I just wrote with because of all the great songs that they'd written was Bobby Braddock. He wrote 'We're Not The Jet Set', 'He Stopped Loving Her Today.'

So when Bobby and I got ready to write, we wrote 'Unwed Fathers.' The night before we got together, I said, "Do you like to start any particular way, Bobby?"

He goes, "You know, if you feel like it, bring a little list of song titles." Just as a way to get started, we can go, "Naaaah . . ." [Laughs] "And that must mean we got a better idea."

I was watching the Superbowl, and I wrote down twenty titles. I used five of those titles in the song. I used the title 'Children Having Children.' I pulled different ones I liked to go with that subject that I liked of 'Unwed Fathers.' Sometimes there's not titles, they're random thoughts you can associate with something else. I don't like to waste paper. [Laughter] I don't like to write and throw it away. I don't like starting over. I may not know the words, I may not know the character's name, I may not know any of that. But I get the picture. It's a matter transferring it to paper.

You said it almost feels like it's dictated to you from somewhere else? Any idea where that is?

No. None. I don't know what the rules are. I don't know if I ever cheated at the game. I don't like to get so close to it. Every once in awhile it's safer to go for a hot dog. [Laughs]

Some of the songs come so fully, it's like their pre-packaged. There have been a couple that came in the middle of the night. And I thought, jeez, I'll never forget *that*. And went back to sleep, and it was gone. You'll hear something years later that another songwriter that you respect writes, and you go, jeez, I think that was the remnants of that song that got sent to me.

Many songwriters feel that songwriting is more a sense of following a song than leading it—

Exactly. Because if you approach it the other way, it seems you are out-guessing it. Like people who are trying to write hit songs are guessing what the public wants. Or worse, what the record executive wants.

One of your most beautiful and poignant songs is 'Souvenirs'.

I wrote that in my car. A '65 Chevelle. Driving to the Fifth Peg. Like the fifth or sixth time playing there. I used to play there just Thursdays after they hired me. They hired me from that open stage the very first time I sang for the crowd.

They invited me back a week later; I did it again for an open stage. That night the owner asked me if I wanted to sing once a week. I didn't know I was auditioning. I didn't know what to do, how long you're supposed to sing or anything. So I went home and wrote a bunch of songs to fill in the time. They told me to do three sets of 45 minutes. About the fifth time I was driving down there I thought, God, the same people are gonna be sitting there. I better have a new song. So I wrote 'Souvenirs' in the car on the way down. Then I thought I'd come up with a melody. And I thought I had come up with a pretty sophisticated melody in my head, and I was surprised to find out it had the same three chords that all my other songs have. [Laughter] Really surprised. I thought I had written a jazz melody.

You've written several songs like that one, really poignant songs about time passing and what we lose in time—

Yeah. Where any of that song came from, I have no idea what the start was.

Was there someone in mind you wrote it to?

I have three brothers, two older, one younger. And one of them was asking me about 'Souvenirs.' He was five years older than me; once we were at a carnival and we were very small, and he got lost for a while and I got very, very scared that I would never see my brother. I remember that. It was a different kind of scared than I had ever experienced before in my life, like being scared by ghosts or creepy stuff. I kept that emotion buried somewhere, and it came out in 'Souvenirs.' How, I don't know. I told him, "I remember you standing there holding a little plastic horse that you either won or somebody gave you. I put it all together in a picture, and that's what came out."

Is it true that 'Bruised Orange' is a title you had long before you wrote the song? You also named your publishing company that.

When I was still a mailman, I had about eight songs, and somebody told me if I wanted to sing them in public, I should think about copyright-ing them. Another fella told me if I just copyrighted them all under one title, as a musical, then I could do it all for five dollars, instead of five dollars per song. So I found this music professor from Northwestern and he would make the sheet music for a couple bucks per song. He'd write it out in music, and I'd include a cassette and lyric sheet and mail it to myself, get it postmarked; that was considered a legal copyright. I put it all under the name *Bruised Orange* [laughs]. Which I used many years later. That's what I called the imaginary musical. They were all songs like 'Sam Stone', 'Blow Up Your TV', 'Paradise'. I had them all under one title. I found it not too long ago, the envelope. I finally opened it. I had to [laughs]. I figured it was safe now. [Laughter].

I listened to the song 'Bruised Orange' last night and realized someone might call it 'Chain of Sorrow', as that's the most prevalent line. How come you chose that?

I liked the title, and the image. I wanted to do something with that image without saying anything about an orange or a bruise in the song. It was based upon something that actually happened. I was an altar boy, and the Northwestern train tracks were not far from the church that I went to. I was going down there one day and there was this big ruckus going on at the train tracks. I had to go shovel the snow off the church steps before Mass. Because they'd sue the church if people fell and broke their legs. So I was going down there to get the snow and ice off. I went over to the train tracks. A kid who had also been an altar boy at the Catholic

Church, I found out later, was walking down the train tracks. Evidently the commuter train came up behind him. They were taking him away in bushel baskets, there was nothing left. There were a bunch of mothers standing around, trying to figure out—'cause it was Sunday morning and all their kids were gone and they didn't know—they all hadn't located their children yet, and didn't know who it was.

I told that story on TV once when it first came out. The family of that son lived near Madison, Wisconsin years and years later—20 years later—just wrote me the nicest letter, told me they recognized the subject. They gave me the date of when it happened, and that would have been around the time. So it was just a vivid memory I had, and I put it together with how I felt about my job as an altar boy. I was supposed to be the maintenance man at church and they were short an altar boy. They baptized me and confirmed me on a Saturday; Sunday I was wearing a robe, lighting a candle. Then I had to go early and shovel the snow as a maintenance man or cut the lawn in the summertime. That's when I bought my first guitar.

Listening to your songs, including great early ones like 'Sabu Visits The Twin Cities', it's evident that you can write about anything in songs, using content nobody else ever has. Was that something you felt?

[Softly] Yeah. [Laughs] Definitely. [Laughs] If I could get away with the song about the veteran coming home, and a chorus like, "There's a hole in Daddy's arm where all the money goes," even as powerful as it turned out to be, then I could write anything. But when I wrote it, it was very *odd*. When I'd sing that chorus, I'd be nervous and by the second time around, there'd be dead silence. And I just figured, yeah, you can write about anything. Anything at all. As a matter of fact, the less familiar, the better.

Many songwriters feel you have to write about yourself. You've shown that isn't the case—unless you feel you're writing about yourself all the time?

There's a certain amount of yourself in it, I'm sure. But as a writer you don't need to be writing about yourself all the time. Maybe you're not that interesting, really. Without an outside thing.

Was there ever content or an idea you couldn't get into a song, that wouldn't work?

More often than not, I can't jump into a song too quick. There's always the danger of painting yourself into a corner. There's no tougher corner to get out of than the ones you paint. Because you can't change the rules if you made up the rules. And then you get to the third verse that needs to be there, and you can't just repeat the first verse. You can't get out of it that way, so how are you going to get out of it? Especially if it's a story song. You'd better be going somewhere [laughs]. I think that's what the listeners are always thinking that, hey, this is precious time I'm giving you, so you'd better be going somewhere. [Laughs] This joke better be funny.

Do you generally write more and then cut stuff out?

No, I edit as I go. Especially when I go to commit it to paper. I prefer a typewriter even to a computer. I don't like it, there's no noise on the computer. I like a typewriter because I am such a slow typist I edit as I am committing it to paper. I like to see the words before me and I go, "Yeah, that's it." They appear before me, and they fit, you know, and I can see the line fits with the previous line and the line after it. I can see the inside of the song as well, not just rhyming the last word so that the song sounds right. I pretty much do that as I go. I don't usually take large parts out. If I get stuck early in a song, I would take it as a sign that I might be writing the chorus and don't know it. Sometimes you're writing the first verse or second verse and you're actually writing what you want to repeat. And you gotta step back a little bit and take a look at what you're doing.

You said that in 'Hello In There' you used all the chords you knew at the time. Have you ever done that with other songs?

Yeah, I still haven't used that many. I think when I wrote *Storm Windows*, somebody had just taught me the Elvis Presley song 'That's When Heartaches Begin'. And it had a Cm(inor) chord. I really wanted to learn the song, so I learned a Cm. And I know how that chord feels. It's the one chord that with a G, I know how it feels, what the emotions are there. So I felt I wanted to write a song that goes there and gets out of it, and that was *Storm Windows*.

Do you remember where the idea of writing 'Sabu'—a song about the famous elephant boy—where that came from?

I know it was from somewhere else. Because it took me several weeks before I would play it for anybody. The whole song came at once, just like it is, fully written. I didn't know whether to show it to anybody or what, whether it was an ugly baby or what.

We were talking about funny songs, and there aren't really that many funny songs that work over many years. The joke wears out. But your funny ones are still funny. Is that hard to do?

I never know until the years pass. [Laughs] I'm surprised as anybody. I pulled the song 'Your Flag Decal Won't Get You Into Heaven Anymore' out of mothballs. I stopped singing that when most of the thing with Viet Nam was over. People asked me about it, after we were in Iraq.

I thought that if George Bush kept tinkering so much about patriotism, that if you talked out against that war, you definitely were a Lefty. When he started with that bullshit, it really got under my skin. So I thought one night I would pull that song back out and start singing it again. I had no idea if it would work as well. And it felt really good.

I have a lot of songs I haven't touched in years. I need to be prodded to bring them out. I only have to play them once or twice to see if they work. It's not even so much the crowd reaction. It's more how I feel when I'm singing the song. I can just tell if I stopped singing that for a reason. Maybe I'll feel that I didn't get everything right in that, or everything I could have. Cause I'll never go back and change a song. I just feel that would violate it. But I've had an amazing track record of my stuff working—at least for me.

We were talking about 'Souvenirs', and you said Steve Goodman used to play on that song, and—

Yeah, I can still hear him playing it. He played a back melody, so that you could *barely* hear the difference of who was playing. On tape or when we did it live. And I realized a large part of what he was doing was making it sound like I was playing the good part. [Laughs]

And that's basically the kind of guy he was. The kind of guy who wouldn't need to shine the light on him, even though he could ham it up with the best of them.

He produced your Bruised Orange *album. What was that like to have him produce?*

He was definitely doing me a favor. I had made the record already, but I didn't have it. I worked with Cowboy Jack Clement, who was a huge mentor to me and the reason why I moved to Nashville. I moved there and we worked for three to four months, solid. And we really enjoyed making the record, but we didn't get it on tape the way we were hearing it in the studio. This was the first one for Asylum Records, and they kept spending money on it. And Jack was on Asylum as well, and his record was about two years late [Laughs]. So these were both of our first records on this label, and here we were working on mine. And we were having a great time. And listening to music, too. It was a very musical summer we spent. Then I got involved with somebody, and it got to be a very sticky affair.

What I'm saying is that I had a record I put my heart and soul into with the songs, gone ahead and made the record, and I didn't have anything to show for it. I had to walk away from the whole thing. So I went out to L.A. and I talked to twenty different producers, really great guys, great producers. Big-time producers. And I just didn't want to do it. I just didn't have the heart to do the record again. And Goodman said he would do it.

I said, "Well, just don't look to me to approve or disapprove. I'm just totally . . . *numb.*" I said I'd come in and do anything, you just tell me what songs to do today and I'll do it, and if you say it's done right,

I'll believe you. I totally put it in his hands. And he handed me back a beautiful record. That's the way that that one went down. It was no fun for Steve, I'm sure. I was not a fun guy to be around. [Laughter] Funny how things turn out. Steve, he was a tough producer to work with.

How so?

Very stubborn. Because he knew me so well. If someone doesn't know me, they kind of keep at a distance. Which is fine with me. But he knew me. So he would push me. Some nights at the studio I'd say, "Steve, get off my back, man." But he knew what he was going for.

Would he criticize your songs?

Yeah. The first time Kristofferson introduced Bob Dylan to Steve and me—this was back in the Village in Carly Simon's apartment, 1971—my first record wasn't coming out for a week. And Kristofferson said, "Come on over," and gave us Carly's address. Carly was opening for Kristofferson at the Bitter End. He said, "I got a surprise for you guys." So we come over and we're sitting in Carly's place. There's a knock on the door and in walks Bob Dylan. At this time, Bob Dylan was not doing any shows. It was after the motorcycle accident, years after, in the early '70s. He had just written 'George Jackson'. You familiar with that song? "Lord, Lord, they cut George Jackson down/Lord, Lord, they laid him in the ground."

So we're passing the guitar around. Kris sings one. I sing one. Bob takes the guitar and says he'd like to play something he just wrote, so he sings that. Goodman looks at him [laughs] and says, "That's great, Bob. It's no 'Masters of War,' though." [Much laughter]. I sang 'Far From Me' and Dylan sang with me. He had an advance copy of my record that Jerry Wexler had sent him. He already knew a couple of the songs. So he showed up at the Bitter End and played harmonica behind me on 'Donald & Lydia' and 'Far From Me'. It was like a dream.

So, yeah, that's Goodman criticizing.

Another great song you wrote with previously untouched content is 'Jesus, The Missing Years'.

I wrote that in a total state of inebriation. I was afraid to look at it for about a week. I knew I had written it, and I was totally surprised that it was as together as it was. I didn't change too much at all. I think I've still got the original transcript, if you wanna call it that. With arrows here and there moving lines around.

On the original record I went all around town trying to find the best recording of a lightning bolt. So I could start to sing with a big clap of thunder. I bought nature albums [laughter]. With the sounds of rain and hurricane, till I finally found a clap of thunder. Put a bunch of echo on the voice just for the title where it goes, 'Jesus, The Missing Years'. Then I play boom-boom-boom and go into this talking thing. I think it was mostly about Hank Williams' 'Luke the Drifter'. I was just trying to emulate that, though I knew Hank Williams would never talk about Jesus that way.

Another unusual collaboration you did was with Phil Spector on 'If You Don't Want My Love'.

The writer for the *L.A. Times*, Robert Hilburn, was trying to get together a book on Spector. He was interviewing him at length over a period of time. I came to town, and Hilburn was a big fan, he would mention my name at the drop of a hat. I mean, if he was doing a Led Zeppelin review, he'd somehow fit my name into it, you know? I was amazed at how much press he'd give me. I ran into him—I think it was when I was out there interviewing all those producers I told you about for *Bruised Orange* before I settled on Goodman. I wasn't talking to Spector about producing, but Hilburn told me he was going out to his house a lot, and said, "Would you like to come over—he likes your songs a lot, you know."

He said, "He's a big fan of 'Donald & Lydia'," and mentioned a couple of others. I said, "Yeah, I'd love to meet him." And you know, *wow!* He is *out* there. Met him a couple of times since then. And now this whole deal went down [Spector's trials for the death of Lana Clarkson], and I don't know, I'm surprised but I'm not.

Did you see the gun?

Oh yeah. He had the gun. He always had it. You'd always see it before the end of the evening.

How did you write a song together?

We'd been there for seven hours, jokin', drinkin'. And by the way, when you go in the house, he's got two bodyguards on his shoulder. Just craziness, you know. This chick came down to say good night and he goes, "Who is the king of rock and roll?" And she said, "You are, Daddy, you are!" [laughs] I'll never forget that.

So I was leaving around four in the morning. All of a sudden Phil sits down at the piano as I was getting my jacket on, and he hands me an electric guitar unplugged. I sit down on the bench next to him. I played him 'That's The Way The World Goes Round', and he really liked it. He said, "Let's do this," and he played the beginning notes of 'If You Don't Want My Love'.

We came up with the first couple lines and he insisted that we repeat them. Over and over. He said it would be very effective. We took 'That's The Way The World Goes Round,' took the melody and turned it inside out. And used that as the basis of 'If You Don't Want My Love'; he played it on piano and I just strummed back on the guitar. We just wrote the thing in less than an hour. And that was on my way out the door. As soon as he sat down and had a musical instrument, he was normal. That's the way he was. He was just a plain old genius.

He'd just finished the Leonard Cohen album [*Death of a Ladies Man*]. It hadn't been released yet. He played it for me in his billiard room, turned the speakers up so high that the balls vibrated across the table. And this is the Leonard Cohen album! [Laughs] I went back playing the song. Didn't know I would do it for the record, but I played it for Goodman, and he said, "You oughta do that for the record. That's great." And I said, "But I don't know if it's done." He said, "It's done. Believe me. I'd tell ya if it wasn't."

So I cut it for *Bruised Orange*. Went back to his house after I cut the record to play it for him. Said he liked it. Said he would've produced it differently, but he liked it. [Laughs] I said, "You can take that up with Goodman sometime." [Laughs]

Do you remember when 'The Late John Garfield Blues' came from?

It was originally called, on paper, 'The Late Sunday Evening Early Monday Morning Blues'. There was a sort of movie that you'd see on Sunday night that you would not see the rest of the nights of the week. I believe it was on WGN. They'd show these old black & white flicks. A lot of my favorite ones were John Garfield movies. I put the two together—the image of him and that kind of odd Sunday time, the Sunday funnies would be laying around and *Parade* magazine. Probably had a big dinner at some point. Your typical Sunday, which was not a typical day at all. It was always different. Lonelier than the other days. And there was the feeling that you had to go to school the next day, or work. So late Sunday night would always be a different time to me. I wanted to pinpoint that, so I chose a John Garfield movie, and I didn't mention the movie at all; I just called it 'The Late John Garfield Blues'. There's an old Jimmy Rodgers melody-wise song I was using. Just the chord change. 'Treasures Untold'. It's a really pretty ballad he wrote. I learned that song early on and I always wanted to use that G to the B7.

Do you have a favourite key?

G.

Yeah, you play a lot in G.

I can fingerpick really good in G. [Laughs] I can pick 'The Star Spangled Banner' in G. I can pick out just about anything I want in the key of G.

I've seen you play a lot in G but with a capo on.

I use the capo up and down the neck, and play in G quite a bit. I only get out of it out of sheer boredom.

Do you feel different keys have different colors or moods?

Yeah. Definitely. It makes a big difference. After I had my throat surgery, I had to drop the key on a lot of my older songs. I was still singing them in the same key I wrote them in. My voice had changed before the surgery. My voice was very nasal; my nose was a more comfortable place to sing out of than my throat. [Laughter]

But my voice dropped quite a bit, and some of my songs, to me, just blossomed in the new key. I got to actually enjoy them as if they were brand new. Which was a really amazing thing. I had no idea changing the key would make such a big difference.

'Donald and Lydia' is your only one which is really about two characters with separate stories who you then bring together. Did that come together naturally or plot it out?

Well, my guide for the song was 'Lonesome Death of Hattie Carol'. Just in terms of the character and what the character's doing. Then the chorus could be a moral for the whole thing. I had the characters in my mind, but I brought them together. Somewhere in boot camp I'd seen the character Donald. In an army town where I was stationed, I think Louisiana, I'd seen Lydia. And mostly they just formed together in my mind.

You're a writer who has written about loneliness effectively—

And the more I sing about it, the more I realize I'm not the only one. I think it's great therapy to sing about the stuff that's goin' on inside you. And other people say, "Gee, I didn't think anybody would ever write about that particular emotion." They tell you you nailed it right on the head. That's a really great feeling.

'The Speed of the Sound of Loneliness' is kind of a later version of the same theme.

That came out all at once. From a broken relationship I was in. I could not understand what went wrong and I had to explain to myself. I did it through this song. The next day I thought, "Jesus, that's beautiful." I didn't recognize it at the time, it was just pouring out of me.

Very cool title.

I really liked it. It must have been a play on the words of *The Loneliness of the Long-Distance Runner*. Probably. I'm guessing. When it was all said and done, I don't know where it came from, but I'm thinking that maybe that's where I got the idea to use "loneliness" like that. Cause it was a long title and kind of abstract. I guess I'm attracted to stuff like that.

You've written a lot of songs out of heartbreak and turmoil. Can you write songs as well when you're happy and things are going well?

Yeah, but usually when you're happy, you don't have time to write a song. Cause you're enjoying your life. But when you're not happy, you have *all the time in the world* to go and write a song.

LOST DOGS AND MIXED BLESSINGS

Michael McCall | 1995 | *Nashville Scene*

Michael McCall moved to Nashville from San Francisco to become the *Nashville Banner*'s chief critic as *Aimless Love* came out. Living in Prine's adopted home, he watched the evolution and growth of the songwriter's fiercely independent label.

Recalling seeing Prine on a record label panel not long after arriving, McCall was impressed by the man's pluck. At a time of "major deal or nothing," Prine made a joke: "I just realized all I had to do was walk out into a field, put my hand on a rock and say, 'I'm a record company.'" McCall recalls thinking, "That intrigued me. The DIY thing, coming out of punk rock—to see someone who was a songwriting legend take that approach to the record business really said something. I remember talking to him later about that, (John) telling me about Ahmet Ertegun with the Rolls Royce outside, realizing he was never gonna be on *that* level. . . . That just wasn't for him or something he was interested in."

McCall, being single, would run into Prine all the time, "out at shows, at [late-night boîte] Faison's, having fun with his friends Don Everly, Roger Cook, all his pals. You'd see him coming out of a movie theater, and he'd stop and talk to you. He didn't have the airs of a star or an artist, just this really humble man. He always wanted to know what you thought or were listening to . . . and unless you did something really bad to him, he was your friend."

When *Lost Dogs and Mixed Blessings* hit the cover of the *Nashville Scene*, it was a moment of triumph for the steadfastly true-to-his-ideals musician. It was also the culmination of a personal life that had been scattered across many late-night-into-early-morning adventures that slowly turned into a homelife that fulfilled Prine in ways he'd never imagined. For McCall, seeing the shift personally was as heartening as the reality of the Howie Epstein–produced record truly giving Prine a larger audience to match his critical acclaim.

McCall, who would go on to be a principal writer and researcher at the Country Music Hall of Fame, would continue to inhabit Prine's world. Years later, he would do one of Prine's first postsurgery interviews. The songwriter's ease of humanity illuminated how to face adversity. What would be horrific to many didn't seem to phase Prine at all.

The journalist recalls of their later encounter, "I'd not seen him since the surgery, and I wasn't quite prepared for how striking [his neck] was up close. I'd seen him from a distance, but you couldn't really tell. Up close, it was a pretty big chunk of his neck, the part that had been cut away. But he wasn't self-conscious at all; didn't seem to have changed who he was one bit. He was friendly and talkative and warm. The more he talked, the less it mattered or you noticed it, really. And it didn't stop his trips to Arnolds, or to shoot pool, and that's when you realized, he was more interested in enjoying life—which he'd always done—than he was worrying about what he might've lost."

Three days after I talked to McCall, an email arrived. Prine, who'd always mirrored his fans' lives with his songs, had left a strong impression on McCall. Sometimes people served to mirror who Prine was back to the songwriter as well. McCall's email:

> He always remembered I grew up in Gary, Indiana, and more than most, he knew what that meant, that Gary was a rough, working-class town. Our first talk, I told him about how, as a kid, I'd sneak off with friends and jump on the South Shore train for a quarter in downtown Gary. We'd ride over to Chicago and just walk around, and usually go to the Sears Tower so we could ride the elevator up and down. He got a kick out of that. We rode over during the 1968 convention, too. I was 11 and stared with wide-eyed fascination at all the hippies in Grant Park. We were there before all the violence started, but the fact that we'd been there, made us pay more attention to it.
>
> Also, for a trip to the Grammys, he saw me at the airport by the curb and said "hey, ride with us." It must've been during my *Banner* years, so pre-Fiona, and it was just him and Al. I can't remember if he was even going to the Grammys, but he may have been. They went out of their way to drop me at whatever hotel I was at. So humble.
>
> Those are the kinds of stories I cherish. They're often the moments we haven't written about that stand out the most, you know? Thanks for letting me share these stories, and for bringing them forward in my memory. There's still a sadness that comes to me whenever John's name or music comes

up. But talking about all this is a good reminder to remember all the good, and to count my many blessings."

—Ed.

Not long ago, John Prine stepped into the Nashville airport believing he shortly would be on his way to New York. Inside, an attendant at the ticket counter informed him that floods in Texas had grounded several planes, and the best the airline could do was fly him to Newark. "I smiled, said, 'fine,' and took my ticket," he recalls.

He hauled his guitar and carry-on bag to the ticket gate, only to discover the flight was overbooked. The attendant told him he would have to fly to LaGuardia airport in Manhattan instead. "I smiled, said, 'fine, that's where I wanted to go in the first place,'" he says. He arrived at LaGuardia. After a long wait at the luggage carousel, he realized his bags didn't fly with him. The attendant told him they must be lost and took his name and how to contact him.

"I used to hate airports," he says. "I used to spend so much time in them because I was always on the road. But it's not like that anymore. Now I go through airports and I kind of look around and say, 'Hey, wow, lookee there.' So I found myself walking around LaGuardia, looking around and whistling. It was 'The Best Things in Life Are Free.' And I thought, 'My life is becoming like a John Prine song.'"

Some songwriters strive for realism. They pluck inspiration from their own lives, or the lives of others, then attempt to capture the poignancy of their epiphany in verse. At their best, such songs contain a kernel of truth or create a flash of recognition. But they're obviously oversimplified; life rarely boils down to aphorisms, no matter what Forrest Gump or the latest radio hit may say. Instead, life clangs along like an urban subway car, barely clinging to unpredictable turns, jerking to sudden stops, lumbering into tentative beginnings, and filling up with an assortment of colorfully odd characters who come and go with unforeseeable randomness. Even the most blessed among us sometimes become separated from our baggage.

In other words, life is a lot like a John Prine song. It's full of incongruous elements that wouldn't seem to work together, but do—sometimes wonderfully, nearly always with an ability to surprise with whimsical charm.

Airport hassles not withstanding, John Prine has plenty of reasons to whistle a cheery tune these days. "I'm 48 years old, and all of a sudden, I've got a family and a band," says the father of Jack Whelan Prine, who will celebrate his seventh month birthday on Tuesday with his mother Fiona Whelan at the couple's Nashville home. These days, Jack's father is as close to being a rock star as he's been in 20 years. He has gray wisps of hair at the end of his shaggy mustache and unkempt head, a head that rarely seems to acquaint itself with a hairbrush. No matter what time of day it is, Prine always looks like he just rolled out of a deep sleep on a couch. He is a sweet-natured, self-effacing, rumpled pudge of a man, and he's enjoying the greatest commercial success of his career.

Prine's new album, *Lost Dogs and Mixed Blessings*, is receiving orders at a faster initial clip than 1991's *The Missing Years*, which became the singer's fastest-selling album since a greatest hits on Atlantic in the mid-1970s. (It is now approaching 400,000 in total sales.) Earlier this month, Prine celebrated the release of *Lost Dogs* with his most elaborate concert tour in 20 years, and the acoustic musician has taken the unusual step of forming an electric band to support him in concert. His success tastes even sweeter because it comes through a record company, Oh Boy, that he co-owns with his longtime manager, Al Bunetta. At Oh Boy, overhead is low—the big promotional item for *Lost Dogs* is a flyswatter with the company's logo on the handle. Therefore, his profit margin is exceedingly higher than it would be at a major record company. Moreover, it's all come as a surprise. "At the start of the '90s, I was thinking I would gradually scale back, kind of slow down and just enjoy it," he says. "Then it all kicked in."

John Prine is one of the most revered singer-songwriters of the last two decades, or as David Fricke put it, "If success can be measured in press clipping tonnage, the cultish good will of devoted fans, and the die-hard respect of his peers, John Prine is a superstar." Truth is, however, he long ago realized he wasn't going to achieve the heights of fame predicted for him following his 1971 release of *John Prine*, one of the most remarkable debut albums in modern popular music. Those initial songs—"Angel from Montgomery," "Sam Stone," "Hello in There," "Paradise," "Illegal Smile," "Spanish Pipedream"—still stun listeners today with their uncommon combination of cleverness and sensitivity. Over the years, he repeatedly proved he could come up with equally memorable material—be it the witty commentary of "Dear Abby" and "Come Back to Us Barbara Lewis Hare Krishna Beauregard," the poignant whimsy of "Fish and Whistle" and "Sabu Visits the Twin Cities Alone," or the tender humanity of "Unwed Fathers" and "The Speed of the Sound of Loneliness." Meanwhile, his entertaining live performances added to his herd of dedicated enthusiasts while reassuring and re-astonishing longtime fans.

By the 1990s, Prine had settled into a comfortable and rather atypical routine for an American recording artist. He put out his own records rather than deal with the promotional politics of big record companies—a revolutionary idea for an older, established performer and one that since has been imitated by veteran rockers, folkies and country singers across the United States. At first, his Oh Boy Records worked off an extensive, computerized mailing list of fans, eventually graduating to a tight, supportive network of distributors that stocked his CDs in record-store bins nationwide, lined up behind the heavily bankrolled disks of Prine and Primus. He toured regularly, sometimes as a solo act, sometimes bringing along a small acoustic group. He had set up a comfortable career for himself that existed outside of the album charts or big-time radio. "I was making records, but the way I was making money was staying on the road constantly," he says. "We were happy with it being small. Even with records that sold 50,000 copies, our overhead was so small that we were out of the red with less than 10,000." His albums of the 1980s—*Aimless Love, German Afternoons, John Prine Live*—were acoustic affairs made at Jack's Tracks studio in Nashville with co-producer Jim Rooney for less than $20,000 each.

Then he got the idea that he wanted to shake up the routine. "I wanted to make one really good record, then not make one for a while," he explains. "Like I said, I was planning on scaling down. But I guess I worked a little harder on it than I meant to."

The result, *The Missing Years*, was produced in Los Angeles by Howie Epstein of Tom Petty and the Heartbreakers and featured such guests as Bruce Springsteen, Petty and Bonnie Raitt. It proved to be the best-selling album of Prine's career. Radio suddenly discovered him; his video of the song "Picture Show," featuring a cameo by duet partner Petty, received regular play on VH-1 and CMT; he received major accolades and feature spreads in *Rolling Stone* and other high-profile pop culture rags.

Suddenly, John Prine was cool, again. "It changed a lot of things as far as being able to pick and choose when to go out on tour," he says with the same unassuming, bewildered shrug that accompanies nearly all of his observations. "The dressing rooms got larger and prettier."

He can't explain the success of *The Missing Years*, he says as if he's still trying to figure it out himself. "I think maybe I was able to do my music thing as well as I've been able to on record," he says. "The closest I came before to representing my stuff was doing a live record. Usually to catch whatever it is I do, I had to do the record live. I thought Howie captured that really good in the studio."

Dan Einstein, vice president of Oh Boy Records and a longtime colleague of Prine's, credits Epstein's modern production flourishes for nudging Prine's music towards a sound that has more in common with albums that get on the radio, but without losing the singer's personality. "The music has become more palatable to a wider audience," Einstein says. "That's not a slam towards anyone else he's worked with. It's just that this was what he needed to bring his music to a new plateau."

Prine measures his success by how it changes his life as a troubadour who goes out and plays songs for his fans. "What it really meant, for me, was that we could play these places that were meant for music to be played in them," he says. "There are these 800-to-4,000 seat theaters all across the country, and that's the perfect place for me. To me, if we can maintain it at that level, well, that would tops for me. No gymnasiums, no arenas. I don't know what we'd do in an arena."

He toured extensively after the album, then he did something really unusual. He stayed home. "Last year I only worked the road for six weeks," he notes. "That's the first time I've done that in 24 years. Over the years, I was constantly on the road. If I was off, it was maybe for two weeks, then back out. It never really seemed like it stopped. Now it's become more concentrated. We go out, do a whole lot of shows in a row, then come home. That's the way I hear everybody else does it." He shrugs, rubs his fingers across his chin, and lets out a deep, slow laugh. It has to be one of the friendliest chuckles on earth.

Apparently, staying home for the first time since he delivered mail for the U.S. Postal Service brought along other changes. Whelan, his fiancé, gave birth to Jack Whelan on Dec. 1, 1994. The couple are expecting a second child in the fall, and Prine is the stepfather of Whelan's 14-year old son Jody. "I guess Fiona and I put the cart before the horse," he says, letting his warm chuckle roll across the room again. "We just got engaged and sometime next year we'll get married."

Prine talks about music with droll ease, always finding the humor in what he does. He doesn't bother to reflect or analyze it too much. Those closest to him say he's reacted well to the new pressures of business and family. "Success hasn't changed him an inch," Einstein says. "That's one of the most admirable things about him. Having a child will change anybody, but John Prine, the man, hasn't changed."

But when Prine starts talking about his newfound family, his shit-eating grin does change. It broadens and lightens, and his conversation grows more animated. "Things are falling right in order, it seems," he says. "I mean, I'm 48 years old, but this actually couldn't have come at a better time for me. I certainly had enough time to do whatever I wanted to. I always knew I wanted a kid. I was married twice before, and I guess we were just young and selfish. If we thought we had a clock to work with, then it would always be later, somewhere down the road. But I had no idea I'd be enjoying having a kid this much."

A week after our interview, Prine is in a Nashville rehearsal hall leading his five-piece band through punched-up arrangements of old favorites and new songs from his recently released *Lost Dogs and Mixed Blessings*, his first electric album since 1979's *Pink Cadillac*. "Basically, we wanted to make a record that was pretty far away from *The Missing Years*," he says. "We figured we could do a *Missing Years, Part 2* somewhere down the line, if we want to. We thought we'd go for something different."

His new band features guitarists Larry Crane, a longtime partner of John Mellencamp's, and a young Nashville newcomer, David Steele, who plays phenomenal slide. Phil Parlapiano, formerly of the Brothers Figaro and a veteran of Prine's Missing Years tour, returns on accordion, harmonium and Hammond organ. David Jacques is on bass and Ed Gaus, an associate of Crane's, is on drums. It's the hardest rocking band Prine has ever taken on tour, and his boyish enthusiasm is obvious as he romps through such new songs as "New Train" and "Ain't Hurting Nobody" and such classics as "That's the Way the World Goes 'Round."

Just before he calls for a break, Whelan arrives with Jack bundled in blankets in a baby stroller. Prine's face shines broadly as he heads quickly towards them, embracing Fiona and kissing her cheek before bending over to shower attention on his son. Crane comes over, gently pokes the baby's belly, and says, "Look at him shine. He's got so much spirit in his eyes." He then flashes a devilish grin at his boss and says, "He's gonna be an outlaw. You can tell." When they returned to their instruments and cranked back up, Prine beamed as he bounced through "Spanish Pipedream," seeming to find particular delight in the words: "Blow up your tv, throw away your paper, go to the country, build you a home. Plant a little garden, eat a lot of peaches, and try to find Jesus on your own."

During the interview, he expressed amazement at his reaction to fatherhood. "I had no idea it would make such a difference. I can't really explain it. Basically, you see yourself. I thought maybe he'd have one of my ears, or something, but here he comes out and he's a dead ringer for me. It really throws you for a loop. It's like starting out totally clean. I can't wait to get home at night and see him. I got this great little family I'm going home to at night."

He's also noticed how he falls into all the familiar patterns. "All of a sudden I'm an expert on this," he laughs. "If I find out somebody else has a baby, I'll corner them and show off my knowledge. I'm carrying pictures, the whole thing. I've learned all the things I'm supposed to do. Mom does them a lot better, but I can change the diapers real quick. It's pretty darn neat that I'm going to have another one in the fall. After that, I might call a halt to it."

Now, however, he's back on more familiar ground, trekking through concert halls across the United States and, eventually, Europe on a tour that will keep him busy through the end of the year. "But I'm looking forward to it—I always do," he says. "But this time, I'm going to miss being home. I've been home every day with the baby since he was born. They change really quick. They change in two, three days time. I'll miss seeing that. But I'm glad people still want to see me sing, too."

That notion, the fact that people find his songs entertaining, is something he professes to have been surprised about from the start. He wrote his first song at 14 on his older brother Dave's guitar. He played a few in the barracks when he worked as a mechanic in the U.S. Army after being drafted in 1966. When he returned to Chicago in 1968, he went back to work delivering mail. "Writing was a hobby for me, just to be able to get away from everything," he says. "I wrote just to please myself. That's what a bored mailman does. It was better than becoming one of those postmen who go back to the office and shoot everybody. (shrug, smile) At least I had an outlet."

Then, one night in 1970, he took the songs he'd written over the previous two years to a club. "I couldn't sing a note," he says. "What I was doing was talking and every once in a while holding out a note." That's all it took. He performed his first amateur's night, got asked to return. On the third week, he noticed people were coming back to see him and bringing friends.

No wonder. In a scruffy, folksy drawl of a voice, he sang one astonishing song after another. In "Sam Stone," he sang of a Viet Nam vet who returned home to his family with shrapnel in his knee and shattered nerves, and with "a purple heart and a monkey on his back." The unforgettable chorus goes, "There's a hole in Daddy's arm where all the money goes. Jesus Christ died for nothing I suppose. Little pictures have big ears, don't stop to count the years. Sweet songs never last too long on broken radios." In "Hello in There," he portrays the life of an elderly couple, then sings, "You know old trees just grow stronger, and old rivers grow wilder every day. Old people just grow lonesome, waiting for someone to say, hello in there, hello."

In "Paradise," he tells of a lush, backroads Kentucky region where his parents were raised, and where he regularly visited as a child, that was ravaged by a coal company. In the chorus, he sings, "Daddy, won't you take me back to Muhlenberg County, down by the green river where paradise lay. Well, I'm sorry my son, but you're too late in asking, Mr. Peabody's coal train has hauled it away." In "Illegal Smile," he created what would become a pothead anthem for the '70s, even though Prine says he wrote it about how, from childhood on, he tended to find humor in things that other people didn't. The chorus goes: "You may see me tonight with an illegal smile. It don't cost very much, but it lasts a long while. Won't you please tell the man I didn't kill anyone. I was trying to have me some fun."

At the time, when everyone else was trying to write like Bob Dylan or old Mississippi bluesmen or show how psychedelic their mind could get, Prine stepped up with a sackful of sweet, smart, completely off-the-wall tunes. "I wasn't so sure they were good," he says, "but I knew they were different." The Old Town club where he started made him a regular performer. Within six months, he was making more money singing three nights a week than he was delivering the mail 40 hours a week. "So, I quit the post office and slept all day and sang three nights a week," he recalls. "I thought I'd been made king. I mean, this is what I wanted to do all my life—sleep 'til noon, walk around in the afternoon and eat a hot dog, then go out at night, drink a couple beers, play some songs and stay up as late as I want."

He met Steve Goodman, another budding songwriter who would provide Arlo Guthrie with the hit "City of New Orleans" in 1972. One night Goodman opened a show for Kris Kristofferson, then persuaded him to go see Prine after they finished. Prine had already finished, but he went back up to sing for Kristofferson, who was floored. He invited Prine onstage the next night, introducing him by saying of the 24-year old ex-mailman, "No way somebody this young can be writing so heavy."

Not so long afterward, Goodman and Prine traveled to New York at Kristofferson's invitation. They went to see Kristofferson perform at the Bitter End. Prine was invited to the stage again, and this time Atlantic Records executive Jerry Wexler was in the audience. Wexler invited Prine to his office the next day. "I sat down and he told me, 'We could go through attorneys or whatever, but right now you have a $25,000 contract with Atlantic Records if you want." Prine accepted it on the spot.

"All this happened so quick," he says. "We weren't in New York for 24 hours and I had a record contract. It was like one day I'm delivering mail, the next I'm in Memphis recording with Elvis Presley's rhythm section. It seemed that fast."

He also saw firsthand how rock 'n' roll changed from an underground business of club, music halls and specialty stores into a corporate behemoth of arenas, strong-armed promoters and record chains. He remembers how he felt walking "the hallowed halls of Atlantic Records, the place where Big Joe Turner, Ray Charles, Aretha Franklin, Wilson Pickett and John Coltrane had resided. Then they moved to Rockefeller Center," he says. "Then they became a part of a big corporation (Warner Bros.)" They became the home of the Rolling Stones and Led Zeppelin, and when Prine turned in albums like *Sweet Revenge* and *Common Sense*, they didn't seem to know what to do with them. He moved to Asylum Records—home of the Eagles and Jackson Browne—and created the outstanding *Bruised Orange* album. Still, compared to the expectations built by the record boom of the '70s, Prine remained a cult act—revered by peers and an intensively loyal but relatively small following. Two more albums—*Pink Cadillac* and *Storm Windows*—revealed Prine's restless creativity and willingness to experiment with different sounds. But rock moved into its new wave and British synthesizer era, and Prine's sales slipped even more.

"I decided to just get out of it," he says. "I just didn't want to get in an elevator again with a bunch of record executives. Some of them were great people, real music fans. A lot of them wished they could be the person who could come up with some marketing idea and figure out how to fit my records in somewhere. It was frustrating for everybody. I didn't want to be in that position where I was blaming stuff on other people. It wasn't healthy."

In the meantime, Prine moved to Nashville. He spent a couple of years writing songs, including collaborating with other writers, something he'd only done sparingly in earlier years. He credits legendary producer Jack Clement, with whom he'd made an album in 1977 that he'd decided to shelve, for planting the idea of starting his own record company. "I figured that if I was going to do it wrong, I might as well do it wrong myself," he says. His company, Oh Boy Records, built slowly yet surely, then skyrocketed with *The Missing Years*. Oh Boy has also put out several volumes of live recordings, *The Best of Mountain Stage*, culled from a popular syndicated TV series, as well as an album by a Nashville-based band, The Bis-quits. Oh Boy will release a debut album by Heather Eatman in August.

Of Oh Boy, Prine says, "I'm not really sure I'd be doing this anymore if we hadn't done it this way. I probably would have been through a couple more record companies by now. The '80s were tough on artists who do something like whatever it is I do. If I'd gone five years with one company and another five with another company, I'd probably be a broken down middle-aged man by now."

He's encouraged by a trend toward other artists creating their own independent labels, citing Nashville's Dead Reckoning Records as a particularly promising idea, with its roster of artists who are working together as a creative team. "Stuff like that can't be anything but healthy for music," he says.

He also sympathizes with those starting out today who, like him, don't fit into an easily identified niche. "It's become such a big business, and it seems like you have to think about it a lot more in business terms," he says. "You have to have management set up and this whole team together before you go to a record company, from what I understand. If that had been the scene when I was starting out, knowing myself and the way I was, I'm not sure I would have pursued it. I got swallowed up in it fast, but it seemed kind of pure. There wasn't a lot of business between me and making a record. If I had to go through getting a manager and putting a business together first, I don't think I would have done it. I would have been put out by it. I still hold a special place for where songs are from—call it the muse or whatever. I know I have to nurture that still. Back then, I really didn't want anything to get in the way of where these songs came from. I thought one of my main enemies was organization and business. I thought it would get in the way of being able to see the song at the end of the trail. I think there are probably some great people out there who don't want to get into the whole thing."

But Prine found a way to work around it, and his pioneering efforts have been rewarded. He's now enjoying the greatest success of his career, and he no longer regrets not following some of his peers to superstar status. "I've seen it happen to people I knew starting out," he says. "Anybody who made it to that big level, they really have to work at it. You don't become a household name by saying, 'Hey, let's go get a couple beers' or 'Want to do an arena show? Nah, lets go fishing.'"

Not that he doesn't sometimes come face-to-face with the spoils of celebrityhood. It's just that it tends to happen in a uniquely John Prine fashion, such as the time he recently hurried into a Kroger's after midnight for a couple of emergency items. "I'm standing in the checkout line, and this guy says, 'John Prine! How 'bout that? Hey, where in the heck do I find 'Paradise'?' You know, (singing) 'Daddy won't you take me back to Muhlenberg County?' Then this guy behind me says, 'Muhlenberg County! I had a friend in the Army from Muhlenberg County. If I remember right, that place in the '50s and '60s was an easy place to get into and a hard place to get out of.' I'm trying to tell the one guy that I personally don't have any copies of that record, that I don't have any control over Atlantic Records. But I can't, because now these two guys are talking to each other and I'm stuck in the middle. So, I just stood there at 12:30 at night in Kroger's and smiled until they were done."

PART VI

Girls and Cancer

DADDY AND THEM SCRIPT EXCERPT

Billy Bob Thornton | 2001 | Free Hazel Films / Industry Entertainment / Miramax / Shooting Gallery

Billy Bob Thornton "got" John Prine. Even before he'd met him, he understood the songwriter's quirky delights and the aw-shucks humor. Thornton loved the songs, but he also loved laughing, almost as much as the kid who never truly got the Muhlenberg County out of his soul.

Hanging out some months before the cancer was diagnosed, Thornton remembers dropping Prine at the Sunset Marquis in West Hollywood, starting to drive home—and being struck with a feeling. Turning around, he knocked on Prine's door and asked, "Are you alright?" With a "yeah, I'm good" for a response, the actor-screenwriter pressed, "You would tell me, right?" When the 1997 Oscar winner eventually heard that Prine had cancer, his mind reeled.

At work on a screenplay about the odd joys and strange ways of a family in Arkansas facing a relative's jailing for armed robbery, Thornton had often found his mind drifting to the folk singer whose songs often contained the same odd dissonances and unbridled love. "I based the character [of Alvie Montgomery] on my Uncle Jack, who was nervous," Thornton says now. "But I wrote the character based on John; I wrote all the lines *for* John. . . ."

Tom Petty was originally slated to play Thornton and Prine's characters' other brother, but the Rock & Roll Hall of Famer was so far behind getting an album written and recorded that he was forced to drop out. It didn't matter. The character of Alvie was as much about showing the world Prine's heart as it was sending up dysfunctional deep Southern families.

"That part was the heart and soul of that family," Thornton says of the quiet brother absorbed in Zane Grey books. "You want to set somebody up to not fail [when you cast a nonactor]; you want to show who *they* are. Funny thing is: John had a way of humor that made it *not* comedy but made it seem like life."

Billed as a dark comedy, marketed as "an all-American story only Oscar-winner Billy Bob Thornton could tell," *Daddy and Them* follows the Montgomerys, a lower-working-class Southern family racked with dysfunction. When the family comes together after an uncle's arrest for armed robbery, ultimately, their uncle's British psychologist wife snaps and reads them the riot act, telling them they need to talk *to* and not *at* each other—and calling them all alcoholics in the process. Silence engulfs the room. Ultimately, Prine—as Alvie, the quiet brother who'd confessed, "I'm pretty much nervous all the time"—starts talking, and he says everything that needs to be said. He sows healing.

"I love that [Alvie] read that psychology book so he could talk to them," Thornton confesses. But perhaps not as much as he loves "In Spite of Ourselves," the end theme that Prine wrote for the film at Thornton's urging. Prine hadn't been writing that year; he'd been battling neck cancer. But when Thornton asked, he said, "Well, I'll try."

With Iris DeMent, Prine delivered a duet that perfectly distilled the characters of *Daddy and Them*. Containing the infamous couplet, "She gets it on like the Easter bunny . . . I caught him once, he was sniffing my undies," the song was as bent as Thornton's script. It would go on to become the title track—and sole original song—on Prine's duet album, which features many of country music's formative females.

"John was like a unicorn, he really was. He used to sit and play his guitar on the back porch when we were shooting, and everyone would be trying to listen. And then the song being a guy singing about the girl and the girl singing about the guy, I thought it couldn't have been any more perfect or true to the characters," Thornton says. "Iris DeMent has such a beautiful, haunting, and odd voice. She captured it, too."

The script pages contained follow Alvin, in the aftermath of the Montgomerys' reckoning, going from room to room, speaking to his family members one by one. In each room, he says exactly what that person not only needs but also deserves to hear. —Ed.

Alvie enters dining room; his mother is at the table.

Alvie: *I'm gonna go buy you a record player, Mama . . . so you can listen to some different music.*

Still staring ahead, Mama: *Boy, that'd be something, wouldn't it, hon?*

Alvie smiles. Turns, exits dining room.

Alvie bursts into darkened bedroom, flipping on the overhead light.

Daddy?

Huh? Oh, oh! I ain'. . .

(Something under covers, clearly asleep, rouses)

(Andy Griffith, as father, emerges from covers, still half-asleep)
I ain't ready yet, Lord. Please. I can't go now. I ain't got no grandkids yet.

Alvie: (leaning in reassuringly)
It's me. It's me, Daddy. It's me.

Father, clearly annoyed:
Alvin, what in the shit are you doing? You scared me half to death. I was havin' a nightmare. I got ganged up on by a bunch of boys.

Alvie:
You might wanna tell somebody about those nightmares sometime.

>>five second pause, as both men regard the other<<

Alvie:
If you'd talk to Mama sometimes. . .

>>Alvie's head shifts, hand wisks away invisible concern<<

she might quit playin' that damn monkey.

Father: *Alvin, you're one of my boys and everything. . . but you are the oddest poor son of a bitch there is.*

>>Alvie bows head, leans in, then exits room<<

[Stereo: "When Johnny Comes Marching Home"]

Alvin quietly opens another door, to a darkened bedroom, whispers:
Ruby?

Ruby?

>>Ruby, clearly asleep, rolls over<<

Ruby sleepily whispers:
Oh, hey, Alvin.

Pulling up on one elbow, she says kindly:
Is something wrong, hon?

Alvie stands up straight, takes in his sister-in-law

Alvie:

*If Claude still wanted to be with Rose or anybody else for that matter . . .
he'd still be with her. Your fear of losin' him makes you want to blame
him. . . for stuff he don't do.*

>>3 beats of silence<<

Alvie:

*Lord knows he's got his problems. Y'all both want to mess things up before
the other one does.*

>>3 more beats of silence<<

He told me one time. . .

(Alvie leans forward a little, lowers voice)

*you look like an old-time movie star. . . so pretty, you're not even <u>real</u>
to him.*

>>2 more beats of silence, Ruby remains in repose, listening<<

Alvie:

Actually, he didn't tell me. He told it to you.

>>1 and ½ beats of silence<<

Alvie (with certainty)

*I just heard it. He talks to you while you're sleepin'. He's just crazy about
you.*
'Night, Ruby.

>> Alvie steps back into hall, closes door behind him

>> Ruby, smiling, tucks arm behind head, settles back in to sleep<<

[Stereo: "When Johnny Comes Marching Home"]

(Bathroom, shot of Claude on the commode, flipping magazine, door opens)

Claude, fiercely
Goddamn it.

(shot of Alvie opening door, cuts to two shot: Claude with magazine on
toilet; Alvie entering and coming closer)

Claude:

What you doin', Alvin?

(tight shot of more annoyed Claude)

Ain't you got somethin' to read or somethin'? Brothers ain't supposed to see brothers on the shitter—I don't even let Ruby watch me take a shit.

(cut to: tight show of Alvie).

Alvie, nodding:

Maybe you ought to sometime.

>>shot of Claude, flipping magazine over to cover his privates, Claude reaches for matches; shot stays on Claude<<

Alvie:

Claude?

Claude fiddles with box of matches, draws one out as he speaks:

What, for God's sake, Alvin?

(tight shot of Alvie)

Ruby wouldn't hurt you for anything in the world. She's crazy about you.

(shot of Claude striking a match, waving it around)

Alvie continues:

Any man in the world oughta be happy as hell . . . to have somebody

(Claude blows out match)

care about 'em that much.

(Claude waves match in the air)

She's had a lot of boyfriends.

(tight shot of Alvie, who continues speaking)

Women whose daddy's run off . . . they do that sometimes. They're lookin' for something.

>>2 beats of silence; Alvie nods a bit, continues speaking<<

She found it.

(cut to shot of Claude on the toilet, with magazine and match, stunned)

You're a lucky man.

(Claude relaxes some, softens as Alvie confesses)

Sure wish I was built like you, lean and everything. Sometimes I think Ruby'd be crazy about you if you was as fat as a hog.

(Claude, half-smiling, tender):
You think so?

Mm-hmm.

(cut to Alvie, nodding a bit)
Alvie:
Sometimes I don't think she's bluffin'.

>>4 beat, pause, sound of critics, kindness on Alvie's face<<
Alvie:
Don't ever let it be too late.

(cut to Alvie, considering, who looks down)
[Sighs]

HOW TO SURVIVE ON AN APPLE PIE DIET

Robert Christgau | October 5, 1999 | *Village Voice / Is It Still Good to Ya?*

By the time *In Spite of Ourselves* was ready, the buzz on Prine's return had moved from rumble to thunder. In New York to tape *Sessions at West 54th* and *Late Night with Conan O'Brien*, Charlie Feldman at BMI decided to throw an intimate celebration for the beloved musician. A glittering cast converged on a private room at Michael's in Midtown Manhattan to toast Prine's return. It was perfect for Prine's inner Ferris Bueller: a fancy dinner with a lot of pretty people, plus his band and friend Iris DeMent. Very few media people were smuggled onto the list for this night.

One of the invited was the *Village Voice*'s Robert Christgau, known as the Dean of American Rock Critics and keeper of the insightful Consumer Guide column. A passionate chronicler of American pop culture as well as music from around the world, his presence was all that was hoped for; no expectation of coverage—of what would ultimately be four whirlwind days in New York—was mentioned.

But funny things happen around John Prine. After spending a night cracking jokes and telling stories, plumbing the news and the human condition, exchanging truths about where they're from, people walk away inspired, feeling like they've met their long lost best friend—or had every notion they've ever had about the quietly philosophical songwriter turned on its head. —Ed.

John Prine and Iris DeMent were seated across from each other at a table for eight in Michael's on West 55th Street. Here BMI had convened a small party to celebrate George Strait's conversion of the obscure Prine copyright "I Just Want To Dance With You" into a hit that paid Prine's hospital bills while he fought off cancer of the neck in 1998. Prine is a genially impish guy who wears his grayish-black hair in a long crew cut. He looks his age whether it's fifty-five, as he told me, or fifty-two, as the books say, but like so many musicians he doesn't act it. He has a story-teller's memory, conjuring details from years back about anything, and without claiming a monopoly or even seeming immodest, he did most of the talking. Among the topics I recall: Prine's collaborator on the Strait song, obsessive Australian-Nashvillian craftsman Roger Cook; God d/b/a Sam Phillips threatening to kick Prine's ass all the way to the Houston clinic that saved his life; a bar for midgets on Roosevelt Road in Chicago; Prine's forthcoming Billy Bob Thornton movie, *Daddy and Them*, which generated the title song of his DeMent-heavy duet cover album, *In Spite of Ourselves*; how to roast pork with German wine; regaining forty lost pounds on an apple pie diet; Prine and his late buddy Steve Goodman's Kris Kristofferson-brokered courtship by Atlantic's Jerry Wexler and Buddah's Neil Bogart, making them the first Chicago artists ever to sign with a major without emigrating first; and—the only time he actually boasted—his skill at buying shoes for his third wife, Fiona.

Early on Prine pulled out snapshots of his two preschool boys—"Irish twins" born ten months apart who were honored guests at their parents' wedding. They're his first kids, and he's officially hooked. Knowing that happy marriages have taken the piss and vinegar out of many songwriters, he mused about how he would cope—"I could become a peeping Tom and write about the neighbors." But although "In Spite of Ourselves" is his only new song in three years, he's too glad to be alive to let that worry him—in 1992, he predicted that the Grammy-winning *The Missing Years* might be his last album, only to produce the even better *Lost Dogs and Mixed Blessings* in 1995. Before long the conversation moved on to Prine's dad, a frequenter of country-music bars who for an extra fifty bucks a month served as president of his machinists' local and always planned to take his boys back to Kentucky. This impossible dream inspired Prine's "Paradise," and Prine told how his father first listened to the acetate from the next room, so it would sound like it was on a jukebox. He died young, at fifty-six, shortly after losing a union election.

I glanced over at DeMent, who had silently pumped her fist at the news that Prine's dad was a union man. To my astonishment, she was trying to wipe tears from her eyes without making a fuss. The guy from BMI leaned over and quietly asked if she was OK. Yes, she nodded, then murmured, "It was just such a moving story." A minute later, she entered the conversation. What she wanted to know was how old Prine was when he realized he was something special. She posed the question in several versions, and Prine listened up good. But without wasting any false modesty, he never really answered. This wasn't something he worried about either.

Afterwards Prine walked DeMent down Fifth Avenue to go watch themselves on Conan O'Brien, where the powers that be had liked "In Spite of Ourselves" so much they didn't bleep out the dirty words. At home, I watched too. Unfortunately for TV purposes, Prine's voice was less mellifluous than ever. Throat radiation can do that to you.

If DeMent had seemed a bit fragile at Michael's, at Town Hall two nights later she bounced out like a trouper, proudly displaying her red thrift-store heels over the footlights. At thirty-eight, the late-blooming DeMent has grown into the role thrust upon her by her big, high, Holiness-steeped soprano. But she's in the middle of a divorce, and the songs aren't coming—her unaccompanied thirty-minute set included only one that postdated 1996's *The Way I Should*. Her speaking voice was an octave lower than the one she sang in. Introducing one of the several songs she's written about her late father, she told how she'd cried at dinner.

DeMent's performance proved that power doesn't always require speed. But half an hour later, Prine burst onstage with rockabilly-looking guitarist Jason Wilbur and balding bassist David Jacques, launched the "Blow up your TV" chorus of the time-tested "Spanish Pipedream," and took over. Even before his voice loosened up he was lit, radiantly explaining why he was "really glad to be here tonight." He'd become a medium for the glow I'd heard him describe Tuesday—the glow that surrounds the things of this world after you've beaten a command to leave it.

Making things glow has always been a Prine specialty anyway. Even at the beginning, he wasn't the "protest" singer he's still said to be: blowing up your TV was a prelude to throwing away your newspaper, eating lots of peaches, and finding Jesus on your own. When the *Rolling Stone Encyclopedia* praises his depictions of "white proletarian America," I wonder whether the writer grew up in a world so rarefied it lacked frying pans, slippers, umbrellas, knick-knack shelves, and four-way stop signs, to name a few of the everyday objects that figure on the four terrific albums that got the young Prine not far enough between 1971 and 1975. Prine is like Bobbie Ann Mason, or early Barry Levinson, or a Nashville songwriter going for quality (which in fact is what he's become). I'd call him an American realist except that often he's also an American humorist, which brings out his omnipresent surrealism—associative leaps from an imagination that's known a normal life's complement of consciousness enhancers, though Prine cut down on his drinking years ago. His realism, his surrealism, and his laugh lines all shoulder the fundamentally celebratory function of language in love—especially language born from the spirit of music. Prine's adoration of the turned cliche ("Some day you'll own a home / That's as big as a house") and the newly minted idiom (lovemaking as "the land of the lost surprise") transfigures even such oppressed proletarians as Donald and Lydia masturbating in two different worlds, or the isolated old wife of "Angel From Montgomery," although not the Vietnam junkie of "Sam Stone," which as Prine's best-known song has always made him seem more maudlin than he is.

I could quote Prine's big houseful of first-rate work forever, make you wish you knew him by heart the way I did when he brought out "Grandpa Was a Carpenter" at Town Hall, which though it had been a decade still had me singing "Voted for Eisenhower / 'Cause Lincoln won the war" on the first chorus. He performed for two hours without sinking below "Sam Stone," an exceedingly well-written piece, and there were plenty more where those came from—Rhino's *Great Days* comp barely falters for forty-one tracks, and after that you can go back to *Sweet Revenge* or *Common Sense*, to name just two. Yet between 1980's *Storm*

Windows and 1992's *The Missing Years*, the quality flagged—his only selection from the period wasn't "I Just Want To Dance With You" but the withering "Unwed Fathers," written with Bobby Braddock, one of the many songsmiths and sidemen who've revved his tune sense since he got to Nashville. Prine's fondness for Braddock types is one reason the novelties and cheating songs of *In Spite of Ourselves* are a perfect way for him to keep his hand in until his muse feels as glad to be alive as he does. The other is that he doesn't have to sing so much. His soft-burred drawl is real lovable once you get to know it, but that doesn't mean Trisha Yearwood and Emmylou Harris and Dolores Keane and Lucinda Williams and Fiona Prine and creaky old Connie Smith and Melba Montgomery aren't welcome additions to his soundscape.

Yet with all due respect, Iris DeMent cuts every one of these ladies. Her four tracks on *In Spite of Ourselves* include two all-time George Jones gems, Braddock's beyond-cornball Tammy feature "(We're Not) The Jet Set" ("We're the old Chevro-let set") and the impossible "Let's Invite Them Over," which had George and Melba spouse-swapping in the c&w top 10 in 1964. DeMent joined Prine about an hour into his set; reticent on "Milwaukee Here I Come," she picked up steam on "Jet Set" and an eye-rolling "Let's Invite Them Over" and owned Yearwood's part on "When Two Worlds Collide." Then it was time for "In Spite of Ourselves," where her first verse begins, "He ain't got laid in a month of Sundays / Caught him once and he was sniffin' my undies." DeMent is rightly known as a good girl. The few sexual references in her writing are indirect. But she sang those lines with an unflappable gusto worthy of Loretta Lynn or Belle Starr and topped Prine throughout, as she was meant to. A good portion of the standing O at the end was for her.

"In Spite of Ourselves," in which a husband and wife who love each other to death paint wildly disparate pictures of their marriage, is the comic masterpiece of someone whose family ways have left his bodily fluids intact. Prine and the band immediately obliterated it with a loud blues and two 1995 copyrights, including the surreal history of a wrecked marriage "Lake Marie," a mostly recited flag-waver that's climaxed his shows since he put it out. It must be daunting for a songwriter in a dry

THE VOICE OF EXPERIENCE

Randy Lewis | April 30, 2000 | *Los Angeles Times*

Robert Hilburn wasn't the only *Los Angeles Times* staffer who recognized John Prine's ability to distill the human condition into moments of vulnerability, loneliness, and unbridled joy. Longtime editor, writer and pop critic Randy Lewis had followed Prine's music throughout the years; upon Hilburn's retirement, he had his turn as the West Coast champion for a songwriter-artist whose ties to Los Angeles dated back to the '70s.

Not only did a healthy chunk of Prine's musical references and collaborators live in Southern California, Prine loved the old Hollywood of Dan Tana's, the Pacific Dining Car, Molly Malone's, and the Troubadour. When it was time to face the media for *In Spite of Ourselves*, Prine's collection of vintage country duets that teamed him with Emmylou Harris, Lucinda Williams, Melba Montgomery, Iris DeMent, Patty Loveless, Irish singer Dolores Keane, his wife Fiona, and more, Lewis filled Hilburn's shoes with a bit of humor and the willingness to dig into Prine's cancer diagnosis, treatment, and impact.

As much a "state of Prine" as an exploration of the songs, it finds the man doing well. Not only had *In Spite* spent more than thirty weeks on the country sales charts, but in spite of cancer, his homelife was the best it'd ever been. Prine's return marked a robust embrace of life. Lewis's piece reflects that and more. —Ed.

John Prine has been lionized by critics and folk-rock aficionados during his three-decade career, and 99.9% of the compliments have to do with the second half of the "singer-songwriter" description that usually accompanies his name.

Rarely does the "singer" part enter the picture. Prine himself makes no bones about the dirt-clod of a voice with which he croaks such uncommonly insightful songs as "Sam Stone," his 1971 look at the toll the Vietnam War exacted on one morphine-addicted soldier, through his whimsically titled but penetrating 1996 song "Humidity Built the Snowman," about the age-old struggle to understand why love evaporates.

Case in point: When a bothersome lump on his neck turned out to be cancerous and a well-meaning radiologist offered to build lead shields to protect his vocal cords during treatment, Prine just laughed and asked, "Have you ever heard me sing?"

So, chalk it up to the mysterious ways of the musical gods that Prine's latest album, "In Spite of Ourselves," is selling as well or better than any of his previous 15, when it consists not of a batch of new Prine tunes for fans to rally around, but of 20- to 50-year-old country songs.

Part of the explanation is the friends Prine brought along for his ride down the back roads of country music. The songs are duets with his favorite female singers, including Emmylou Harris, Trisha Yearwood, Patty Loveless, Iris DeMent, Melba Montgomery, Lucinda Williams, Dolores Keane and Connie Smith.

"There are a lot of singers you hear and go, 'Wow!' because they have such great voices," says Loveless, who sings the 1952 Webb Pierce hit "Back Street Affair" with Prine. "At the same time, [vocal] perfection is not always desirable—it's the feeling you try to get across and the emotion, and that's what John does so well."

Adds DeMent, who harmonizes on four of the album's songs and will open for him and sing with him when they play UCLA's Royce Hall on Thursday: "John definitely knows how to deliver his songs, and in my book, that makes him a singer."

The album has sold 115,000 copies since September, according to SoundScan, and has spent 30 weeks on Billboard's country albums chart. "The response has been phenomenal," says Prine, who has been used to selling around 75,000 copies of each of the albums he's released on the Oh Boy Records label he started 15 years ago. (The label's logo bears a striking resemblance to the Big Boy restaurant mascot, an icon of Americana that keeps popping up in Prine's album artwork and press materials.) "It was something I've been meaning do to for quite a few years," he says. "I just finally figured that if I'm ever going to do a record like this, I'd just have to get in there and do it."

When he started recording in the fall of 1997, it looked as if the album would be done in a few weeks. That's when he found out he had neck cancer, which put the album on hold for about 19 months. "I'd never had a serious health problem before," Prine, 53, says. "If I had to go to the doctor, it was like, 'Lay off of this' or 'Take three of these.'" Shopping for a cancer treatment turned out to be far more complicated. "I was talking to six or seven different doctors, and they all had radically different remedies," he says. "One wanted to do nothing but big doses of chemo, another guy wanted to do node surgery, another was big on radiation."

The man he credits for delivering him from cancer is the same man who delivered Elvis Presley to the world—Sun Records founder Sam Phillips. "I got a call out of the blue from [Sam's son] Knox Phillips, because he'd had the same thing I had," Prine says. "Sam got on the phone and said I should drop everything I'm doing, go down to this place in Texas where Knox had gone. . . . The last thing he said to me is that 'If you don't go down there immediately, I'm going to come to Nashville and kick your ass every inch of the way.' So I said, 'Yes, Mr. Phillips, I will go and talk to those people.'"

The treatment he underwent at the University of Texas M.D. Anderson Cancer Center in Houston worked, and Prine says he has tested cancer-free for almost two years now.

He did, however, get bitten by the acting bug while going through treatment. He's co-starring with Billy Bob Thornton and Andy Griffith in Thornton's new film "Daddy and Them," which Miramax has slated for late summer release. He also wrote "In Spite of Ourselves" for the movie, which is the only Prine composition on his latest album.

Now the only pressure Prine is feeling is what to write about for a new album he wants to record in the fall. "I've never been so content in my life. All my new songs are probably going to sound like 'Zip-a-Dee-Doo-Dah,'" he says with a chuckle. "I have the best home life I've had, probably since I got out of high school. I've got a great wife and kids. . . .

"Everything's good, but even more so since I recovered from cancer. You can't help but go through something like that and not have everything seem brighter than it was before."

PART VII

Fair & Square and Awesome

JOHN PRINE—TO BELIEVE IN THIS LIVING

Lloyd Sachs | May 1, 2005 | *No Depression*

Launched in 1995 as a place for fans of alt-country and other roots music, *No Depression* was the *New Yorker* for organic music. Unafraid to deep dive, willing to let major features go five thousand words, the Grant Alden and Peter Blackstock–founded quarterly became a must-read publication that brought like-minded music fans together.

Lloyd Sachs, who wrote Prine's 2005 cover story, was perfect for the job. He knew Prine's songs and how his projects created a narrative arc. And as a longtime Chicagoan, Sachs understood how Midwestern values shaped how Prine saw the world. As an adjunct professor, film and music critic, and radio host, the *Chicago Sun-Times* columnist viewed the intersection points in Prine's music from a multitude of perspectives. Quietly working on *American Country: Bluegrass, Honky-Tonk, and Crossover Sounds*, he was also immersed in many of Prine's favorite artists.

Prine had largely withdrawn from original songs following *Lost Dogs and Mixed Blessings* a decade before, but *Fair & Square* reestablished him as a creative force to reckoned with. With this much-coveted *No Depression* cover to begin the cycle of press, *Fair & Square* ultimately delivered Prine his second Grammy Award. —Ed.

I'm floating through an outmoded Chicago newspaper database that gets used these days about as frequently as rotary phones, looking for bits and pieces about one of the Windy City's favorite singing and songwriting sons. The keywords "John Prine" bring up the expected reviews and articles, some co-billing him with his dear buddy Steve Goodman, as in "Prine, Goodman Battle Show Biz Tradition" from July 20, 1978. There are featurey parsings of personality like "Behind Prine's Woes Lurks Lot Of Humor" (from the same week), and articles you would pursue if you thought they lived up to their promise, like "Why Is John Prine Singing?", a Chicago Tribune query from January 21, 1979.

And then, interspersed among the links, are a number of seamy tabloid headlines, including "2 Hurt In Fire, Mother Charged" and "Bond Set In Murder, Arson Plot" and "Cabdriver, 18, Shot To Death." Why they come up is of less interest than what they evoke. Prine may be the guy who wrote "It's A Big Old Goofy World", but as anyone who has spent any time with his songs knows, mundane violence, mainly emotional but sometimes physical, seeps through them. He's an intrepid reporter on silent sufferers who have been cut out of life's rewards, who can't fit in, who are neglected by fathers and mothers and Big Brother, who don't have that fifth season to explain the other four.

Sometimes, the violence is front and center. "Lake Marie", one of Prine's masterpieces, was inspired in part by a series of grisly murders he remembers the Chicago news media having a field day with when he was a kid. "Saw it on the news, on the TV news in a black and white video," he sings. "You know what blood looks like in a black and white video? Shadows. Shadows, that's exactly what it looks like." And that's what it sounds like when the Vietnam veteran in "Sam Stone" shoots all that money in his arm, or when the kid with two first names in "Six O'Clock News" ends up with his brains on the sidewalk.

"I felt I had to tell funny stories before I went into those songs, just to, you know, let up on the crowd," says Prine, reflecting on his early days of performing. "I thought they were so sad or something, that they were in such a miserable place. That's why I came up with some of the humorous songs, too, just so I could get back to the sad ones."

None of this is to say it isn't a big old goofy world. On a sunshiny March day in Nashville, where Prine has lived for 25 years, it was Meat Loaf Friday, meaning Prine's favorite food was one of the specials at a local eatery. Yesterday, somewhere else, was Meat Loaf Thursday. He keeps track of where there's a meat loaf special every day of the week.

Sad to report, the place he went to on Meat Loaf Tuesday closed up shop recently, but hey, it's a big town. Unlike Los Angeles, Nashville may not have a restaurant that serves potatoes eleven different ways—have I mentioned he's also big on spuds? But it does know how to fry. Everything.

Prine moved here in 1980, after his first marriage ran aground. His career was in a serious rut, and he was on the verge of a permanent split from the major labels. Perched on a chair in the office of his longtime business partner, Al Bunetta, in the modest Music Row headquarters of Oh Boy, the independent label of which he is "nighttime president," Prine was in a low-key mode. Could be he was saving up energy for his dinner-hour assignment: taking his kids, who are 9 and 10, to Vin Diesel's The Pacifier.

Fatherhood dropped in on him after he married his third wife, Fiona, whom he met during a trip to Dublin, where she was the business manager of a recording studio. They conducted a long-distance romance over five years before getting hitched (they planned to celebrate their anniversary by attending a Bob Dylan/Merle Haggard concert in Chicago). She and her son moved to Nashville. The Prines spend as much time as they can on the old sod, in a small cottage they bought on Ireland's west coast, near Galway.

"It all happened at a great time," Prine said. "I was 49 when the first kid came along. It just, like, keeps me off the street, that's for sure. It also makes it legitimate for me to go to toy stores. Used to be, I could never buy anything because I had no one to buy anything for.

"I don't know if I would have appreciated it as much in another time of my life. The stuff I thought was interesting and all the stuff I did, all the partying I did—I would have hated to miss it being with my kids. It used to be all I'd do was sleep late, walk around and think about ideas for songs. Now, I've got a family, a wife, a whole thing going on. I have to put aside time to write."

The originals on Fair & Square, Prine's first album of new material in nearly a decade (released April 26 on Oh Boy), were written over a period of five years. That's quite a different pace from early in his career, when he turned out four albums in a little more than four years for Atlantic, having signed to deliver an impossible ten in ten. ("They were looking for publishing," he says. "Whether anyone was gonna become a James Taylor or not, they were getting in on it somehow.")

If the early songs that stopped people in their seats with their quick-cutting insight and genius turns of phrase had a certain airtight quality, his new efforts have a more relaxed, ruminative quality. On the sunset-streaked "Taking A Walk", which boasts radiant harmony vocals by Mindy Smith and Pat McLaughlin, and the infectious, easy-rolling opener, "Glory Of True Love", Prine brings a graceful, dyed-in-the-bone wisdom to themes of love, loss and dislocation. There's resignation in the songs (which include a cover of Texas legend Blaze Foley's "Clay Pigeons"), but no small amount of resolve: "Radio's on/Windows rolled up/And my mind's rolled down," he sings on "Long Monday", written with one of his longtime cronies, Keith Sykes. "Headlights shining/Like silver moons/Rollin' on the ground."

Prine, who overcame his initial disinclination to co-write songs to become the most openly collaborative of the great singer-songwriters— he's shared credits with everyone from Goodman and John Mellencamp to Bobby Bare and Lee Clayton to a stable of regulars including Sykes, McLaughlin and Roger Cooke—produced Fair & Square himself, along with engineer Gary Paczosa. Though he has a co-producing credit on other Oh Boy releases, he considers this his first real effort at the helm. Working with his regular accompanists, guitarist Jason Wilber and bassist Dave Jacques, and old hands including Phil Parlapiano on accordion, organ and piano and Dan Dugmore on steel guitar, Prine arrives at such a natural, spacious, dare we say organic sound, you wish he had gotten serious as a producer before.

As a singer, Prine sounds freer and more relaxed than ever. Whereas the young John, beholden as he was to folk tradition, could sound a bit stiff and sober even when cracking wise, the older John has grown into a living-room kind of voice, where there are all kinds of crannies for his listeners to find comfort.

It wasn't just living that altered his pipes. An uncommon form of cancer had a say in it as well. In 1998, after he had started making In Spite Of Ourselves, an offbeat series of country covers featuring duets with the likes of Iris DeMent, Melba Montgomery and Trisha Yearwood, he found out that the bothersome lump on his neck that doctors had dismissed as nothing was in fact something. Having seen Goodman stave off leukemia for years longer than anyone said he could (he died in 1984), Prine wasn't scared by the disease, but he was unsettled by the fact that no two physicians could agree on what to do about it.

He was saved from manic doubt by an out-of-the-blue call from Knox Phillips, who had produced Prine's 1979 album *Pink Cadillac* with his brother Jerry and famous father Sam. Having heard through the grapevine about Prine's condition and his frustrating trials, he directed him to a health center in Houston where he'd had his own neck cancer successfully treated. Prine was resistant, but a threatening call from Sam sealed the deal, and saved his life.

The treatments transformed Prine physically. He lost a chunk of real estate between his head and shoulder and had his bite refashioned. He also has put on a bunch of weight. But if someone else in the same situation might dwell on the down side, or wear a turtleneck ("That's just not John," says Bunetta), Prine plays up the positives.

"I'm sure part of it is being grateful for being able to do it at all, but a lot of it was, 'Jeez, I have this new voice,'" he says. "My voice dropped as a result of the treatments, and it seemed friendlier to me than ever; it seemed like an extension of my conversational voice. Maybe I always had it and didn't know it, because I know I used to talk way down here, and then I'd go to sing and I'd sing the song where I wrote it, I'd sing it way up here, and through my nose on top of that.

"Anyway, I had to change the key on all the songs because of my new voice, which turned out to be a real gift for me. The old songs became new to me again. If I had known all I had to do was change the key, I woulda done that years ago. From day one since I started performing again, it's never been the same for me onstage. To have that sack full of songs and to discover them again—I couldn't ask for anything better."

Prine, who re-recorded his early classics for his 2000 album Souvenirs—not only to test-drive his new voice, which sometimes slurs a bit, but also to own masters of the songs—enjoys telling of how he laughed off his doctors' offer to put a shield around his vocal cords during radiation treatments. "I said if I could talk, I could sing, because that's all I could do in the first place. I play the guitar and talk, and talk a little faster, and hold a note at the end of the line, and I said that basically became my singing voice. My definition of singing is how spirited it is, how believable, not whether or not you can hit the note."

As much as he runs down his vocal talents, having fallen so short of his childhood desires to croon like Jim Reeves, he knows, like so many other craggy-voiced songwriters Bob Dylan gave license to trill, that the power of his personal expression transcends whatever stylistic i's he can't dot or t's he can't cross. Opposite a full-bodied weeping willow such as Melba Montgomery, his instrument can seem a bit twiggish, but when he's in his own backyard, in his element, he's an untouchable.

Covers of his songs are many and varied, including Bonnie Raitt's "Angel From Montgomery", Bette Midler's "Hello In There", Johnny Cash's "Unwed Fathers", the Everly Brothers' "Paradise", Norah Jones' "That's The Way That The World Goes 'Round", and let's not forget Swamp Dogg's "Sam Stone". But most of his interpreters play things too straight up, if not with too much sentimentality (something Prine himself has been accused of), to serve his rascally sensibility and oblique poetry.

Kris Kristofferson, one of Prine's early champions, marvels over the elusiveness of lines like, "As soon as I passed through the moonlight/She hopped into some foreign sports car" (from "The Great Compromise"). Joe Ely, who came under Prine's influence while with the original incarnation of the Flatlanders, admires his craft. "It's one thing to write lyrics and another to have the whole melody and the way you sing it work with the song," Ely observes. "When John finishes a song, he knows how to present it. He figures it out while he's putting it together. There are very few people who can do that."

Few pop artists are as thoroughly well-liked as Prine is—not only by his fans, many of whom, after he and Bunetta started Oh Boy as a mail-order business, sent in money for albums Prine hadn't even started; not only by fellow artists, who, in addition to covering his songs, appearing on his albums and citing him in interviews, have put his name into more than a dozen of their own tunes (including the moody Minnesota trio Low's "John Prine"); not only by poet laureate Ted Kooser, who pre-ambled his recent onstage interview with Prine at the Library of Congress by comparing him to short story master Raymond Carver for making "monuments" of ordinary lives; but also, just possibly, by the large gallery of characters in his compositions.

I'm referring to Donald and Lydia and Iron Ore Betty, to Barbara Lewis Hare Krishna Beauregard and Linda who went to Mars, to Forbidden Jimmy, who "got a mighty sore tooth from biting too many dimes in a telephone booth," to Dear Abby, who showed up in a novelty tune named after her—one that inspired a fan to actually write to her pretending to be the guy in the song whose stomach made noises whenever he kissed. Sabu is in there, too, and so is Jesus. To their eternal gratitude, Prine has never abandoned them, stretching his concerts to two and a half hours so he can play the old songs along with the new.

Prine seems always to have made people happy. "I was such a good kid, childless couples used to borrow me," he said, recalling his formative years in Maywood, an economically mixed western suburb of Chicago. "They'd loan me out for a night. You could just sit me somewhere and I'd be there an hour later when you came back. Though I ended up having a little brother, I was supposed to have been the baby. I had two older brothers and I could do no wrong whatsoever. Everybody picked me up when they came in the door and swang me around. It was a really great childhood."

His father, a tool and die man and union head who left Kentucky to get away from the coal mines, had a big collection of country 78s and "loved to go to honky-tonks and play the jukebox. He'd take us with him to hillbilly bars, set me up, order an orange pop for me, go play the jukebox and give me money for the pinball machine." Prine's maternal grandfather played guitar with Merle Travis. Young John took a liking to Hank Williams and Roy Acuff and moved on to other country and bluegrass and honky-tonk stylists from there.

Taking a page, and informal lessons, from his older brother Dave, a fiddler who was featured on his early albums, he hung around the Old Town School of Folk Music. He began learning to play songs at 14, when "I was trying to impress a girl." One of them was "Twist And Shout". The other was one of his own songs, which he remembers as "a Hank Williams throwaway." He found it easier to play his own stuff than learn somebody else's. Two other originals from that early period, "Sour Grapes" and "The Frying Pan", ended up on his second album, Diamonds in the Rough.

He lost interest in music for a while. But having been pressed into playing tunes for his mates in the Army—drafted out of high school at 17, he was stationed in Germany at the height of Vietnam—he began making up songs to amuse himself during his rounds as a mail carrier, a job he held for six years in Maywood.

No one knew about his commitment to songwriting—not his wife, Ann Carol, whom he'd married in 1966, not his brothers, not his parents. His announced his talents in 1969 at a club near the Old Town called the Fifth Peg, having scored a job auditioning with three originals: "Sam Stone", about a war veteran's drug troubles; "Hello in There", a tearful ballad about neglected old people; and "Paradise," which depicted the ravaging of his father's hometown in Kentucky by strip miners. "I wrote it to show I could write stuff my father knew about," he said.

Movie critic Roger Ebert, who also did some music writing back then, was among the first to call attention to Prine after catching him in October 1970. Legend (with help from Prine) has rewritten the details a bit: Ebert didn't walk out on a movie to get some popcorn and overhear people talking about this guy from Maywood singing and so headed over to the Fifth Peg. He had heard about Prine—and, he conjectured recently, probably had seen him—before. And the headline over Ebert's column in the Sun-Times wasn't the Variety-worthy "Singing Mailman Delivers the Message," but rather the awkward "Singing Mailman Who Delivers a Powerful Message in a Few Words."

"He appears on stage with such modesty he almost seems to be backing into the spotlight," wrote Ebert. "He sings rather quietly, and his guitar work is good, but he doesn't show off. He starts slow. But after a song or two, even the drunks in the room begin to listen to his lyrics. And then he has you."

In the summer of 1971, Prine won over Kristofferson, who was riding high as one of the new leaders of the new country, after Goodman talked him into seeing Prine's act at the Earl of Old Town. Goodman was opening for Kristofferson at the Quiet Knight, where he played one of Prine's songs. By the time Kristofferson and Goodman made it to the Earl—along with the unlikely third wheel of Paul Anka, who was singing Kristofferson's "Help Me Make It Through The Night" as part of his nightclub act at the Empire Room—everyone had gone, chairs were on tables, and Prine was asleep in a booth. Or, as Prine recalls, under it.

Kristofferson asked Prine to sing, and heard seven songs. He then asked him to sing them all again and add some others. "If he was nervous, it didn't show," Kristofferson said recently via email. "His performance was as natural as breathing. And his songs simply blew us away."

The songs carried Prine to New York, where Kristofferson got him and Goodman (who was about to release his first album on Buddha) onto his gig at the Bitter End. Prine played the late set, for the door. Legendary Atlantic Records producer Jerry Wexler, who had helped launch the careers of Ray Charles and Aretha Franklin, heard Prine and signed him. Later that year, Atlantic released Prine's self-titled debut, with liner notes by Kristofferson and a thank you to Anka (who attempted to become Prine's manager). The new "next Dylan" was born.

On the cover of the album, which was recorded in Memphis, Prine is sitting on a bale of hay, looking like anything but a Chicago guy. "I thought they coulda had me on a bus or something," he said. "I had never sat on a bale of hay in my life." The photographer assured him he was shooting a close-up and using the hay only as "an interesting pattern to put behind my face." In the end, Prine cottoned to the image. "Maybe he saw the hick inside me trying to get out."

Produced by Arif Mardin, John Prine certainly was marked by the rural inflections and sensibility passed down by his parents. Would the songs—emotional knife-twisters such as "Hello In There" and larkish lifestyle commentaries such as "Spanish Pipedream", in which a topless dancer offers "level-headed" advice to "Blow up your TV, throw away your paper/Go to the country, build you a home"—have caused such a stir if they weren't coming from a kid of 24 who didn't have any right to be passing on such wisdom?

"Hey, I just figured I knew about what I was writing about, but that doesn't make me smart," said Prine. "To be able to have those insights about people, that doesn't mean you have any answers. All you're able to do is give the police a good description of the guy who robbed the place. You might even tell a few courts about them, but that doesn't mean you can tell them where he lives or why he did it.

"In certain ways, I only wrote those songs because I was as innocent as I was about the world. But I could see these things going on and they stuck with me evidently, or I couldn't have written them down and they couldn't have touched nerves the way they did.

"But, I don't know, it was only after that that I was shown the world. All of a sudden, I was able to travel all over and meet all different people. After all these years of doing that, I wasn't so sure that I didn't like the world that I started out with better than the one I saw after years and years."

Prine was perfectly happy working with Mardin, who also produced Diamonds In The Rough and Sweet Revenge, his second and third albums. "Truly, I think he was a genius as a producer," Prine says. "He had never heard of a steel guitar before he worked with me. And the day we brought Leo LeBlanc in the studio, Arif sat there for a good two hours, just asking Leo to play standards and stuff, and he couldn't get over how it reminded him of string arrangements. I thought we were rolling along fine."

But for his fourth album, 1975's Common Sense, Prine picked as his producer Steve Cropper, famed Stax and Booker T & the MGs guitarist, "out of the air, thinking you were supposed to try different things with different producers. I didn't know there'd been all this bad blood between him and Atlantic, so Atlantic took it as a slap in the face."

Recorded in Memphis and Los Angeles, Common Sense made no secret of its commercial designs. It had a big sound, Memphis horns, and backup vocals by an L.A. posse of Jackson Browne, Glenn Frey and J.D. Souther. But for its professional polish, it was a rebellious effort in signaling Prine's desire to go off in a different direction.

As you might gather from his description of the album's title cut in his notes to Rhino's Prine anthology, Great Days, he wasn't in the brightest of spirits: "It's a song about the American dream only existing in the hearts and minds of immigrants until they live here long enough for democracy to make them cold, cynical and indifferent, like all us native

Americans." The obscure bent of tunes such as "Saddle in the Rain", in which he "dreamed they locked God up/Down in my basement/And he waited there for me/To have this accident/So he could drink my wine/ And eat me like a sacrament," didn't help sell the album. After Common Sense tanked at the box office, it made sense for Prine to move on.

"In the short time I was there, Atlantic really changed from what it was when I was a record buyer," Prine laments. "That's who I thought I was signing with when Wexler signed me. Jerry retired about three years after I was there, and then they signed Led Zeppelin, and then they signed the Stones, and Ahmet [Ertegun, the label's founder] just started traveling the world, and between Zeppelin and the Stones, that was it.

"Jerry had an idea of why he was signing me, and why he started a Nashville label. There was something stirring with this kind of music and he wanted to pursue it. With Jerry gone, I went to Ahmet and asked him if he had any ideas of about what he'd like me to do after four records. I said I don't feel like anyone knows or cares what I'm doing here; they just kept giving me money to make records. I just felt lost."

Feeling constricted as a songwriter, he made a conscious decision to go beyond the story-songs that were his bread and butter. "I thought if every time I do an album, I come up with twelve new characters, sooner or later I'll have like an entire city, you know, of people," he said with a laugh. "They came so easy for me, they were gonna get trite. So I tried to write anything but, just to stretch out."

With his marriage headed for an end—his wife reportedly wasn't happy about her life as a musician's better half—he headed to Nashville. Newly signed to Asylum, he hooked up with Cowboy Jack Clement, the famed producer, studio founder and label head. Once a cog in the Sun Records machine, Clement spent the summer of '77 producing Prine and working on his own first album. He completed that debut, All I Want to Do in Life (which didn't yield a sequel until last year's Guess Things Happen That Way), but the songs he recorded with Prine remained unfinished. "We had some great music, and we had some great tapes," Prine said. "But we didn't have a record."

"John is one of my favorite people, and it was a productive time for him," recalls Clement. "We did a lot of experimenting and messing around, him and me playing guitars, which I thought was the direction to pursue. But he had things going on. We'd start working on a song and he'd start singing something else. He had a crush on the bass player, Rachel [Peer], who he married later. That was part of the distraction, but there were other things, too."

Forced to start over at ground zero, a grueling prospect for any artist in any field, Prine turned to Goodman for help back in Chicago. "He said, 'Just show up with your guitar and sing the songs however you want to sing them,'" Prine relates. "'I'll surround you with musicians and you'll have a beautiful record.'"

Which is what a lot of people called *Bruised Orange*, the only album he has recorded in the Windy City. Streaked with whimsy and lifted by hometown energy, it boasted instantly appealing tunes such as "That's the Way That the World Goes 'Round" and "Fish And Whistle". It had Corky Siegel playing harmonica and a turn by the great Jethro Burns on mandolin; it had a song co-written by Phil Spector; it had strings and voices and photos by Victor Skrebneski. What it didn't have was what Prine was hearing in his head.

"It was really far from what Cowboy and I were doing," he admits. "I thought I'd made this record once already, and I couldn't find it in me to go back and make it again." For better or worse, Goodman prodded him forward. "It wasn't a time period I liked being around Steve. He was like Edward G. Robinson as your producer. He wouldn't mind if I argued everyday, but I didn't have it in me. We made a deal we'd go in and do this, though, so I listened to him."

When it came time to go on the road, Prine decided to forgo the usual suspects in putting together a band. With the help of guitarist John Burns, Jethro's talented son, he rounded up other reliables from the Chicago scene, including keyboardist and harpist Howard Levy and drummer Angie Varias. When they hit the road, they hit it hard.

"John was into this band," Varias remembers. "He was playing with new enthusiasm. He wanted to do Elvis songs and old Johnny Cash and rockabilly and rootsy stuff. He couldn't get enough of that music."

"When Asylum asked for another record," says Prine, "I said, well, I'm gonna give them a record. I'll give them the record I was gonna make before I made *Bruised Orange*. And so I wrote some songs for it and we ended up going over to Memphis to work at Sam's place with Knox and Jerry Phillips. We got an apartment not far from there, Johnny Burns and all the guys, and we recorded six nights a week. We'd go in at six at night and leave at six in the morning. Once Sam heard what was going on, he'd be in there at 4 a.m., his devil eyes flashing."

"We did that for I don't know how long—we ended up with something like 500 hours of tape—and took the best of what we had, and Asylum just about had a heart attack. They called me out to L.A. and one of the heads there said, 'John, what you've got here is not what I think you want.' This is a problem. He tells me what I want and it's not on that tape.

"I said, well, that's what I want. And I said, that's expensive noise on there. We did a lot of things to get the noise on those tapes. At the time, Steely Dan and the Eagles were the kinds of records out there, and the sounds were highly digital. That was the popular sound for the records that sold, and this was not that at all."

Pink Cadillac will forever be another commercial blip on Prine's resume—a cousin to those "uncharacteristic" departures Neil Young got sued by his label for making. Artistically, though, it was a high point in Prine's career. Scrapping the singer-songwriter aesthetic for a raw bar-band approach, he heated up old tunes such as "Baby Let's Play House", bit off as much of Floyd Tillman's "This Cold War With You" as he could chew, poured his rakish car collector's soul into his own "Automobile", and spared no hope on the bleak and biting "Down by the Side of the Road". The sound of *Pink Cadillac* was jarring, the playing loose and jagged, the attitude one of going for broke.

It shouldn't have come as any surprise that it wouldn't be well-received at Asylum, where "everyone in the office dressed like the Cars, with skinny ties and shiny suits," Varias says. What do you do when your best work is brushed aside by a label to which you're under contract to deliver another record?

"I just more or less picked stuff I didn't record on *Pink Cadillac*, went down to Muscle Shoals, recorded it, gave it to 'em and left," Prine summarizes. "That was the end of my major-label days." His appropriate parting lyric: "Silence is golden/'Til it screams/Right through your bones."

Nursing his wounds back in Nashville, Prine wasn't worried about the future. If he kept on as a performer—as opposed to, say, becoming a fisherman, which he reportedly had considered at one point—he'd have no trouble supporting himself. "I knew I could go out and play till I was 140 if I wanted to," he says, "just me and my Martin, playing John Prine songs, and make a good living doing it."

Fans being fans, though, they like to have keepsakes from their favorites. Bunetta had had some success starting a mail-order label for Goodman. He and Prine decided to have a go at starting one up for him. Named after the Buddy Holly song ("All of my life, I've been waitin'/ Tonight there'll be no hesitatin'/Oh boy!"), with a logo that borrowed the curl from the cherubic figurehead for the old Big Boy burger chain, Oh Boy started out with modest aims. Prine's first release was a red vinyl 45 of "I Saw Mommy Kissing Santa Claus" and "Silver Bells".

Encouraged by the holiday single's small but successful run, he followed it in 1984 with the full-length *Aimless Love*, which included "The Oldest Baby in the World" and "People Puttin' People Down", and then 1986's bluegrass-oriented *German Afternoons*, Clement's favorite Prine album, which included "Speed of the Sound of Loneliness" and "I Just Want to Dance with You".

As Oh Boy grew, its mail-order sales increasingly gave way to store sales. Prine and Bunetta had on their hands a trailblazer for the artist-run indie labels. But amidst Oh Boy's strong start—Prine scored his first Grammy nomination for *German Afternoons* and his second for the 1988 release John Prine Live—he was going through another divorce and was again entertaining thoughts of quitting the business.

He had a chance to do so when Sony made an offer to acquire Oh Boy. "I turned it down because I didn't want to go mess with all that stuff," he says. "I didn't want to be around it. Still today, if I gotta go visit somebody or take a meeting in a building that houses a major label . . . that feeling just crawls all over me."

Playing an inspired game of "if you can't beat 'em, join 'em," in terms of going after pop's brass ring, he got a Heartbreaker, bassist Howie Epstein, to produce his next album, 1991's The Missing Years. An all-star affair with a crisp state-of-the-art sound, it featured most of the

Heartbreakers, with leader Tom Petty, Bruce Springsteen, Bonnie Raitt and Phil Everly on background vocals.

How do you spell sweet revenge? The Missing Years sold nearly a quarter of a million copies—five times Prine's previous best efforts—and won a Grammy for Best Contemporary Folk Album. How could it not, with rhyming phrases like "Exactly-odo" and "Quasimodo" (on "The Sins of Memphisto") and pearls of plainspoken philosophy like "I tell you funny stories/Why can't you treat me nice" (on "Great Rain")?

The ascension of John Prine continued. Having co-written one of the tunes on The Missing Years with John Mellencamp, he took a small role in Mellencamp's 1992 film Falling From Grace. (A few years later, he was Billy Bob Thornton's "Zen hillbilly" brother in Thornton's unreleasable Daddy and Them.) Lost Dogs & Mixed Blessings, an underrated Epstein production even if it did draw another Grammy nomination, came out in 1995, delivering "Lake Marie" and the always applicable "Quit Hollerin' at Me".

Prine's success has translated into success for others. As talent scout at Oh Boy—the guy who listens to the tapes and CDs that get sent in, mainly while he's on tour driving a rental car—he has signed the sharp-witted Todd Snider (following Snider's mid-'90s major-label stint) and the odd-witted Dan Reeder (an American living in Germany who paints doors for a living).

Life is good for Prine, and one can assume it will get only better with the release of Fair & Square. There is, however, a small matter of politics intruding upon his contentment. More than three decades after needling the Reader's Digest crowd with "Your Flag Decal Won't Get You Into Heaven Anymore", he is drawing negative feedback for Bush-bashing lyrics on the new album's fifth track, "Some Humans Ain't Human".

The song begins as a general indictment of "jealousy and stupidity" and abruptly shifts into higher critical gear. "Have you ever noticed/When you're feeling good," Prine says, speaking the words, "There's always a pigeon/That'll come shit on your hood/Or you're feeling your freedom/And the world's off your back/Some cowboy from Texas/Starts his own war in Iraq." The gutsy payoff: "Some humans ain't human/Some people ain't kind/They lie through their teeth/With their head up their behind."

"I've been performing the song since the day I wrote it," Prine says. "I wrote it in Ireland last August. Two days after that, I came back to the U.S. and started to perform it, in Washington, D.C. I've been getting mail and comments from people after the shows, really strange stuff.

"When you get letters that say I've been listening to your music for 35 years and that song would offend them, I wonder what they thought I was singing about in my other songs. If nothing else, I'm glad I wrote it because it seems the way the climate is, if you're not saying anything, you're showing support for the administration.

"It's a more blatant comment than I ordinarily would make," he continues. "But I was really mad at the Bush administration. I was trying to write something lighter, but they made me lose my sense of humor. Sometimes you gotta call a spade a spade."

Back in those flaky 1970s, commenting on Prine's efforts as a "protest singer," the Chicago Today newspaper waxed approvingly over his "bizarre occupation in this time of no commitment from pop musicians." Prine isn't alone in the new century in rallying people to the cause. But in ways both goofy and sober, he's at the head of the class in showing us how it's done.

A LITERARY EVENING WITH TED KOOSER AND JOHN PRINE

Ted Kooser | March 9, 2005 | Library of Congress

No one had ever thought to bring a singer-songwriter to the Library of Congress when thirteenth US Poet Laureate Ted Kooser landed on the notion of having Prine join him for an evening of songs and conversation. Discussing process, motivation, many of the characters in Prine's songs, and the way life shapes how artists face the world and in turn their art, the pair delved into what makes words matter.

Billed as "A Literary Evening with Ted Kooser and John Prine," the 127-minute program was summarized as "a lively discussion between the songwriter and the poet as they compared and contrasted the emotional appeal of the lyrics of popular songs with the appeal of contemporary poetry." More a meeting of like-minded creators with a few Prine classics sprinkled in, the discussion created commonality between two seemingly different art forms.

Kooser confessed to buying Prine's self-titled debut as a young man. The Pulitzer Prize–winning poet and teacher explored the shadows and poured light onto the emotional clarity of Prine's work. Clearly conversant in Prine's catalogue, the two-time NEA fellow and Pushcart Prize winner shared one of his own poems during the exchange.

The significance of a kid who hated school appearing at the Library of Congress wasn't lost on the man about to release *Fair & Square*. Bringing his wife, Fiona, along with sons Jody, Jack, and Tommy, John marveled at the places life had taken him and the way songs can fall together, and he looked to honor the poet's recognition of his work.

Currently a professor emeritus at the University of Nebraska, Kooser shares Prine's Midwestern roots and sensibilities. Known for his conversational poems, collaborations with Jim Harrison, and ability to capture the heartland in his work, the writer from Ames, Iowa, opens the door for a comprehensive consideration of Prine's career. —Ed.

Ted Kooser: You're seated tonight in the most beautifully decorated building in the United States. It's a real privilege we could put this together here. Mr. Jefferson, in need of a little money way back when, decided he would sell his books to the Congress thinking that they needed to know a little something. And look what's become of it all. It's a marvelous collection here.

For those of you who've been following country and folk music, less than one hundred yards from where we are here is the American Folklife Center and the Archive of American Folk Song and Folk Life Reading Room. When you come back someday, you can go down there and you could listen to or watch actually, the last two videotapes of the Martha White Flower Show from 1968 with Lester Flatt and Earl Scruggs, Carl Perkins, Johnny Cash, and June Carter Cash. The Folklife Center is a marvelous collection of material, folk songs, storytelling, oral history, dance, you name it. The kind of treasures that Alan Lomax and others collected over the years.

Now, just three years after those Martha White episodes were taped in 1968, a young mail carrier was playing and singing his remarkable songs on Thursday nights in a backstreet bar in Chicago. He's with us tonight, another American for the Library of Congress. One of the privileges of being Poet Laureate is the opportunity to choose a few programs for the library.

Within days of receiving my appointment, I began to dream about tonight's event, wondering if I could persuade our special guests to come here. Then I did a poetry reading in Knoxville and met a man who's here tonight, RB Morris, who knew somebody, who knew somebody, who knew somebody. R. B. actually knows John Prine. So he put it together. And somehow it all came together. I thank that man and John Prine's staff, Al Bunetta, Josh Swan and others—and I especially want to thank the staff of the Library of Congress for all their help in getting this evening set up.

Poets like me are especially sensitive when people begin to talk about great poetry, wanting to be great ourselves, of course, and trying to figure out how to get there. And during the past thirty or forty years, there's been a lot of talk about which of our songwriters was the real poet of the

American people. I bought John Prine's first album on LP when it was released, played it as soon as I got home, and knew at once here was a truly original writer, unequalled, and a genuine poet of the American people.

I noticed, I looked at that record just before I left home in Nebraska, and I paid $5.89 for it; things have kind of gone up a little bit over the years. I've often thought about how our guest's songs could be seen as literary works and have concluded that they're very much like the short stories of the late great Raymond Carver, stories about the most ordinary people elevated through Carver's art to almost heroic status. John Prine has taken ordinary people and made monuments of them, treating them with great respect and love. I may be an incurable optimist, but I believe that most people are living as best they can. Trying to live good lives, sometimes against enormous odds. All over this country are good people like John Prine's "Big Old Goofy Man Dancing with That Big Old Goofy Girl," or others, having made bad choices and fallen on hard times like "Barbara Lewis Hari Krishna Beauregard."

No distinguished literary poet of our time ever even came close to capturing the plight of Vietnam veterans better than our guest did in one of his very first songs, "Sam Stone." We're here tonight to hear about writing songs and about living life and about the courage of good people and to listen to an American master talk and play. I'm deeply honored to have with me in this magnificent institution dedicated to the best in American art and thought, somebody I've been hoping to meet for thirty-five years. John Prine.

John Prine: Thank you. I asked Tanya if it would be okay if I started out with a song, because that's the only way I know how to start something off. [*Prine performs "Fish and Whistle."*]

Kooser: I want everybody in the audience to know we haven't rehearsed this at all. So tonight is a very freeform evening. We're going to rely on you a little bit later to give us some questions and so on. I spent the last few weeks going through John Prine's lyrics; I downloaded them all off the Internet and read them all again and again and, you know, there's such a wealth of material. I don't think we're going to have any trouble filling up an hour and a half here. I wanted to start with, to—tell us a little bit for those people who don't know about your background, how you got started in songwriting and your early career in Chicago, and so on.

Prine: Well, I learned to play the guitar when I was fourteen years old. My brother Dave taught me. He was a fiddle player, and he needed a rhythm guitar player. So, he taught me three chords. And after I learned my first couple of songs, I found it easier to make up songs than to try and learn my favorite ones. They would never sound anywhere near as good as the record sounded. . . .

Then I discovered girls. So I would make up songs to try and impress them, which didn't always work. I did that for a while, was more or less a hobby I kept to myself. The group I hung around with, the fellows, they didn't know I could play the guitar or make up songs. So, I did it off and on for a while, and then kind of dropped it.

Went in the army, got drafted when I was right out of high school. Seventeen, I spent a couple of years in army over in Germany. It was the height of Vietnam and [the army] decided to send me to Germany. Now, I took my guitar with me over there, and I found a renewed interest in it. The fellas would wake me up at night when they come in from drinking and ask me to play a few country songs on the guitar. And it became, it made a lot of friends for me in the army. I started to write a few songs again.

As soon as I got out of the army and went back to the post office, because that was the safest job at the time. And it was good benefits working for the government. So, I was a mailman for six years. I always say once you got a regular route and you know what street you're on, you've got a lot of time on your hands. It's like being in a library with no books, so, I would make up songs to amuse myself. And some of them would stick with me. That's the way I wrote what became my first song, so I ended up singing publicly.

Kooser: I always wondered if the mailman really read the postcards.

Prine: I read everything.

Kooser: Yeah.

Prine: If there was ketchup on page fifty-seven of *Time* magazine, it was me. I read it at lunch.

Kooser: Tell us a bit about Chicago, when you were just getting started.

Prine: It's terribly cold [*laughter*] and windy. I was born and raised on the west side of Chicago, Maywood, Illinois. That's the post office I worked out of.

Maywood was a factory town. The American Can Company was the main—that was where my dad worked, where a lot of people that lived in Maywood worked. My father had come from rural Kentucky, western Kentucky. Him and my mother were both from there, from Muhlenberg County. They settled in Maywood; my dad worked for the American Can. He started working there in the '30s, helped start the Steel Workers Union, a local one there at the American Can. *That* became his life's work actually, the work with the union. He only got $50 a month for doing that, but that was what he really enjoyed. He's a tool and die maker, but he was president of the Union for fourteen years and vice president for another fifteen. So, he was a union man through and through.

Kooser: Your song "Paradise," I've known for many, many years, it was about your home ground and everything; but I never read it, never heard it quite the same way, as after I read about [how] your father had always wanted to go back. It's that yearning to go back that really is the power behind that I think.

Prine: My father loved Country & Western music. When I learned to play the guitar, he would—I'd sit in the kitchen and he'd ask me to play Hank Williams and Roy Acuff songs, Jimmie Rodgers songs, Webb Pierce.

So, when I got around to writing, I remembered that when I was away in the army. My dad had sent me a letter and a little clipping from the newspaper saying they finally tore down their town of Paradise, which was where they would—that's where my mom and dad were from—they would take me and my brothers when we were kids.

It had two general stores, and this one old fella, Bobby Shorte, would sit around, tell us ghost stories all the time. All there was to do is go fishing for catfish. And when I was away in the army, my dad sent me a letter, telling me that Peabody Coal had bought up what was left of the town, moved the people out and tore the town down, because they were going to strip mine where the town was. The joke was that people sold their houses to him, but everybody knew there's nothing there except sulfur. It took Peabody twenty years and millions of dollars to find out that there wasn't any coal right where the town was.

Kooser: That's great. Still laughing at it down there probably.

Prine: Except it was awful pretty down there—and strip mining, as you know, really takes away the whole identity. It didn't look like anything. They had to reclaim it after years and years. Actually, the government started enforcing, they made the coal companies go back and reclaim the land; but the trees look like you're from Seattle or something. It never looked the same down there. They got some manmade lakes and everything; it's pretty and all, but it doesn't look anything like it used to.

Kooser: Do you remember what you were reading as a kid as far as books and stuff like that?

Prine: Yeah, because I read a whole lot as a kid, and I don't anymore. For not any particular reason, I just find it really difficult to get through a book anymore. I read a lot of Steinbeck when I was in high school. I read just about everything except *Grapes of Wrath*. Because I liked the movie so much, I didn't think the book could be better than the movie. [*Laughter.*]

Kooser: You were right. [*Laughter.*]

Prine: For reading one particular author, he was it for me. I liked them, all of his characters and his descriptions of everything. I used to mess around when I first got out of high school, every once in a while, with the short stories, you know. You know, I really liked working with song lyrics.

Kooser: I've never really understood how songs got written. Do you?

Prine: Sometimes the best ones come together at the exact same time—and it takes about as long to write as it does to sing it.

Kooser: Is that right?

Prine: That's the best songs. They come along like a dream or something; you just got to hurry up and respond to it. Because if you mess around at all, the song will either bypass you or it'll be harder and harder to remember that moment.

Kooser: Do you set aside a time where you just sort of sit and wait for that to happen?

Prine: I've just learned to become patient. Sometimes it doesn't come for a very long time. When I first started writing. I don't know if this had much to do with [it] or not, but I used to really, really get into another world, just walking down the street delivering the mail or sometimes driving a car. You know, I should be paying attention to the road but—

Kooser: Yeah.

Prine: —I know I get very far away. I try and explain to some friends that once I had one of these spells when I was about thirteen. I told my parents about it and they sent me to an eye doctor. [*Laughter.*] I just told them sometimes I felt very far away yet, felt like I could see things as if I was looking down into the room. This went on for a good long while.

Kooser: I read someplace or somebody told me part of the meaning behind "Illegal Smile" is staring off into space like that, right?

Prine: Yeah, I wasn't—the song got a reputation for smoking marijuana. But at first, that's not what it was about. It was, I'd just be walking down the street with kind of a half grin on my face, because my little world was fine. And, and I called it "An Illegal Smile."

Kooser: Actually writing poems has always been pretty much the same thing for me. You sort of go into a trance, and you're just, they're waiting for something to happen. My parents have a photo of me when I was a little boy, staring off into space, and it was the same sort of thing. I just get one and would get lost. I think that may be part of the way you get work done is you got to show up for work, you know, got to be there waiting for the geese to come flying in.

Prine: I learned the hard way when that song came to me in the middle of the night, and I got up and walked around a little bit, humming it. I didn't pick up the guitar at all. Didn't pick up a piece of paper. Love the song. Went right back to bed. Got up the next morning, couldn't remember it.

Kooser: "Souvenirs," you wrote on the way to the bar to sing, right?

Prine: Made it up in the car. I thought I had written a melody I couldn't play. I'm not a very accomplished guitar player, and I had myself convinced I'd written a melody with a bunch of jazz chords. Jazz chords to me are anything it takes more than three fingers to hold. [*Laughter.*]

I got down to the club and couldn't wait to take my guitar out to find out if I could even get close to it. It was the exact same three chords I always play. [*Laughter.*]

Kooser: Well, you feel like playing a little something else for us?

Prine: Maybe I'll play "Souvenirs." I had a good friend, Steve Goodman from Chicago. [*Applause.*] He used to play the heck out of it and sing it with me. He had a way of doing it that always made it sound like I was playing the really good, the fancy parts. It was always him, you know. [*Performs "Souvenirs."*]

Prine: I got away in that song with making up a word. You know if you were writing on the computer, it would tell you you'd spelled it wrong.

Kooser: You've made up a lot of words, I think.

Prine: I love words, therefore, I like to every once in a while, if I can't find one that it says what I want to, then I'll make up one—and see if I can get away with it.

Kooser: And you love rhyming, too. I just—the rhymes are always so marvelous. What's that one with a *sake*?

Prine: I was being kind of cocky with a head full of sake. . . .

Kooser: Yeah. Yeah. Yeah. Instance after instance, of really wonderful rhymes. Sometimes I get the feeling the rhyme comes first, then the line sort of fills in behind the rhyme because you're having such a good time with the rhymes.

Prine: I do get carried away just with words, sometimes. It's really fun to see how many you can bounce on top of each other. It's like a house of cards, until they all come tumbling down.

Kooser: Well, they all come tumbling down. In my introduction, I mentioned "It's a Big Old Goofy World." One of the things I like about that song is that it's a whole string of clichés. Now, most writers will say, "Well, geez, you don't want to use clichés for anything . . . ," but you got: work like a dog, quiet as a mouse, eats like a horse, cute little dish, smokes like a chimney, drinks like a fish, everything you could throw in there as a clichés, which is really a lot of fun.

Prine: My mother helped me with that. . . I hadn't written a song in so long when I wrote that song, I was sure that maybe the last time I wrote was the last song. I was really stuck, and I was over visiting my mother. She liked to work crossword puzzles, and she would buy the easy ones, you know, because she likes to work by quantity. And sometimes in these crossword puzzle books, they would have other games in there. One was these assemblies.

We were sitting on the couch together one day; my mother was telling me some things she used when she was a little girl in Kentucky—and some of them were just hilarious. You know, they'd have to do with somebody's name on the street. Anyway, I got thinking about them, tried to put them all into a song and see if it would work.

Kooser: Another thing about the spirit of your music is that you really come off as having a good time with it. Even in the songs that are the most serious, it's clear you're really enjoying what you're doing.

Looking back over all these years of singing and writing songs, can you see where changes in your life are reflected? I mean, big changes in your life, how do they show up in your songwriting. . .

Prine: For me, it takes a while. I have to absorb losing somebody or a relationship. It all has to soak in. I hardly ever write out of anger or misunderstanding right away. I may get mad but don't go writing a song. That's not what I do. I kind of—let everything sit for a while and stew. Eventually it'll come out somehow. It'll come out in an emotion somewhere.

Kooser: But if you kind of put it off—if you went into an angry moment, does the time cleanse some of that anger out of you?

Prine: Usually.

Kooser: Well, the song seems so emotionally balanced that way. There are obviously some angry songs, but "Your Flag Decal Won't Get You Into Heaven Anymore" is a very important political song. Yet it it doesn't—it seems to be sympathetic with those people. Am I wrong about that?

Prine: I think you have to be, especially if you're poking fun at somebody or something somewhat sympathetic. Otherwise you're not doing anything but just poking fun.

Kooser: I read once you start singing for money, it just changes everything.

Prine: It's easy the first couple years to think that you're just messing around and actually getting money for it. . . After a while, even if you impose the time limit on yourself, say, "I've got to sit down and write today." You know, "should've had a record last week" or last year; all of a sudden, it's a job.

I try and balance the job with the fun. I've been in Nashville for twenty-five years. There's a lot of cowriting goes on there. Something I never thought of when I first started. I thought, "How can I write these personal songs with somebody else?"

But these people that became my close friends, they were songwriters, too. We'd be shooting pool, somebody would go, "I got a great idea." You start knocking it back and forth, and before you know it, you're writing a song. At best, when you're writing with somebody else, it comes out something you wouldn't have done on your own or they wouldn't have. A third thing happens there.

Then sometimes, it becomes a real struggle to finish it. That's when you're depending on craft solely, and there's no particular passion coming from the individual.

So, yeah, I'd really like to hear you read something Ted.

Kooser: I could read some. I've got a poem about a tattoo that is sort of the kind of subject that I kind of figure I see in some of your songs.

The tattoos. I don't know how many tattoos we have in the audience tonight.

I won't ask you to raise your hands, but you know what they look like when they get really old. This is a poem about seeing a man at a yard sale with a very old tattoo. [*Recites "Tattoo."*] Thank you. [*Applause.*] Thank you. Is that the kind of character you'd notice?

Prine: I got in a pool hall when I was a teenager, and there was a man who'd come in once a month—and he had a purple head. The story went when he was a young guy he went out, he was in the navy and got drunk. His buddies took him out. They shaved his head and he got tattoos all over. And later on, they all ran together. It's just red and blue. All this ink on top of his head.

Kooser: Have the meanings of your songs changed over the years, to you?

Prine: Not completely, but they've deepened. Some early songs I wrote, if somebody were to ask me years ago if I would have thought "Sam Stone" would have been a song that was sung for thirty years, I would have bet against it.

I thought it was just a bad dream from Vietnam that had just . . . couldn't get it together. That song over the years, the veterans that come to our shows, that song, it won't let go. [*Performs "Sam Stone."*]

Kooser: Here's a question. What is the song "Mexican Home" about?

Prine: Just a feeling I was trying to capture. "Mexican Home." When the song began with one of those spells I used to have; I hadn't had one in years and years. I had one when I was about twenty-three, and I pull the car over and tried to write down what I was feeling, because it was such a strange way to look at the world.

A lot of times after I write a song, I never figure out an answer until somebody asks me. Usually, especially with a song like that, where it doesn't seem to be about any particular subject, I just try and capture an emotion that was very strong to me. It's more about something approaching, something sort of that endangers, something not good.

That's all I was trying to capture in that song. Then if I get done with something like that and sing it a couple times, it feels good, then it's a song. But I have a real difficult time trying to take the song apart and explain different parts of it.

Kooser: Which singer-songwriters are you listening to today?

Prine: I still like my old favorites. Bob Dylan always does it for me. Van Morrison I love to this day from his early stuff right on. Listening to a lot of Gordon Lightfoot lately.

I always knew Gordon Lightfoot was a really great songwriter, but his stuff sounds better and better all the time. It's just so, so good. Next to a really good contemporary folk song is a Gordon Lightfoot song.

And Kristofferson. When I first heard of him, I thought it was something I'd always heard, but nobody ever wrote it like that. Nobody ever put it down on paper. His stuff was so lyrical that I read the lyrics to Kristofferson songs before I ever heard them. I knew what the melody was because the lyric had the melody in it. A lot of times, when you don't get the words and music together, you write a lyric that's what I would call a Chuck Berry lyric, where every syllable has a beat to it.

Kooser: I remember one of Kristofferson's lines, "Maybe I'll never believe in forever again . . ." I thought, "God, I wish I'd written that line." It's just such a gorgeous line. He's particularly good. Is there a role for protest music anymore?

Prine: I'd say there's a full-time job. [*Applause.*]

Kooser: That's a good answer. [*Laughter.*] "Mr. Prine," this one starts, "there's so much talk in contemporary politics about values. You and your songs represent American values better than any other. Will you get involved in the current political dialogue and tell the fanatical right what real values are?"

Prine: That would be difficult. You'd have to, if that's what you set out to do as a songwriter, I would say most of you would fail. You got to keep in mind that politics don't come first, even for the people whose politics you don't like.

Maybe they get the same kind of white shirt on, you know? That might be your song. If you're looking for the big picture, you got to get a really small frame sometimes.

Usually, protest songs, they're self-serving. They're written for that crowd that already agrees with you. You're preaching to the choir. But occasionally, a protest song gets written that they'll hear it before they realize what you just did, then they're done. Then they get up and walk out, but at least they don't leave until it's over.

Kooser: What you just said is very interesting, because I've told students, they're trying to write poetry, that you can't start with a big idea, that you have to start with some little snatch of something.

If you have a big idea, the big idea will sort of emerge through the small things.

Prine: Exactly.

Kooser: How 'bout another song?

Prine: My boys are here tonight; I promised I wouldn't put them to sleep.

I wrote this on my mail route where I was a postman in Westchester, Illinois. One of the publications all of us mailmen really disliked was *Reader's Digest.*

The reason being *Reader's Digest* were small as a letter, but they were thick. So you couldn't put them with your magazines. You had to carry them like you would your letters. With about five or six *Reader's Digest,* you had a bundle of mail. So instead of having, say, 17 bundles of mail for your whole mail route, you would have about 213 when a *Reader's Digest* came, because they were so fat.

We didn't like to see them come. They were like the Columbia Record Club. You just picked it up in the dentist office, you'd subscribe to it. You know? Just about everybody got a *Reader's Digest.* So, one month, this was around 1969, for no particular reason, they gave every customer a decal of the American flag that was just about the size of the *Reader's Digest.* I thought, "Wow, that's really odd."

There was no explanation whatsoever. They didn't say, "This is for you because we feel strongly about this"—they just put it in there. Next day I went on my mail route, stickers were everywhere. Bumpers of cars, front doors, mailboxes, and they weren't just put on, they were like *that.* Like that ought to *show them,* you know? So I wrote this. [*Performs "Your Flag Decal Won't Get You into Heaven Anymore."*]

Kooser: One of the people in the audience says, "Being sick teaches things to write about. How about you?" John Prine and I are survivors of exactly the same kind of cancer. He was about six months ahead of me going under treatment. And here we are. . .

So, we decided we might be willing to talk a bit about that just to underline the fact people do get over things like this and . . . [_Applause._] Well, thank you. When I asked John earlier, if he felt like talking about this, he said when he was very sick that he didn't want to talk about it then, all he was concerned about then was getting over it.

But he doesn't mind talking about it now, nor do I. What happened to me—and I guess happened to you—surviving something like that means _everything_ becomes extremely vivid and alive. At least it did for me. I've written more really good work since I was ill than I ever wrote before. Everything kind of came into focus for me, I suppose you had a similar experience.

Prine: Exactly. That all happened and everything I'd done before that experience, all my older songs, songs I'd sung thousands times, I wasn't tired of them. They became, it was like a getting a paint job. All of a sudden, they were coming out of my mouth.

I knew these songs really well. Some of them I felt like I was hearing for the first time. It was one thing to write them, but I was actually hearing this song for sometimes the first time—and it was an amazing experience. It was kind of like, to me, the army in a way. It was something I hated going through. But I wouldn't want to have missed it for the world. It really was an experience that taught me a few lessons I needed to be taught.

Kooser: For me, I never was a real smartass. But it was a tremendous dose of humility delivered very quickly. You sit in those oncology waiting rooms with those people, and it's a quite a marvelous experience, a leveling experience. Nobody in those rooms is any better than anybody else.

Have some of the newer songs since then been influenced by that? I was wondering about "New Train." Was that a song you wrote since you were sick?

Prine: No, I wrote that before.

Kooser: It has this sort of tone of being about dying. That's why I wondered.

Prine: I was more or less writing about starting over, about you know, it's a new life.

Kooser: It's a beautiful song.

Prine: Thank you. As far as the way the cancer affected it, it's like the really big things in your life. It's still soaking in the effect of going through the experience. My wife and I went through it totally together. We went through the whole thing.

It was really amazing the people you meet and the feelings you go through. The scariest part for me was when I found out the doctors—it wasn't like going to a doctor for a cold. He didn't say, "Well, take two of these, lay down," you know. Each doctor had a different treatment. That's what scared me, that "Well, what the heck do I do here?"

They all are telling me totally something different. So, where do you go? Once I found the right doctor I trusted and was able to sit back and just say, "OK, what do you want me to do?" It was a really big relief. I would think most people that go through anything of that— [*Guitar falls.*] That guitar didn't like what I was saying.

Kooser: It changed me completely. But I think for the better. It's a terrible thing you have to go through but, you know, here we are, which is wonderful.

During the course of [treatment], he said, "I'm going to have to take out a sizable chunk of your tongue. Do you have to do any public speaking?" I said, "Well, nothing I really care all that much about." I could certainly quit it; my wife said, "Well, you know, he is a poet. He does poetry readings from time to time." I didn't think any more about it. Ten days later, we got back to the hospital and went to see the doctor. He mentioned he'd been to the library and checked out all my books and read them. I mean, you got a doctor when they're willing to read your terrible poems from years ago.

So, this one's a two-part question. "When writing new material that feels overly familiar, like something you've done before, with too many common elements, what process do you use to carve out a new angle?" Part two. "When performing old songs, do you fight temptation to alter words sometimes, just as you might tweak a musical arrangement?"

Prine: The first part of the question is: I usually don't let it go that far.

There's too many everyday things I'd rather go do than work on a bad song or a mediocre one. I don't think I'd go down the avenue of writing about something I'd written before.

Kooser: "Hello in There" is not only about old people, I think it is the *very best* song ever written about old people. It has such a true feeling for old people. Want to play it?

Prine: When I wrote this, I don't think I approached it as I thought I was going to write a song about old people. I heard John Lennon sing the song "Across the Universe," how he's got a bit of echo on his voice and the guitar.

I listened to the song but twenty times in a row, and I thought, "Man, it sounds so needed."

It really sounds like you're singing through a hollow log or something. I was thinking about what you would say if you stuck your head in that hollow log. "Hello, hello in there . . ." you know. And that developed into a song about old people.

That's, that's a process there. [*Applause. Prine performs "Hello in There."*] Thank you. [*Applause.*] Thank you. [*More applause.*]

That's one of my personal favorites. It's come back to me in spades over the years, and I always, ever since I can remember, I always liked old people. Yeah. I hope I'll be one someday. [*Laughter, applause.*]

Kooser: We hope you are too, yeah. Last question. Someone asked, "Of all the places you've traveled, which one is your favorite and why?"

Prine: Ireland, because that's where I met my wife. She's here tonight. We go back there quite often. Just a beautiful, beautiful place.

Kooser: I want to thank everybody for coming. I've felt a really warm response from this audience—and maybe if we're really lucky, we can talk John into playing one last tune to get us out of here.

Prine: Doesn't have to be a happy one, huh? [*Plays "Sam Stone."*] Ted Kooser, thanks a lot for inviting me down. God bless. [*Applause.*]

Voice-Over: This has been a presentation of the Library of Congress.

JOHN PRINE: FAIR AND SQUARE

Jesse Kornbluth | January 1, 2005 | HeadButler

If *In Spite of Ourselves* was the first post-cancer, post-radiation project, one that let Prine record classic country duets with some of his favorite female singers, *Fair & Square* marked his return to "being John Prine."

Recording across some railroad tracks in an older industrial patch at the Butcher Shoppe, adjacent to Nashville's gentrifying Germantown neighborhood, Prine and longtime Jack Clement engineer David Ferguson set up shop. "Ferg" was not only a friend but also a bridge to Prine's Nashville roots, as well as a man who'd recorded Johnny Cash's *American Recordings*, portions of U2's *Rattle and Hum*, bluegrass icon Mac Wiseman, and Country Music Hall of Famer Charley Pride.

Prine enlisted Gary Paczosa, known for his production and engineering work with progressive country and bluegrass stars Alison Krauss, Dolly Parton, Sarah Jarosz, Blue Highway, Kelly Willis, Chris Thile, and Nickel Creek, to enhance the acoustic presence of the dozen songs that make up the album, plus three bonus tracks. Opening with the quick-strumming "Glory of True Love," with accordion wheezing, mandolin flourishes and the kind of twin-guitar discourse that suggests classic Appalachian-tinged country, Prine signaled a vitality that thrilled his fans.

Having been through his battle with neck cancer, the now sixty-year-old songwriter was feeling frisky. With a cover of the late Blaze Foley's "Clay Pigeons" and closing with the Carter Family's "Bear Creek Blues," *Fair & Square* sees Prine pulling his focus back a bit—writing about life in more philosophical terms, slightly less political, definitely more in love and reflective about how lives are engaged and invested.

USA Today photographed Prine in the bar of the Hotel Edison for a major feature, once again demonstrating the power and reach of the humble folkie who eschewed fame jockeying. A concert at Carnegie Hall sold out long before the songwriter hit New York City. There was Lloyd Sachs's wonderful *No Depression* cover story.

But Prine was just as revelatory and present in unlikely pieces. Longtime *Vanity Fair* contributor Jesse Kornbluth's HeadButler was just establishing itself as a thinking person's one-stop culture shop when the pair spoke. Erudite, quippy and exceptionally quick, Prine wasn't the man the *New York Times Magazine*, *Architectural Digest*, and *Tatler* normally spoke to.

"But the best interviews aren't a question-and-answer back-and-forth," Kornbluth says. "They're real conversations without a checklist on a clipboard. You really see the other person, and even better is when the answers are completely unexpected.

"Beyond being one of the most original songwriters who ever lived, I don't think one thing Prine said would've been what I was thinking he would say. We talked about vegetables, comic books, the state of the world, and it just flowed. . . . And where some people know how to play humble, John Prine was this massive talent for the ages, but he never once felt the need to let me know that. It wasn't humility, it was just this kindness and bemusement about the world outside him—and I was in on the joke."

Comfortable profiling superstars Robin Williams, Tom Cruise, John Cheever, Linda Ronstadt, and Michael J. Fox and Tracy Pollan, Kornbluth has a keen curiosity that made him perfect for interviewing someone who'd rather not talk about himself. "I had a lawyer tell me the best stuff in interviews is the first two hours, after that, it all starts coming apart," Kornbluth recalls. "I've found truly the best stuff is before you get started or after you're done.

"John Prine, who is so curious about the world around him, was great the whole time. But then it was only forty-five minutes, so technically, I had another hour and fifteen before the wheels came off." —Ed.

A classic song doesn't belong to its creator. It's ours. We take it into our lives and use it for our purposes and sing it in the car or the shower— we own it so completely we might as well have written and recorded it ourselves. "My favorite song." It's like that.

What are the elements of a classic song? No one can quite say. But some people seem to have the knack of not trying to write them—and then rolling them out with frightening regularity. Like John Prine.

Prine was once a prodigy, the next savior of the music business. At a tender age, he was introduced to Kris Kristofferson, and the next thing he knew, Kristofferson had called him up on stage. Prine sang a few songs on a borrowed guitar. Kristofferson announced, "No way somebody this young can be writing so heavy. John Prine is so good, we may have to break his thumbs." The legendary producer, Jerry Wexler, was in the audience. The following day, he offered Prine a recording contract.

Prine is such a natural songwriter that on his first album he used two songs he wrote when he was fourteen. At 19, he wrote "Hello in There," a song about senior citizens that will bring audiences to tears until the end of time. For thirty years, he went his own way, pleasing himself and, in the process, delighting his loyal audience. And now, on the cusp of 60, he has a new CD that is studded with classics.

These songs have an inevitability about them; it seems there's no other way they could have been recorded. I could cite examples until I bore you to death, but let's look at the first few stanzas of "Long Monday," the song I can't get out of my head:

[*Lyrics from "Long Monday" listed, concluding with . . .*]
Gonna be a long Monday
Stuck like the tick of a clock
That's come unwound—again

First, the lyric line: It's more spoken than sung. Which gives you the feeling that anyone—namely: you—could "sing" it (but maybe no one could sing it better than a guy who's fought off neck cancer). Second, the subject: Many of us have been blessed by relationships that make a weekend fly. And then "long Monday"—you just know he's going to stretch that "long" out, don't you? And how about those last two lines? Isn't that "again"—almost an afterthought, really—a killer?

Prine's CD is so satisfying, so easy to put on the machine and play all day, so damn comfortable that it almost seemed that Prine had intimate access to my head. It was like, "These are my songs. This is how I feel. So how did this guy in Nashville come to write and sing them?" That was when I decided that I wanted to talk to John Prine. That's usually a terrible idea—in my experience, you do best never to meet your heroes. But this thing could be arranged, and, in short order, I discovered that the smart, laid-back, endlessly amused persona of John Prine on "Fair & Square" is very close to the actual person I was talking to. Here are the Greatest Hits of that conversation:

HB: Why do these songs sound so familiar?

JP: Because this was the most comfortable I've ever been in the studio. I sang these songs in concert over the last 3 years. I knew they fit, I knew people liked them.

HB: "Hello In There" was an instant classic. Forty years later, can you bear to perform it?

JP: More than any other song, it gets stronger every day for me. I never tire of singing it. I don't know how I came up with such a pretty melody. It was an exercise—to use every chord I had ever heard. I paid a guy five bucks to write it out so I could publish it. I couldn't believe it when he played it on piano.

HB: Some of these new songs are so funny, do you laugh while you write them?

JP: I laugh at the funny lines—hey, I laugh at even the serious stuff. When it's going well, I feel like I'm taking dictation. But I don't have hundreds of songs waiting—you've heard them all.

HB: Do they come out in a rush?

JP: I type so slow I can edit as I write.

HB: You say you're lazy. Do you feel guilty when you go for months and don't write?

JP: I'm not Catholic, I'm not Jewish—I can talk myself out of feeling guilty. Because it's easier to not write. I only love the songs I have to write. I trust a song like that—a song straight from the gut. There are some really good songs that, if you don't write them down, someone else will.

HB: On "Fair & Square," there's a political song, "Some Humans Ain't Human"—but it's mostly funny, with only one direct reference to the President.

JP: I always felt that way about protest and politics—include it in your conversation instead of raving about it.

HB: How does that song go over in the red states?

JP: When I'm first singing about some issue, people change the subject. Later, it seems about right.

HB: What's your daily media intake?

JP: I hardly read at all. My wife reads three books at a time, but I read "Archie and Veronica"—in the comic book form.

HB: Who do you listen to?

JP: I buy a lot of CDs, and I listen to them once. But Van [Morrison] or Bob [Dylan] or Merle [Haggard]—I listen carefully to all of those.

HB: Taking care of yourself?

JP: I have a poor diet—I'm a meat and potatoes guy. That has something to do with how I see things. There are no peas on my plate.

"No peas on my plate" is a throwaway line from a song John Prine will never write. No loss. The songs he wrote will do just fine. Not country. Not rock. Not folk. Just . . . songs. With no gimmicks. I guess if you write classics, that's good enough.

UNPUBLISHED INTERVIEW WITH JOHN PRINE AND MAC WISEMAN

Andy Ellis | 2007 | Interview Transcript

In some ways, *Standard Songs for Average People* isn't a major record to casual Prine fans. Not a single original song, but the pairing with sweet-voiced bluegrass legend Mac Wiseman was a valentine to the music of Prine's childhood.

The follow-up to the Grammy-winning *Fair & Square* might not have capitalized on Prine's momentum, but the fourteen-song collection of old country jukebox classics and a Southern gospel song was a labor of love. Recording with Prine's core road band and noted bluegrassers Tim O'Brien on banjo and guitar, Ronnie McCoury on mandolin, Stuart Duncan on fiddle, plus the legendary Cowboy Jack Clement on dobro and acoustic guitar, Joey Miskulin on accordion, and the iconic Carol Lee Singers, the sixty-year-old Prine and eighty-one-year-old Wiseman melted time and reanimated the neon-lit taverns favored by Prine's father.

Whether the lament of love versus class divide in "Saginaw, Michigan," Bob Wills's lilting reminder of good times enjoyed in "Don't Be Ashamed of Your Age," the true-life bluegrass of "Death of Floyd Collins," or Bing Crosby's "Where the Blue of the Night," *Standard Songs* showed more than diversity, offering a sense that truly loving music—and musicians—creates a blissful cocktail of styles. Homage was paid to the raw emotions of Hank Williams with Leon Payne's "The Blue Side of Lonesome," friend Tom T. Hall with a philosophical postcard from Miami International Airport "Old Dogs, Children and Watermelon Wine," and Kris Kristofferson with a loping "Just the Other Side of Nowhere."

USA Today opened its review, "Old-fashioned folk—there's nothing special about *Standard Songs for Average People*—except for everything." The *Nashville Scene* suggests, "Prine's jagged voice evokes the acoustic storytellers of his generation who used personality and phrasing to give their tales color. Wiseman, a bluegrass pioneer, is the Frank Sinatra of mountain music, a smooth and adventurous crooner whose mellifluous tone rides atop mandolins and fiddles like cirrus clouds skimming tall pines and deep hollows," while the *Raleigh News and Observer* offered, "Hearing John Prine and Mac Wiseman sing together is like having a front row seat to the yin and yang of today's Grand Ole Opry."

Nominated for Recorded Event of the Year at the International Bluegrass Music Association's awards, *Standard Songs* was a masterwork of old-time music. Demonstrating Prine's increasing role as a Nashville institution, *Premier Guitar* editor Andy Ellis was dispatched to interview Prine and Wiseman for the Country Music Association's *CMA Close Up*, a magazine helmed at the time by former *Musician* editor-in-chief Bob Doerschuk. Ellis was a writer who could thread the needle of the exceptional musicianship and the camaraderie between not just the two vocalists but also the players bringing these songs to life.

On the day Prine and Wiseman were set to perform the entire album at Nashville's hallowed Station Inn, Ellis found both men chatty and mutually admiring. For the first time, Ellis shares his entire remarkable conversation with the two gentlemen. —Ed.

Mac Wiseman: How're you doing?

John Prine: Well, I've spent almost the entire day in the gym, and I don't ever do that. Liftin' weights . . . tires you out, but get a good night's sleep after. . . .

Andy Ellis: Describe the sessions. . . .

Prine: I think the most we cut in one day was four, and that was a really good day. A lot of times we'd quit in the early afternoon. . . . If we were ahead with one or two songs me and Mac had ready to sing, and the band knew them, we'd cut four every time we went in. Because every time we quit, we'd go, "Man, we're rollin'. Where are the songs?" They'd get on the Internet, try to get the lyrics and everything, and try to get a couple more.

Ellis: Walk in with a list of possible songs for that day, arrange them, then and there? Discover the keys and tempos as you learned the song?

Prine: Yeah.

Wiseman: That was how we worked out the songs.

Ellis: Was there a larger list than wound up on the record?

Prine: As far as fully cut, there was only one or two we cut we didn't include. We usually knew by the second time we sang it if we thought it was worth it or not. There were really good songs, but for some reason they weren't working. After we cut the first four songs, we had something to measure up to.

Ellis: It's an eclectic group of songs, especially "Old Cape Cod."

Wiseman: That's John's. He brought that one. It had been a favorite of mine for a long time, but John deserves all the credit for getting that on the list and into the CD.

Prine: "Old Cape Cod" was one of those songs. I liked the echo, and the background voices, and the strings as much as I did Patty Page on that. It was a little record that you walk into a place in New England and pop on, and man, [*snaps fingers*] it just lights up the room. I said, "Mac, I'd like to do 'Old Cape Cod'." For a while we were calling ourselves the "old Cape codgers." [*Laughs.*] When Mac and I were cutting, the band was sitting all around us. There might have been a baffle here or there, but everybody could see everybody's eyes; the stuff the guys were playing pretty much determined the arrangements.

Wiseman: I was amazed because many of those aren't easy songs to play.

Prine: It's a good thing I didn't have to play them on my guitar. I'd still be learning the chords to "Old Cape Cod." It turns out there were nothing but diminished chords and those ones you have to hold five fingers on. The song had all kinds of those. For me, the Carol Lee Singers really made that song. When we put them on as an overdub, that's when the song . . . It was a real good version up until then, but when they got on it, man, it sounded like *a record.*

Ellis: On several of the other songs, they add an old-school country music vibe.

Wiseman: They do, because they're from that kind of background. Carol Lee [Cooper] being the daughter of Wilma Lee [Cooper] and Stoney

[Cooper]. Her parents were doing this music when she was born. I knew her when she was just a little girl.

Prine: She comes up with the vocal arrangement so quickly, and she'll give you three or four different choices. Like, "Are you going this way?" Then they'll all come in to illustrate. Or "Do you want more of these oohs in there?" or "Do you want us singing the words?" To me, it was like having a full orchestra at your disposal, all day long. Only we're telling them to play "Old McDonald," or something. [*Laughs.*] We'd order in ribs. and they'd sing anything and everything we wanted.

Ellis: How many vocalists?

Prine: Four of 'em, two guys, Carol Lee, and another girl. It's a huge sound. The bass singer gets way down.

Ellis: The album has clean, open sound, rather than the pushed sound of today's music. It's how much we're missing in terms of musical richness.

Wiseman: That was the kind of feeling John and I had when we did these songs. As far as the arrangements, we'd go through a song, and John would say, "Why don't you take those lines?" Or vice versa. We'd try it. I might say, "I'm coming in on the chorus, why don't you take the last two lines in the verse?"

Prine: Some songs, the words are so good, I think we wanted to jump in and claim a section. "Saginaw, Michigan," I knew some parts I wanted to sing. And Mac, when we got to "Old Dogs, Children and Watermelon Wine," Mac got to sing. "I was sittin' in Miami . . ." Man, I would have *loved* to have done that. But even more so, I loved to hear Mac sing that line. [*Laughs.*]

Ellis: John, do you find it harder to record covers than your own songs, or the other way around?

Prine: For me, it's more gratifying right then and there to sing covers. I'm basically a big fan. I love being in the studio when I'm enjoying myself—when it's not work. And it's not work at all when I'm singing covers.

When I've got something I've written, I worry it. I worry the thing right up to where I finally get something I'm satisfied with. Sometimes when I take one of my songs into the studio, I don't know whether it's done or not. There are a couple of songs you might have been singing on the road, and you know they're done; then there's a couple you don't know if you ought to expose them yet. You get 'em in the studio and you start playing with them, and it's different. But going in and singing your favorite songs—and especially sitting across a table singing with Mac Wiseman all day—that was nothing but pleasure. It was like Christmas morning for me.

Wiseman: Likewise with me, and I mean that. The environment was so comfortable, and the way John would interpret a song, to me that was . . . subliminally, that is what feels comfortable with the listener. Most of the time, he can't put his finger on why he likes that, but it's either something he goes, "Well, hell I can sing that," like they do in the clubs. Or, it's like the old saying, and I've watched it through the years, "Once a hit, always a hit." Because it has some secret ingredient that appealed to the masses. And generations don't make any difference. People don't change, we just get a new batch, you know? A new audience comes along, that's the reason these standards are so everlasting.

Ellis: It's impossible to identify exactly why the standards are everlasting, because if we could, we'd all write standards and be extremely wealthy. But are there aspects of these standards—especially now that you've recorded a set of them, that you can identify?

Prine: Mainly, we just like them . . . It doesn't matter whether a song was written a year ago or 40 years ago, if it was a pop song, or a country song, or bluegrass. I said just make a list of what we think we might want to sing. . . .

But the narrative thing in "Old Dogs, Children, and Watermelon Wine," I knew if we both got into telling the story, part of it's narration and part of it's you're the character in it; it's a really good song for that. A great story.

Ellis: Was it Cowboy Jack Clement's idea to do this record?

Prine: It was a good seven years ago (and these days when I say seven, it's probably ten or twelve), but I'd been over to visit with Cowboy one day, and he said, "Mac Wiseman was over the other day. Do you know Mac?" I said, "Well, I'm a big fan, but I don't know Mac."

He says, "Well, I mentioned your name and Mac likes you."

And I said, "You mean Mac Wiseman knows I'm alive?" [*Laughs.*]

Cowboy says, "Man, you guys ought to get together and record some songs." When Cowboy says something, I know he's not just talking off of the top of his hat, you know? I thought about it, and went, "Man, that would be great," but jeez, I don't know if I could sing with Mac Wiseman. "How would I do that?"

Then Fergy started talking about it a couple of years ago, and I thought, "I'm not going to let the opportunity pass me by." So Fergy kept workin' us both, until we did get together. And for me, from day one, I knew it was the right thing.

Wiseman: It was so natural, you know, and so easy and so comfortable. It was a labor of love, but there wasn't any labor in it.

Prine: If I could make records like this all the time, I'd be making records five days a week.

BACKTALK WITH JOHN PRINE

Alex Rawls | December 1, 2002 | *OffBeat Magazine*

Oh Boy Records was approaching two decades in business when Alex Rawls interviewed Prine for *OffBeat*, the New Orleans–based music magazine that celebrates the Louisiana music and entertainment scene to this day. Rawls measured what life for Prine—who was slightly between projects at the time—was like on an indie, as well as how the hard-touring musician was managing a fairly engaged family life.

Measuring how Prine's songs' meanings and urgency may have shifted, the pair looked at the reality of America through the prism of his songs. What emerges is a clear picture of Prine's recognition that Oh Boy was perfect for how he wanted to do business: no rancor expressed towards the majors, but a philosophical notion that not all careers are one-size-fits-all.

With New Orleans's rich music culture, this glimpse into a truly successful artist-driven label must have been instructive to many of the Louisiana-based musicians and artists who read *OffBeat*. Rawls understood the dual needs of Prine fans and other readers.

While Rawls moved on from his time as the monthly's editor, interest in New Orleans and its music from both local and global readers via its online ideation has sustained *OffBeat* as a vital source of informed coverage. —Ed.

It was only in retrospect I realized I talked to John Prine on the eleventh hour of the eleventh day of the eleventh month. While President George W. Bush spent Veterans' Day getting America ready to make new veterans, Prine talked about "Sam Stone," his sympathetic depiction of a heroin-addicted veteran as a result of his time in Vietnam. Since *John*

Prine came out in 1971, he has made a career of writing songs that treat even the most marginal people with the sort of warmth, intelligence and good humor we all wish we had on a more regular basis.

His career suffered two significant interruptions, both health-related. When good friend Steve Goodman, best known for writing "The City of New Orleans," died of leukemia in 1984, Prine took some time off, then a few years ago he was diagnosed with neck cancer, not throat cancer as has sometimes been misreported. Though he feared the effects of treatment on his voice, *Souvenirs*—a 2000 collection of re-recordings of some of his classic songs—shows that if anything, his voice has grown warmer and more sympathetic.

You were hailed as a "New Dylan" when you started? How did you feel about that?

At first I took it as a compliment, but when it wouldn't go away, I didn't care for it. Back then, I guess they were looking for a new Bob Dylan—by "they" I don't mean the record companies; I mean the media in general—because Dylan was laying low and he wasn't making any records. Every singer/songwriter that came along that had something to say, they wanted to stick that label on them, but after a while the label stuck and you couldn't get rid of it. It was like flypaper. It was something that you didn't know how it got started so you didn't know how to put it away.

How has your relationship to "Sam Stone" changed over the thirty years of playing it?

If somebody were to ask me back then after I was singing for a couple of years and things were still going on in Vietnam how long some songs would be timely, that's one I probably would have bet wouldn't. But I kept on singing it and people kept on requesting it. I never felt it was old. After so many years, it even started to get as relevant or more relevant because the problem never actually went away.

It wasn't as topical as I thought it was. I was right in the midst of it in 1969 and America was heavily involved [in Vietnam] by then. We had as many troops as we'd ever have there. I was in the army in '66 and

'67; I got drafted just after they went from 23,000 troops in Vietnam to 500,000. It was still a conflict; we were "protecting our interests." That's what the whole deal was. It wasn't a war, and here they are sending a half-million kids over there.

I was surprised to see recent set lists and see how many old songs you still do; why do you still do those songs?

They feel good. If I get tired of anything, I put it on the shelf for a couple of years then bring it back out. If it feels good, I'll play it; if it doesn't, I won't.

Why did you record *Souvenirs*?

Ever since I've had Oh Boy! Records [the label Prine co-owns], over in Europe I've had problems with different distributors. You lease a record to them, then a year later you find out they didn't do a good job on it, so every time I make a new record I have to go to a new distribution deal over there. I didn't like the distribution I was getting on the continent in Germany, France and Belgium. Italy—it didn't seem like I was getting anything there, so I signed a deal with a German record company to do my next couple of Oh Boy! Records. The guy said Germans were just starting to get interested in American roots music and if he had any kind of collection of my old, classic songs, it would do well. We recorded the album for over there, but when we got done recording it, it sounded pretty good so we went ahead and put it out over here.

Did any of these versions sound significantly different to you? Did you learn anything about any of the songs recording them again?

They were songs I was doing live all the time. I went into the studio with my band and we laid them down the way we do them live. We didn't have to have any talks about arrangements. They sounded better when I recorded them than I thought they would. I thought they'd sound a little tired to my ears, but they sound pretty darned good.

I never did like some of the early versions. I was still trying to find my voice. I don't want to complain, but I started in this business before

I meant to. It was just a hobby—songwriting—and I didn't sing for anybody. None of my friends knew I played the guitar, I just got up at that club that night for the heck of it and got offered a job at the club. Six months later, I had a record contract.

Things are not supposed to happen that way, as you know. I don't feel in retrospect like I was ready to go into a studio and make records. I would rather have just kept on writing and had a whole lot of material. I was so nervous on my first album—I found out I was cutting with Elvis Presley's band in Memphis—and I went, "What am I doing here? I'm a mailman!" I can hear how nervous I was when I listen to that record and it makes me uncomfortable to hear my voice on it, so I'm glad to have these new versions so at least I can listen to them if nobody else does.

You've taken some time between albums of new songs. Why so long?

I don't see any reason to go in the studio unless you've got 10 really good songs. I don't believe in putting a lot of filler on an album. It doesn't really matter how long you take as long as you come up with a good record.

Are you a slow writer?

Yes and no. When I start writing, I can write three that I really like, then go eight months and not be able to put "Once upon a time" together. You feel like you're writing for the first time sometimes.

I got two little boys—a seven- and an eight-year-old. One's in second grade. A couple weeks ago, his teacher asked me to come in and talk to the class of second-graders about the subject of writer's block! She didn't know how ironic it was. I guess they had a little project where they were writing something and they were going to go through the same efforts you'd go through to get something published, and some of them couldn't get started on their stories. She picks me to come in and give a speech on writer's block, so that's what I'm preparing now—how to tell a second-grader about writer's block.

Talking to second-graders has to be a lot like talking to other musicians.

Yeah, except they might be a little more mature.

Do you ever worry that the well's run dry?

I used to, back when I was about two to three albums into this whole thing. I worried then—"Jeez, what happened? I used to write all the time." In retrospect, it had become my job, and I had to decide how to make it fun again. See, it was my hobby before, and all of a sudden the record company is calling, saying, "Hey, it's July and you said you'd give us a record by April." I took all the pressure out it when I started my own record company.

Where do songs start for you?

I don't know. If I did, I'd move there. [laughing] I haven't got any more idea now than I did 32 years ago. My best ones are out of some sort of whimsical thing that happens, or I see something or I hear a phrase and it sticks with me. I can go searching, I can read, I can go to movies and not begin to get a song anywhere out of it. I co-write once in a while, but I do that because when I'm writing with somebody else, I depend more on being a craftsman and don't just write off the top of my head. It's not a way I would write by myself, but if you get the right combination, somebody pulls something out of you. I don't do that with too many different people. I like to do that with someone I like to spend the afternoon with, so if you don't get anything, at least you had a good time.

Who's an example?

My buddy Roger Cook. Roger is nothing but a commercial songwriter. He started his career with "Long, Cool Woman (in a Black Dress)." I think his biggest hit was "I'd Like to Teach the World to Sing." That gives you an idea of the spectrum of this guy's stuff. He writes some great songs, but they're really commercial. He's just a buddy of mine, we play dominoes and shoot snooker together. We spend all this time together and we're both songwriters so we might as well write once in a while. I've got three Number Ones out of it. I didn't put any effort hardly at all into it because he's always writing and I'm never writing.

In the interview with John Hiatt you did for *Sessions on West 54th*, you told the story about "Lake Marie," the homework you did before writing it; is that common?

Sometimes it's more like detective work. If I actually look into something and get some knowledge about something, maybe it'll spark the idea, you know? I knew I wanted to write a song that started off almost like statistics about this place, but I didn't know what place it would be, then I picked Lake Marie. Then I decided to go hunting for the history of Lake Marie just because I wanted the song to start that way. Whatever happened after that, it didn't have to stick to the truth because I wasn't looking for the truth in that sort of way; I was looking for the truth under the story. I found there were these two ugly sisters and they named the two lakes after them [Lake Marie and Lake Elizabeth, in Illinois]. That was enough to get the song started.

I'm working on a different one now. I've been working on this one off and on for seven years. Are you familiar with Birmingham, Alabama?

Sure.

You know the iron man up there? [the 56-foot Vulcan on the summit of Red Mountain: the world's largest cast metal statue] I'm writing a song, "The Iron Man From Birmingham." A construction guy wrote a book about it, but I'm almost coming from a Biblical place. They took this darned thing down and moved it to St. Louis. They used to have it with a giant pickle in its hands, but the main thing that interested me is when they had a light in its hands that would turn red when there was a traffic fatality. That to me is Biblical, you know? I'm trying to fit all this together; I'm reading newspaper articles and things about the Vulcans so I can get a line and direct it to this mother and son that are going to be the second part of it. I'm hoping I can get it finished for the next record.

You started Oh Boy! in 1983; what in your experiences with major labels made you prefer to start your own?

I wasn't the kind of recording artist who went around complaining, "My label doesn't know what they're doing, they're screwing up my career."

It wasn't that way. I just didn't feel we were ever on the same wavelength. I thought, "What am I doing this for?" Anytime I've taken my guitar and got in my car or got an airplane and gone somewhere, I've never had any problem connecting with these people that come to see me, they remain dedicated after they come and see me. If don't come to their town for five years, when I do come back, they come and see me. That's something I can depend on. I decided to start my own company and take care of the people that take care of me.

I took radio out of the equation altogether. We act as if there is no radio; I'm not going to worry about why radio doesn't play my songs. I keep on going on a grass roots level of singing for Joe Blow and his sister. Hopefully they'll tell their cousins and bring them to the show next time.

Once I found out this interview was going to happen, I talked to friends and had three or four people tell me their John Prine stories. One friend saw you in '84 in Alaska.

I just got back from there for the first time since '84 a few weeks ago. Nothing but natural disasters going on the whole time we were there—earthquakes and rain, 15 inches of rain in a day and a half. It was more like your weather.

What are the advantages of having your own label?

The whole thing feels better from the onset. When I go to write a song and I finish something, there's this elation before anybody else in the world hears my song. A lot of times when you write something, you write it quick and you know it's good already. You feel like more of a messenger, like the song just came to you. It's a really great feeling to feel like you're the only one who knows about this song; it's an even better feeling to be able to show it to the public. Now I don't have to go through any channels to do this. I know how to do each step. I know how to get my band, I know how to go in the studio, I know how to get the thing recorded, and once it gets to sounding good, get it pressed up and go out and sell it and proudly put my name on it. It's a good feeling all the way around.

When you were at a major label, did you periodically wonder what the label people thought of your songs?

No, they never tried to question the material at all. Neither Asylum nor Atlantic questioned my material unless I did covers; they wondered why I didn't do more of my own songs, which they had a piece of the publishing. No wonder! I didn't know that at the time.

I did *Pink Cadillac* in Memphis with Knox Phillips, and Sam Phillips came in and produced three cuts on the record. I handed it in to Asylum and the guy—one of the vice-presidents—listened, and said to me, "John, what you have here is not what you want." I sat there thinking, "Did I hear what I just heard?" He wouldn't admit he didn't like it. This was at a time when the general sound of all records were as clean and technological as Steely Dan. Here I'd gone and made as rough a record as I could with noise all over the place. Noise that we paid for. We blew up amplifiers inside of echo chambers. We got Sam Phillips to get away from the bank for a day to come over and produce. I handed it in with a big grin on my face, "Here, look at this." They didn't understand it at all.

What are the disadvantages of having your own label?

For anybody who's tried to do it, distribution is the toughest. Distributors are also having their own problems at the same time; you don't know it but they might have their worst problems while you're enjoying your best time, expecting to sell a lot of records and the distributor goes bankrupt. That happens all the time. In the last five years, because of the trend of the small-time outfits selling out under the big umbrellas of the corporations, a lot of the small, independent distributors have gone that way. We had to watch it. I didn't want to get back in any way with the majors, even if I was calling the shots. I didn't want them to be a part of what I've got going on. You don't make a million bucks, but each dollar you make, you're really proud of. It's like having your own bread shop; every loaf of bread that goes out the door you're proud of.

How does it feel to go from a counterculture figure to an icon of the Americana genre without significantly changing your music?

It feels like you're getting old! They have all these names for you: "living legend," "icon."

You tour in short bursts these days.

I tour in short bursts because of my children. Them and my health. I'm in good health, but I want to keep it that way. The road will wear you out; if your body gets worn down, your mind gets worn down. It doesn't become fun anymore. I go out weekends, and I have a band that loves it because they can work during the week in clubs around town or on their own projects.

Also, even though I get a lot of different age groups, the main age group will be people my age, and they can only afford to get out on weekends. We're taking a chance if we play a 2,500-seat concert hall on a Wednesday. We're taking a chance that people would like to come but can't get it together with a babysitter, or just can't get it together. We do it on account of that, but mainly I want to be home for my kids during the week to take them to school each morning and pick them up. It's a normal life for them and me.

A friend who says he can't listen to your music without getting drunk wanted me to ask: whatever happened to Donald and Lydia?

If I ever find out, I'll write a sequel. I don't know if they ended up happily ever after after a beginning like that, but if they did, they probably lived in separate towns.

JOHN PRINE: FOR BETTER, OR WORSE, OR BETTER, & BETTER

Holly Gleason | September 12, 2016 | *Contributor* **(Nashville)**

If you find something you love, do it again. Or so Prine believed when he returned to the studio for 2016's *For Better, or Worse*, another collection of classic country duets with the next wave of female country stars. A cavalcade of Grammy queens, including Alison Krauss, Miranda Lambert, Kacey Musgraves, Kathy Mattea, Susan Tedeschi, and Lee Ann Womack, plus longtime duet partner Iris DeMent and Fiona Prine.

Drawing on Hank Williams Sr., Loretta Lynn, Conway Twitty, Jessi Colter, Flatt & Scruggs, Buck Owens, Waylon Jennings, and a recent vintage Vince Gill song, the covers were warmer and more settled; even the unrequited and cheating songs had a twinkle in the eye.

Having faced cancer twice and losing longtime manager Al Bunetta, Prine seemed resolved to find things that made him happy. Accepting his role as Americana icon, the sort of songwriter that younger roots artists—from My Morning Jacket's Jim James to Margot Price, Isbell, Sturgill Simpson, and Tyler Childers—invoke with the same fervor Rogers Waters, Bruce Springsteen, and Bob Dylan do, Prine brings a coziness to how he responds to the blessings and concerns about a shifting world.

Published around the time *For Better, or Worse* released, this conversation roams far and wide, whether it's Miss Piggy and Kermit the Frog singing "In Spite of Ourselves" as they reunited after a contentious breakup, Prine singing for President Obama at the Grand Canyon for the hundred-year anniversary of the national parks, or the songwriter's charity efforts for Nashville's Room at the Inn and Thistle Farms, as well as the Campaign for a Landmine Free World. Prine settled in for a far-ranging conversation with the *Contributor*, the International Network of Street Papers publication that gives homeless people a job that stabilizes them enough to allow the vendors to secure housing. —Ed.

"There's too many volatile things going on in the world," says the always topical songwriting legend John Prine. Hitting on his fountain of inspiration, he adds, "It's always good for journalists, comedians and folk singers. This country is in a very odd place right now, paranoid really . . . take traveling around, talking to strangers. Just saying, 'Hello. How are you?' or 'Nice day, isn't it?' People are scared to talk to you.

"I just came back from Canada, and people are so very nice, warm. They don't have this fear driven into them like we do."

Prine, who releases "For Better, Or Worse" on Sept. 30, is a student of the world around him. He has served in the military overseas, delivered mail, spent time with his grandparents in Kentucky and written songs that capture major truths about the human condition in three minutes, often by illuminating a handful of moments in a few people's lives,

By observing and writing, he's built a career and body of work that make us all feel more, well, human. Indeed, those songs earned Prine a 2016 PEN Award (which promotes literature and defends freedom of expression worldwide) alongside equally singular Tom Waits. It can be said no one brings the empathy to outsiders, lost souls, broken people and the forgotten quite like the Grammy-winner from Maywood, Ill.

"Angel from Montgomery" captures the emptiness of a woman ignored in her marriage; "Sam Stone" considers the junkie Vietnam veteran so strung out on his memories and drugs that he overdoses; "Hello in There" peers on an elderly couple left behind by life. Then there's "Paradise," lamenting Peabody Coal's strip-mining in Muhlenberg County, recently vindicated by the Supreme Court in a suit filed by Peabody Coal to have the song removed from pending litigation against them.

With a chuckle, the very first singer/songwriter to ever read his work at the Library of Congress marvels, "All I was trying to do is tell the story about my mom's hometown. If you were there, you saw the world's largest shovel, tearing up this little town. The federal judge said my lyrics not only didn't defame them, they were the truth . . . he went on to quote them in his own summary."

Not that John Prine ever intended to be a crusader. The aw-shucks Midwesterner is more live-and-let-live by nature, but his idea of living includes making sure a society grown calloused doesn't just throw people away. By showing—through the people in the songs—not telling, he's built a wealth of work that speaks to those margin dwellers he thinks matter (and occasionally skewers some of the ones he thinks could be doing a better job, like Fair & Square's "Some Humans Aren't Human").

Prine was the kind of kid in school who was a dreamer with an active sense of creativity. As he says, "I really enjoyed English when I had a teacher who knew enough to leave you alone and let you follow your imagination. If they wanted me to memorize verbs, not so much, but if they asked me to write dialogue for two characters on an escalator, I'd go to town."

On the verge of 70, that strong streak of whimsy and play remains. On For Better, Or Worse, Prine teams with another group of integrity roots singers to cull the vintage country songbook. After longtime duet partner Iris DeMent kicks things off with the bouncy sarcasm of "Who's Gonna Take the Garbage Out," Susan Tedeschi, Alison Krauss and Amanda Shires join Prine for "Color of the Blues," "Falling In Love Again" and "Dim Lights, Thick Smoke, and Loud, Loud Music."

"I love singing with girls," Prine enthuses, as much a fan of the individual vocalists as the vintage country they reclaim. "I could make those duet records all day, every day! Opera, all French, Spanish. To all the girls I've sung before! Because I really like the sound of a guy and a girl going back and forth, you know? I'm not a 'bro' sort of guy."

Making the endeavour particularly sweet, after the death of his long-time manager, Oh Boy! Records has evolved into the family business. His Irish bride Fiona, who once ran U2's Windmill Studios, now serves as his manager, and son Jody stepped in to run the label.

"That's what I'm really working for now," he admits. "Everything I do is for the kids and the grandkids, which feels nice. I've got my family helping with the business. In fact, Fiona's got me working harder than ever!"

For Better, Or Worse boasts its share of CMA Female Vocalists of the Year with Krauss, Miranda Lambert, Kathy Mattea and Lee Ann Womack. It also includes Grammy winner Kacey Musgraves, critics' faves Holly Williams, Morgane Stapleton and the lovely Fiona Prine.

"When this started, Fiona and Jody told me I was doing the fourth side of "In Spite of Ourselves" for vinyl, so I did five songs," Prine confides. "Then they said, 'If you do another nine, we're going to make it its own release.' How do you argue with that thinking?"

Prine has always been sympatico with women. Whether it's the past her prime barfly looking for love in "The Oldest Baby in the World," the heroine of "Angel from Montgomery" or the heavy girl with the oddball beau in "Donald & Lydia," he tempers his vision of those slightly broken females with kindness, awareness and a strong dose of empathy.

"Life's that way, and who's to say?" Prine says of the women in his songs. "(Angel)'s husband wasn't abusive to her, he just didn't talk much or pay her any attention, and it quietly drove her crazy—back then people didn't want to get divorced because of the kids or the stigma.

"I always thought I was writing more observations, anyway. The songs were the way people lived, how it looked to me, felt to me, smelled. And a lot of these songs, too, are about relationships, not so much man and woman, but more man to man or person to person."

Discovered by Kris Kristofferson, when Prine's best friend Steve Goodman opened for him, the soon-to-be-movie star flew the pair of Chicago folkies to New York where they signed to big-time record deals. Looking back, Prine marvels at how quickly he went from invisible mailman to "the new Dylan," losing his ability to observe unnoticed.

Still, he's done OK. Twenty albums—not including retrospectives—later, Prine remains a teller of truths and an impaler of, well, jerks. Getting ready to meet a friend at the Golden Cue for happy hour—"What happier place is there? All that neon just brings out the lies in people," he says of the soon-to-be-closed billiards parlor in the Melrose neighborhood—he talks politics tempered with common sense.

"I don't want to pick on one person," Prine says. "I like to let people draw their own conclusions. Part of what the listener gets from the songs—that's part of the song, what they bring to it. I never want to hit people over the head, but maybe give them something they've seen before, maybe in different colors or another way. When you do that, they might see things differently."

Pausing, his voice drops a little. Ever a gentleman, that doesn't mean he's wide-eyed and believes all people's intentions mirror his. "I'm opinionated as anybody. I see people and envision what their life is like. I might be totally wrong, but as a writer, I try to come up with a good story. Raw imagination and good instincts might surprise you."

He certainly wouldn't have imagined playing the 100th Anniversary of the National Parks at the Grand Canyon with Emmylou Harris and President Barack Obama. Nor would he have envisioned "In Spite of Ourselves" being the song that reunited Miss Piggy and Kermit the Frog.

"Loads of people write me letters they got married to that song," he says about the song that paints relationships in teeny, but exceedingly accurate, detail. "But Kermit and Miss Piggy? It was the first time they talked in over a year! They had to change a few words, but they sang it—and it brought them together."

With a gleam in his eye, Prine confides, "People say Jack White did it, hanging with Kermit and talking about women. But I know it was the song that broke the ice."

Wherever he is, he hopes to find the best part—and he also believes to honor being alive, one must be true to the world around them, leave it a better place. Merriment Prine cherishes. After three bouts with cancer, he takes every moment seriously.

The craggy-voiced songwriter with a proclivity for old time music with bluegrass undertones has done charity shows for Room in The Inn, Thistle Farms and Campaign for a Landmine Free World. Without missing a beat, he offers a perspective that has its dignity in place. "I know homeless people aren't bums, Holly. They all got screwed out of something, ended up on the streets because of the times we live in—and nobody wants to talk about that part.

"That's kind of why I wrote 'Come Back To Us, Barbara Lewis (Hare Krishna Beauregard).' She probably came from wealth of some kind, ran off to be a hippie, joined a religious cult, got married. She tried so many things, she forgot what she was looking for. It happens. It just does."

Happy hour is drawing even nearer; Prine has people to meet and eight ball to shoot. He's already started writing new songs—"the regular records aren't nearly as fun," he concedes—thinking about what kind of solo project he might make. Through all the tough times, challenges and losses, he's managed to maintain some grace; it seems in many ways as if he's never been happier. But that doesn't mean he's lost sight of the thread.

PEN AWARD PRESENTATION

John Mellencamp | September 19, 2016 | John F. Kennedy Presidential Library

A lot had happened by the time John Mellencamp took the stage at Boston's John F. Kennedy Presidential Library for the 2016 PEN New England Song Lyrics of Literary Excellence Award. Tapped to present John Prine with the evening's award, he opened the ceremony with an a cappella version of Prine's promotion-skewering take on the dehumanizing aspects of celebrity, "Sabu Visits the Twin Cities Alone," marveling that the 1978 song's lyrics were "sophisticated" but "simple."

Prine was awarded alongside Tom Waits and Kathleen Brennan, with the honorees determined by a panel consisting of Bono, Salman Rushdie, Rosanne Cash, Pulitzer Prize-wining poet Paul Muldoon, Elvis Costello, former US Poet Laureate Natasha Trethewey, and Emmy-winning television producer and former *Musician* editor Bill Flanagan. Chuck Berry and Leonard Cohen received the initial biennial award in 2012, followed by Kris Kristofferson and Randy Newman in 2014.

As Rosanne Cash told *Rolling Stone, Prine, Waits, and Brennan had "contributed* definitive works to the American canon. That's basically it. You can't imagine a broad version of the American songbook without the songs these people have written."

Most people didn't realize how much Prine, the tacit songwriter from Maywood, Illinois, meant to Mellencamp, the rocker from Seymour, Indiana. When 1982's *American Fool* made Mellencamp a platinum-certified superstar with era-defining slices of middle America in "Hurt So Good," "Hand to Hold On To," and "Jack & Diane," one of the first things he did was invite the industry-eschewing Prine to Indiana to write songs. Recorded with a Casio keyboard and marimba, their acerbic, almost cha-cha "Jackie O" invokes Jaqueline Kennedy Onassis as a dig at a stuck-up, name-dropping girl. The track may float on a sweet melody, but it's a thwarted young man's takedown of a girl with a rich daddy who can't be bothered. It appeared on 1983's *Uh-huh*, the first album that appended Mellencamp's actual surname to his early stage name, John Cougar. Recorded in Jackson Country, Indiana, *Uh-huh* delivered rock radio staples, from the scrappy "Authority Song" to the Rolling Stones–evoking "Crumblin' Down" and the anthemic "Pink Houses."

In spite of the heavyweight Mellencamp-Prine pairing, many critics deemed "Jackie O" slight, given Prine's reputation and Mellencamp's nine-week run at number one on *Billboard*'s Top 200 Albums chart. Surely the pair had more to offer than that fluffy morsel.

When Prine entered the studio to record *The Missing Years* with producer Howie Epstein, he wanted to rock harder. He was looking not to abandon the singer-songwriter ethos but to toughen up his sound as Jackson Browne had since *Running on Empty*. By plugging in, Prine and Epstein could reach farther in terms of guitar tones, sonics, and density of production.

Key to Prine's plan for the album was "Take a Look at My Heart," the other song from his Mellencamp cowriting sessions. The track lands with a jaunty strut, with vowels slightly flattened, accordion underneath, mandolin flourishes for punctuation, and a bent-note guitar part on top. Prine exhorts his old girlfriend's new boyfriend to wise up before he lands facedown in a special hell he can't begin to imagine. Good-natured but clearheaded, this is one man looking out for another. Dyspeptic enough to mirror Mellencamp's vitriolic side, Prine's wink-and-nudge warning is wry: "You don't know what you're getting into, she's gonna tear you apart / You're goin' places I been to, take a look at my heart. . . ."

One night early in the *Missing Years* sessions, Prine was having dinner at Dan Tana's, the old-school Italian restaurant a few doors away from the legendary Troudadour. Bruce Springsteen happened by the table; the pair got to talking, Springsteen saying he'd love to hear what they were doing. According to the Springsteen blog E Street Shuffle, the Jersey rocker left Prine his number, saying, "When you guys get into the record and have something to play, please invite me over. I'd just love to play guitar or harmonica or sing or whatever."

"Whatever" turned out to be a weathered harmony vocal that ratified the song's intention. At a time when Mellencamp and Springsteen were battling it out on radio, road, and retail, "Take a Look at My Heart" brought them together on the album that recast how the industry saw Prine.

Prine darted in and out of Mellencamp's life. Having started Farm Aid to help the Midwest's family farmers with Willie Nelson and Neil Young, Prine was a fixture on the all-star benefit shows. In 1987, the night before the third Farm Aid, Prine joined Mellencamp and Lou Reed for a loose surprise show at Bloomington's Bluebird Nightclub on Seventh and Walnut.

To call Prine Mellencamp's *patron* might be too strong a word, but the intense rock star sought Prine out. With Larry McMurtry's script for *Falling from Grace* (1992), Mellencamp made his directing *and* acting debut as Bud Parkes, a country superstar returning home and getting caught in a love triangle with his wife (Mariel Hemingway) and an old flame left behind (Kay Lenz). Filmed in Mellencamp's hometown of Seymour, Indiana, in July of 1990, the film also featured Prine, playing struggling brother-in-law Mitch Cutler.

Prine's "All the Best" was part of a soundtrack that included Nanci Griffith, Lisa Germano, and Janis Ian. More noteworthy, Prine, Mellencamp, Joe Ely, James McMurtry, and Dwight Yoakam formed the Buzzin' Cousins for the one-off track "Sweet Suzanne." Mellencamp joked about the roots music supergroup's name to *New York Daily News* writer David Hinckley for a piece in January 16, 1992's *Chicago Tribune*, "We wanted to spoof the (Traveling) Wilburys. Why not?"

Not to suggest time didn't pull the two men apart. It did.

But when the call from the PEN awards came, Mellencamp suited up and showed up for his mentor, hero, and friend. His speech shows a vulnerable man instead of cocky rock star; self-aware and willing to tell more than just hard truth, Mellencamp embodied the emotional fortitude so many of Prine's songs turn on.

And when Prine died, Mellencamp was one of the first to express his sadness on social media. He wrote on Instagram: "Losing John Prine is like losing Moses. He stood on top of the hill and he gave us words of wisdom and truth. John Prine and I wrote songs together and we made a movie together. We laughed together, and he spent many a lost weekend at my house.

"John Prine's name is written in the stars. And we should all be happy that he has left us with such wonderful songs and records, just like Moses leaving tablets, that remind us what it is to be a good person and a great songwriter." —Ed.

John Mellencamp: [Sings parts of "Sabu Visits the Twin Cities Alone."] Who writes songs like that? Sophisticated. Simple. Two people come to mind: God and John Prine. John has a very likable way of having melodies you can sing along with and words that you can dissect.

John and I have known each other for a long time. John used to come and stay with me, a lot of times. My favorite time . . . John and I tried to write songs together a couple times, and I knew in like five minutes: I was just dead weight. "Why don't you just write the damn song? I'm no help here."

One time John came to my house. The people who work for me said, "John Prine's here . . ." I said, "He *is*?" They said, "He's up in the guest house. John was there for ten days. I never saw him. So I called him up. I think we were supposed to write songs or something. I called him up, and they said, "He left." So I called him up and said, "John, where did you go? I didn't see you for like ten days." He goes, "Well, John, I think we're on different time schedules." [*Laughs.*] We're on different time schedules.

John and I made a movie together once. It was the first day of shooting. I was directing, you can imagine how well that was going. I'd never directed a movie; John had never acted in a movie. I really just went around and hired my friends. I don't think he even read for the part, right, John? I just said, "Hey, you wanna do this?" "Yeah, sure, I'll do it."

So, it was the first day. We had a lot of money for kids to spend. We landed this jet. All Prine's gotta do is get out of this car, say hello to somebody getting off the plane. Prine is so nervous, that I go, "Action," he gets out of the car and he slams—excuse my language—the fucking car door on his hand. This much of his hand [*Mellencamp clamps the fingers of one hand across where the fingers meet the knuckles of the other hand —Ed.*] is *in* the car door, and he's trying to walk. He's so nervous that he doesn't even know his hand is stuck in the door.

I walked over and unlocked it and opened the door. He said, "Awww, man, my hand was in the door. . . ."

I said, "Yeah, yeah, I know. . . ."

He went like this [waves his hand up and down a bit], shook it off, shot the scene. Never complained and acted like it didn't happen. If that had been me, I'd've been crying, going to the hospital. All kinds of stuff. But not Prine.

John taught me a lot of things, whether he knew it or not, just listening to his songs.

And I have to tell you guys: John Prine was one wild little boy when he was a kid. He was one wild fella. He was a natural-born earthshaker, that guy. And he did. He shook it up.

I know goddamn good and well the record companies had no idea what to do with John Prine. What shall we do with a guy who writes like this? He's not country. He's not rock. What are we gonna do with him? And he just said, "The hell with you. I'm gonna do, I'm gonna do what I wanna do." And he did it.

I'm sort of ashamed of myself, because John and I had a really nice, easy rapport between us for many years. But when John got, I didn't know how to handle it. So I just quit talking to him. That's the way I handled it, not very well.

I thought about calling him a hundred times and talking to him. And every time I thought about him, I could just see that John Prine smile, he had that smile and that laugh that just made you want to laugh along with him, you know. John, I'm sorry for not calling you all those years ago . . . but seeing you again after ten years, I feel like five minutes went by.

So, listen, John Prine has been a great inspiration for all of us. I'm proud to have spent the time that I have spent with him. I've gotten to know him personally. I can tell you . . . If you want to give me the hook, give me the hook, because I have 15,000 stories about John Prine. [*Laughs.*] But John, I love you, and I am proud of you, and congratulations.

PART VIII

Rearview: The Innocent Years

JOHN PRINE: INNOCENT DAYS

Holly Gleason | November 23, 2011 | *Paste*

I'd run into John at the grocery store, especially when the local H. G. Hills was in a little strip mall near the Bluebird. Or more horrifying, I'd be in my pajamas late at night in Kroger's frozen food section, looking for ice cream on a lost-hours deadline. I'd hear humming and turn—and there he was.

"Hey, Holly . . . ," he'd say, like a little kid. "What're you doing?"

Maybe it was Baja Burrito, the indie California-style Mexican place near all the studios in Berry Hill. Facedown in a salad, trying to edit copy, I could feel the energy. "This seat taken?" Just like the high school cafeteria.

"Never" was the only answer.

John was always about joy, fun, the—as he wrote in "In Spite of Ourselves"—"big door prize."

"You're never gonna believe this," he said. "We found a bunch of my old demos."

"But you don't *do* demos . . . ," I replied.

"Yeah, but these are from Chicago! I recorded them at WRMT when I was starting out. I asked if I could maybe get a few songs down when I did Studs Terkel's show. . . . There was a show from the Fifth Peg, too."

Someone sent me the music. It was startling, both the aw-shucks innocence and how fully formed a writer Prine was before he was ever knighted "the new Dylan."

To be able to ask Prine the questions—to weigh what he knew about who he was—was too delicious to resist. I reached out to Josh Jackson at *Paste*; they were happy to let me write about it.

They're the kind of recordings many artists prefer to bury, but Prine released the unearthed demos as *The Singing Mailman Delivers*. The album is a portal to a time when

Prine's nasal bray was even flatter and his earnestness was on full display, pairing studio performances with a live set before a local audience who recognized their hometown son was creating something special. As you listen, time melts into a subzero Chicago night, breath turning to self-generated plumes before you. –Ed.

Blame the wife.

"Fiona made me clean out the garage," John Prine confesses with a chuckle that's equal parts warm breeze, cold beer and fried chicken. "I cursed her every day. . . . But she was firm. She said she wasn't moving the stuff to the new house.

"She got a dumpster—and sent me to the garage. Boxes from my first marriage, boxes from my second marriage . . . boxes from before I moved to Tennessee. Boxes and boxes and boxes . . . and in one of them . . ."

. . . were several reel-to-reel tapes, long forgotten but dating back before the iconic American songwriter was discovered by Kris Kristofferson and signed by Jerry Wexler to Atlantic Records in New York. One set of recordings were made after an interview with Studs Terkel at WFMT; the other was an early show at Chicago's Fifth Peg, where the man still walking a mail route in Chicago would sing his songs three nights a week.

"All those years, I'd wished I had something from the Fifth Peg. . . . Because I *know* how those nights felt, but to be able to listen to it, to hear it? I'd've given an arm to have even had a cassette of a night there; then there it was on reel to reel tape in pristine shape even before we had them treated."

The wonder in Prine's voice is palpable. The quality of the music is striking.

"Hello in There." "Paradise." "Angel From Montgomery." "Great Society Conflict Veteran's Blues" (later known as "Sam Stone"). "Illegal Smile." "Spanish Pipedream." "Blue Umbrella." "Souvenirs." They're all there on his new retrospective album *The Singing Mailman Delivers*—fully formed, but infused with a wide-eyed soul-searching and a folkiness that's equal parts bluegrass and Bob Dylan.

"I was struck by how innocent I was," Prine admits. "When I started, I *was* that innocent—and it was amazing how quickly that was gone. I was signed, dined and thrown back and forth between both coasts in less than a year.

"I was never able to get back to that guy, but I never forgot him. You just can't see things that way anymore. Where I was from, how I was raised, those things never leave you, but the innocence? Once it's gone, it's gone."

Prine, who had been in the service in Germany and came home to deliver the mail, never meant to be a voice of his generation. That was for other people, but he did hate the biting dogs and brutal cold he encountered on his route. Most people didn't even know he wrote songs.

"I wasn't doing this for attention or to be on a record," he explains. "*That* was such a different world! People whose records you bought? Or saw on TV? I didn't aspire to that. . . . I never even thought about it being a place I couldn't get to or be a part of; that was just something else! Honestly, I just wanted to get off work and get home, have fun. Write songs, and all that. But there was no end game. Heck, I didn't even think about a game: I just wanted to write and play those songs."

So much so, most of Prine's friends had no idea. A few knew he played guitar. Only one buddy knew *anything* about the songs. He was an artist; Prine would go over to his studio and write while he painted, then they'd show each other what they'd created.

"When I got up that night at the Fifth Peg, it was an open mic night and the people were just awful. I thought, 'I can do better than this. . . .' I'd been at the Old Town School [of Folk Music], learning bluegrass. Those are my classmates in the audience. They introduced me as 'Davey Prine's little brother. . . .'

"I went up there and played 'Sam Stone' and a few others; they didn't even applaud. They looked at me. All I could think was, 'Wow, I'm screwed. . . . What do I do *now*? cause it was so quiet. Then the place just exploded."

The songs no one knew he was writing were written along Prine's mail route. In part to entertain himself, in part to take a break in the little shelters along the way, in part to work out things that were running around his mind. It wasn't Voice of a Generation stuff; it was Prine's own inventory.

"I didn't talk about the stuff I was writing about," Prine says in that rasp. "I thought about it all the time, but never said anything. People would *never* have expected those songs from me. But I saw these things all around me, and nobody ever talked about them. That was the big thing: nobody ever talked about them. They were taboo.

"I knew there were a lot of GIs out there, who came out of the war and they weren't quite right . . . ['Sam Stone']. I knew there were homes nobody was talking to each other, which became 'Angel from Montgomery.' . . . I knew kids who didn't have fathers, and nobody ever acknowledged it, which became '6 O'Clock News.'. . . I saw all that. I knew, and I couldn't figure out why no one would say anything."

John Prine pauses, taking stock. He's not a crusader. He laughs about some journalist asking him "Why there aren't more political songs?" then says, "Heck, I don't write political songs. . . ." Though if you know him—his politic is humanity.

"In the end, people want the truth," the Grammy-winner explains. "The second you start second-guessing or writing 'to' them, you're screwed. You can't *make* 'em authentic. People think through marketing they can deliver what people want, but [people] know."

So John Prine, the singing mailman, kept delivering mail, watching the people, puzzling about life and writing his songs. When film critic Roger Ebert ducked out of a bad movie and into the Fifth Peg for a drink, he saw the dark-haired folkie—and decided to write about him instead. The people came.

Studs Terkel asked him to do his radio show. "He was working on his book called *Working*. I told him about my dad, and he wanted to interview him—but [Dad] died before they did it."

The engineer on that show agreed to let Prine record some of his songs after the interview. That document became the first disc of *Singing Mailman*. The engineer, who also hosted the local folk radio show called "The Midnight Special," introduced him to another local folkie, Steve Goodman, who'd become Prine's best friend.

"It was magical," Prine says of the time. "My dad came to see me at a point. I remember him standing up in the bar, going 'That's *my* boy!' He'd come in with a couple union buddies. . . .

"And then going to see Kris [Kristofferson] in New York. . . . Getting off the plane at 7 and going down to the Bottom Line where Carly Simon was opening. Every record company person was there. Getting up, singing a few songs—and having a record contract on Jerry Wexler's desk at 10 the next morning!

"I remember walking around on our way down there—and I'm from Chicago— looking at those skyscrapers, thinking, 'Whoa . . .' It wasn't real."

Except it was. And it did. And then even more happened. Four decades later, John Prine still sells out multiple nights at Nashville's storied Ryman Auditorium, as well as annual shows at Washington, D.C.'s Wolf Trap and Los Angeles' Wilshire Theatre. His songs—especially songs like "Paradise" and "Angel from Montgomery"—have become such a part of the culture, many assume they're traditional folk songs. He was the first songwriter to read at the Library of Congress. It still doesn't make much sense to him.

With a documentary in the works, directed by noted photographer/ filmmaker Jim Shea, *The Singing Mailman Delivers* was meant to be a companion piece. "But when we found the stuff from the Fifth Peg, I got excited. That's what makes this interesting to me: I was able to capture that innocence in a way you know [it's real].

"It was there on the tape—and there in the pictures. It was me in the beginning of all this, where these songs really came from. Me talking not because I was entertaining, but because I didn't want to go from a song where somebody killed themselves to an even sadder song. It didn't seem right. . . ."

And yet, somehow, listening all these years later, it's more than right—it's perfect.

PART IX

Prime of an Americana Icon

TREE OF FORGIVENESS ALBUM RELEASE SPECIAL

Dave Cobb | April 2018 | *Outlaw Country*, SiriusXM

John Prine was having such a good time, touring with a new wave of artists, enjoying his family and making people happy, he might not have made another record. But Fiona Prine knew it was time; she spoke with emerging uberproducer Dave Cobb.

Cobb, who'd been on a roll with award-winning and genre-defying albums for Jason Isbell, Chris Stapleton, and Brandi Carlile, seemed the perfect choice. Sensitive to songs but a fan of finding the soul in the recording, if anyone could midwife Prine's first album in almost a decade and a half, Cobbs could.

The Tree of Forgiveness was magic. Whether the power-strumming opener "Knockin' on Your Screen Door"; the minor-keyed and foreboding "Caravan of Fools"; the retro-whimsical "Egg & Daughter Nite, Lincoln, Nebraska 1967 (Crazy Bone)," with its barrel house piano and walking upright bass; or the yearning invitation "Summer's End," Cobb created temperate musical environs for the songs. Sensitive but not wimpy, it was a modern classic.

Prine had always been a favorite of SiriusXM's *Outlaw Country*, and program director Jeremy Tepper wanted something special to launch *Tree* when it was released in 2018. No stranger to the network's playlists, Cobb himself was a perfect pick to host a special dedicated to what would be Prine's final studio recording. The 2020 Grammy nominee for Producer of the Year crafted a conversation with his friend that was like stopping by Arnold's on meatloaf day. —Ed.

[*John Prine sings "Knocking on Your Screen Door."*]

John Prine: Hi, this is John Prine. I'm here on SiriusXM. I'm talking about my new album, *The Tree of Forgiveness*, and I'm sitting here talking with the pal that produced this fine album.

This is Dave Cobb.

Dave Cobb: Hi! This is Dave Cobb. I'm here talking with John, hanging out!

Prine: Well, that was the opening song they just played, "Knocking on Your Screen Door."

Cobb: You know what I like about your songs? There's usually food in the lyric. [*Laughing.*]

Prine: You're right. I have to have food! The promise of food somewhere in the song. I was cowriting with Pat McLaughlin and Dan Auerbach and Dave Ferguson. Dave Ferguson was the guy who got us all together in one room to write, and we were writing one song after another, and I said, "Hey, don't you guys ever eat?" So we go get in the Cadillac and went and got a big bag of White Castle. Came back and wrote three more songs. There's gotta be food somehow.

Cobb: Literally every time I hear your lyrics, there's usually something about ham. This one has sweet potato pies. There's always a theme, pretty much ties in with Arnold's Diner.

Prine: Pretty much. Either going there or leaving there.

Cobb: It's right on. Do they have meat loaf Friday there?

Prine: Again, I have a million neck ties at home, and each of them, I can tell you what restaurant I wore them to, because they got different sauces on the front. [*Laughing.*]

Cobb: Your signature cocktail. You should tell them about that, man.

Prine: I've turned everybody on to my favorite cocktail. It's called a Handsome Johnny, and I named it kind of after myself. But I thought Handsome Johnny sounded kinda like a Rob Roy or a Manhattan. You know I kind of... Now, every bar you go to has a cocktail list, but twenty years ago when I started drinking Handsome Johnnies, people wouldn't make you a Rob Roy or a Manhattan; they said it was old school. So, now they've come back around again. There's actually a couple of bars in Nashville that have Handsome Johnnies that'll be on your receipt.

Cobb: Tell them what it is. . . .

Prine: It's Smirnoff Vodka, red Smirnoff, *not* blue. If you get too good a vodka, it kills the bubbles in your ginger ale. I use diet ginger ale because the other kind's too sweet after a while. You don't want to get diabetes from drinking! And in the wintertime, I drop a lime in it. Don't squeeze it, just drop it in from about 6 inches above; in the summertime, a lemon . . .

Cobb: It's gotta be six inches, right? Can't be seven or eight, gotta be perfectly . . .

Prine: Yeah, right. Literally. You live long enough, you know what six inches is. [*Laughing.*]

Cobb: I think the record was also enhanced by KFC. You had a lot of KFC [Kentucky Fried Chicken] with your Handsome Johnnies.

Prine: One night, you guys asked me . . . We'd been eating that pretty good food, and you guys asked me what I wanted. I thought, "I'm really hungry for some fried chicken from KFC," and everybody did a little dance. *Yeah.*

Cobb: Favorite of all time.

Prine: Let's see, which song are we going to play now? Oh, "Summer's End." That's one of my favorites.

Cobb: That's my very favorite on the album I think.

Prine: Wow. I tell you, Dave, what I really liked about the way you and I work together and the ideas you had, you left a lot of space there for my songs. And then you put these . . . like that mellotron part on this. "Summer's End" sounds like a bunch of, sounds like we hired a room full of strings, and everybody hit the right note at the right time.

Cobb: When I heard the chorus for the first time, that "Come on home . . ." lyric, it's crushing. I remember Brandy Carlile coming in and singing that. You know, now it's called the "Come on Home Song" 'cause of that chorus. It's such a beautifully simple lyric, but it resonates.

Prine: I was never good at titling songs. . . . I always picked the wrong title. You should maybe let the audience pick the title 'cause they're going to call the song "Come on Home," you know. Keep fooling them. Keep 'em coming back.

[*Prine sings "Summer's End" then "Boundless Love."*]

Prine: Hi, this is John Prine, right here on Outlaw Country. On SiriusXM.

[*Prine sings "Caravan of Fools."*]

Prine: Hi, this is John Prine, on SiriusXM, sitting here talking with Producer Dave Cobb about my new record *The Tree of Forgiveness.*

"Caravan of Fools," I wrote with Pat McLaughlin and Dan Auerbach; none of us discussed what the song was about. To me, it's about impending doom. Like when you start a song in a minor key, you're already admitting that somebody's sick or somebody's about to die, you know? Happy songs don't work in minor keys, you know, starting in E minor and say "we're getting married in the morning. . . ."

Cobb: That's a scary song, that "Caravan of Fools," though. . . .

Prine: It is! Ominous. It's so . . . the voice and guitar are so huge, I don't know how you got it sounding that big. You must have put me in a shoebox or something.

Cobb: Pro-Tools. No, that's that way you sing it. Man. There's nothing hiding behind the curtain.

Prine: I thought it was really cool, over at Studio A. I didn't really know that much about it, but when I walked in . . . It just felt right. I like really big areas; I like breathing in a corner, or being in the center of the room with plenty of room around me. That's why I brought my Christmas tree down, 'cause when I found out we could turn all the little lights up and sing to the Christmas tree, that's when things got . . .

Cobb: You did, didn't you?

Prine: That's when things got really warm in there! We got some really warm vocals. Jack Clement took me to—we cut something in the '70s over at Woodland. That room had the same sort of feeling; you walked in and it was just cool. You could tell some really cool music had went on there, a lot of people had probably just hung around over at Woodland. There's a couple of studios around town that have that feel, if they haven't been torn down.

Cobb: The thing about Studio A is the guy who bought the place has a bunch of pictures. He's done all this research, but there's more pictures of the parties than there are the sessions. So I think it was pretty much a party palace.

Prine: Well, we did our share of parties.

Cobb: Yeah, yeah . . .

Prine: This is John Prine, I'm here on SiriusXM, sitting here with producer Dave Cobb about my new record *The Tree of Forgiveness.*

This next song has kind of a misleading title to it. I wanted to get the history behind the song; it's called "Egg & Daughter Nite, Lincoln, Nebraska 1967." Then, it's also known as "Crazy Bone." I was fishing North Central Arkansas, where I've been going since I was 14 years old. My buddy John Earl—John used to be the guitar tech for the Everly Brothers, me and him were sitting in a boat floating down a river, drinking cold beer, and the fish ain't biting. So, John gets to telling me a shaggy dog story about when he was a teenager in Nebraska. He said they used to go hang out down at the roller rink on Thursday nights.

The boys called it Egg and Daughter Nite 'cause the egg farmers would come to town and drop their daughters at the roller rink, and the city boys—the big city of Norfolk, Nebraska—they were all wise, and kind of, you know, whatever boys and girls do. The farmers would go off and sell the eggs, come back and pick their daughters up later. And I just thought, "Egg and Daughter Nite," that'd make a great name for a song.

So, I explained the story two years later to Pat McLaughlin, and I said, "Pat, how in the hell can I tell that in a song?" Pat said, "Easy." He grabs his guitar, and goes, "If you're stuck up in Alaska, you should be in Nebraska, on a Thursday when it's Egg and Daughter Nite."

I thought, "How come it takes me so long to tell the story when Pat can do it in two lines?" So we just attacked the song, and it's actually true if you look it up, there was such a thing as Egg and Daughter Night. I thought my buddy made it up entirely just to pass the time on the river.

So, this is it. "Egg and Daughter Nite, Lincoln Nebraska." I got the name of the town wrong, it should be Norfolk, but there's a line that says "If they knew what you was thinkin', they'da run you outta Lincoln," and I didn't want to change that line. This is "Crazy Bone."

[*"Egg & Daughter Nite Lincoln Nebraska 1967," "No Ordinary Blue," "God Only Knows" play.*]

Prine: Hi this is John Prine, here on SiriusXM. We're talking about my new album *The Tree of Forgiveness.*

Along about 1978, I was out in Los Angeles, talking to different producers to do what became my *Bruised Orange* record. I ran into Robert Hilburn, from the *Los Angeles Times.* Bob had been an early supporter, so I knew him pretty good. I asked what he was up to, and he said he was trying to write a book on Phil Spector; he was interviewing him every day. I said "How's that?" He said, "Pretty crazy." He says, "You want to go up and meet him?" I said, "Well, sure. I'd love to meet Phil Spector, but he wouldn't know who I was." And Bob says, "Oh, he was quoting 'Donald and Lydia' the other night." I said, "You mean he knows one of my songs?" I couldn't believe it.

So, I went up to his house. Sure enough, things were pretty crazy. Phil has a three piece suit on with a show girl under each arm; he's got a gun, two bodyguards. One little swarthy guy, and another big guy that looked like Chewabaca that went everywhere . . . If Phil went to the bathroom, the bodyguards went with him. This is his own home.

We come in the door, and it's probably oh, the middle of March, and he's got a Christmas tree up. Now, I don't want to say anything about that, because I have had a Christmas tree up too, but this was a live one. I said, "Phil, I like Christmas, too, but this is a fire hazard."

Just then, his kids come down the steps in pajamas. He goes, "Who's the king of rock and roll?" They both grab his legs and go, "You are, daddy! You are!"

Okay. This is how I arrive at Phil Spector's house. [*Laughing.*] He shows his jukebox to us, and plays Wilbur Harris and "Kansas City" about fifty times. Later on in the evening, I call a cab and I decide, "This is fun and everything, but I better get out of here." I'm heading for the door, and Phil's walking me to the door. We pass by a piano. He sits down at the piano, hands me an electric guitar; it's not plugged in. And we write a song in thirty minutes. "If You Don't Want My Love."

So, I went to Chicago, and recorded "If You Don't Want My Love." Six months later I come back, and I want to play it for Phil, so he can see how the song turned out. I go back up to his house, and we go through the same crazy stuff all over again. I'm leaving that night, I play the song, and I get my jacket; I'm heading for the taxi, and he sets at the piano again, hands me the guitar again, and we wrote half of the song "God Only Knows."

I put it up with my unfinished lyrics. I brought it out a couple of times over the years because I really liked the chord progression on it. When I got around to doing this project, and I knew I was going in the studio with you, Dave, I thought it would be nice to finish this. So one night when I was holed up at the Omni, I wrote another verse and a bridge I took from the child's prayer. And it all seemed to work. You liked it live, so . . . Really great playing—Jason Isbell played mandolin, Amanda Shires, really nice. Well, since we both got guitars, why don't we play one, Dave?

[*Prine and Cobb sing "The Lonesome Friends of Science."*]

Cobb: Man, if I wanted to play an old song, say ah "Freebird". . . [*Laughing.*]

Prine: [*Laughing.*] Were you around when I did "Freebird?"

Cobb: "Hello in There," that's the one. . . .

Prine: OK, that's really old. That was every chord I knew at the time. Someone taught me . . .

Cobb: Same key, wasn't it?

Prine: "Nobody Knows You When You're Down and Out" had about seven or eight chords in it, so I took all the new chords I'd learned—and somebody'd taught me a B minor, and I thought that was just . . . I had to put it into a song. So, I put every chord I knew into it, and it came out as "Hello in There." I didn't even think about what order I was putting the chords in; I just kept playing them all over and over. Word just kinda fell out. . . .

John plays "Hello in There."

Cobb: That's the fancy chord right there. . . . That song kills me.

Prine: I like that one, the melody. I didn't have any idea where I was driving to and I stayed on the road the whole way. And I was still really into giving names to my characters. When the guy's wondering, he didn't know what to do with himself, the wife sits around all day and stares at the screen door. So he's retired, and he thinks he'll call one of his buddies from work, well, I didn't know what to call the buddy, so there's this lady at 4 or 5 every afternoon, she'd call her dog in for dinner. And the dog's name was Rudy. [*Laughs.*]

She's across the street. I'm sitting there with my guitar, in my mailman outfit, waiting. And my wife didn't come home from work till 6:00, and I'm going, "What can I call this guy?," I hear "Oh Rudy! Rudy, come in!" And I thought, "That's it! His buddy's name is Rudy." I used to keep a baby book with names. When I was writing. I'd pick up this old baby book.

Cobb: Get a baby book, you can write songs exactly like John Prine! That's it . . .

Prine: That, and three chords! [*Laughing.*]

Hey, I'm still John Prine, and I'm still here on SiriusXM. Me and Dave Cobb been talking about [how] we worked together on my new record *The Tree of Forgiveness*. Dave, you did a beautiful job; I love this record. It sounds better and better every day. I can't wait 'til we unleash it on the public.

This is the last song on the album. This had to finish the record, there was nothing we could follow this song with. I had a chorus, and the chorus went: "I'm going to get a cocktail, Vodka and ginger ale . . . Smoke a cigarette that's nine miles long."

Well, I had to quit smoking twenty years ago, because I lost half my neck to cancer—and the doctor told me, "You better quit smoking now." I miss it every day now. I really loved smoking. I smoked from the time I was fourteen, till I . . . how old was I? Anyway, I smoked thirty-five years. A pack a day of Marlboro reds. I just miss it. I see somebody outside a restaurant, and they're getting ready to fire it up. I'll run over and stand next to them so I can smell that first puff that they're taking. You know?

So, I thought, "How can I use this in a song, smoking a cigarette that's 9 miles long? Where can I smoke?" I thought the only place I could possibly still smoke is heaven 'cause they're not going to have "No Smoking" signs. . . . They're not going to have no cancer! Why would they have heaven if they have cancer? So, I thought, "I might have to write a song about heaven in order to smoke a cigarette that's nine miles long. . ." That's how self-serving this song is.

Cobb: My favorite part of this song is the line your dad told you all the time. You say it, because you laugh every time you say it. That was my favorite thing about being in the studio, every time you told this one line of this song, you'd laugh. (*Prine laughing.*) We've probably heard it 50 times, and every single time . . .

Prine: My daddy had two pieces of advice he gave to me and my three brothers. He must have said this, if he said it once, he said it a thousand times. He'd say, "Buddy, when you're dead, you're a dead peckerhead." [*Laughing.*]

I've got to use that in a song sometime, you know? And anyway, it's a good song. And Fiona prodded me along to come up with this recitation; my wife Fiona, told me, "Don't forget about your mom's sisters. You gotta mention them in the song." They're all the reason we have a family reunion every year; it's the reason I see all my cousins every year and we're such a close family because of her eight sisters. They're all gone now; the last one passed about 4 years ago.

But they were a real force of nature, these girls were. They grew up in Paradise, Kentucky, and basically never had nothing, married really good, colorful characters. We had a really good family reunion, I mean,

JOHN PRINE IS STILL SINGING ABOUT HEAVEN AND MORTALITY— AND SOUNDING AS VITAL AS EVER

Randy Lewis | May 16, 2018 | *Los Angeles Times*

When Prine emerged with *The Tree of Forgiveness*, his first true collection of songs since *Fair & Square*, the critics scrambled to find new ways to praise the songs, the lyrical turns, the delicate balance of emotional transparency and hilarity. Pitchfork, *Spin*, *Wall Street Journal*, *New Yorker*, *Relix*, and PopMatters joined the more expected *New York Times*, *Lone Star Music*, *Rolling Stone*, and NPR in lavishing the ten-song collection with kudos.

As "of the moment" as ever, Prine was the toast of hipster artists—2010's *Broken Hearts & Dirty Windows: Songs of John Prine* featured Drive-By Truckers, Justin Vernon, the Avett Brothers, Lambchop, Deer Tick, and Old Crow Medicine Show—while sharing stages with a checklist of Americana must-sees, from Jason Isbell, Sturgill Simpson, and Tyler Childers to Margo Price, Amanda Shires, and Sara Watkins. Even more than revering the classics, Prine was inspired by the younger artists.

The *L. A. Times*' Randy Lewis took the occasion to look beyond the songs. The pair got together at Prine's hotel during release week and discussed subliminal themes of death and the afterlife with delight. Whether unpacking his own creative process, praising Taylor Swift and a generation of young songwriters with "good, grounded ideas," confessing how much he misses smoking, or laughing about Prine-ing up a song with lines like "fry me some pork chops" and "a heart like an old washing machine," Prine kept the conversation light even as it addressed heavy things.

Once Lewis and Prine established trust, nothing was too silly or dishy—it was just true. Even the tale about a young Kacey Musgraves, fresh from Golden, Texas, trying to get Prine high reflects the playfulness that permeated this moment of Prine's life. —Ed.

"The doctor in Houston said, 'I can't tell you your history of smoking did this to you. But wouldn't it be a great time to stop?' I said, 'You know, you're right,'" Prine said. "I had two little kids, they were 2 and 1 at the time. I thought, I'm lucky to be getting by with this cancer thing.

"So I gave it up," he added. "But I never gave up thinking about it. When I see people in a bar fire up, I go over and stand next to them, or if they're standing outside a restaurant, I just kind of stand near enough so I can get that initial blast.

"I thought, 'Where in the hell can I smoke cigarettes? It's not going to be anywhere down here.' So I thought, maybe when I get to heaven I can smoke cigarettes," he said. "That's how I came up with the [lyrical reference to a] cigarette nine miles long and the rest of the thing."

Prine was opening a window into his creative process that's every bit as acute today as it was when he put out his 1971 self-titled debut album, still regarded as one of the most auspicious arrivals in pop music history.

"When I Get to Heaven" is among 10 new songs that address issues of aging and mortality, although Prine said it was a surprise to him when he sat back after the record was done and soaked in the new collection.

"I thought I had 10 songs I believed in," he said with the permanent growl that's been with him since he beat the cancer by sacrificing a significant part of the right side of his neck. "But I didn't think any of them had anything to do with each other, or that there was any kind of theme running through the record."

It shows up in songs as light-hearted as "When I Get to Heaven" and as darkly foreboding as "Caravan of Fools," which he wrote with the Black Keys' guitarist, singer and songwriter, Dan Auerbach, and one of his frequent collaborators, Pat McLaughlin.

"The only time I ever think about getting old is when I look in the mirror," said Prine. "I feel pretty good about it, actually. I can remember other times in my life when I haven't been this settled. It's a really good feeling."

Prine has plenty to feel good about these days. In the month since it was released, "The Tree of Forgiveness" has sold more than 70,000 total equivalent sales, according to the Nielsen sales monitoring service, and has garnered mostly positive reviews.

Prine said he thought another song he wrote with Auerbach, "Boundless Love," was initially for Auerbach's 2017 solo album, "Waiting on a Song."

Then Prine decided to record it himself. "I called Dan and told him, 'I'm going to have to John Prine this song up.'

"He said 'What do you mean?,'" Prine said. "I said, 'Well, there's a part where the guy wants to come home and he asks [his woman] if she'll make him some food. I said I'm going to make it 'fry me some pork chops.'

"Then I replaced the second verse with 'I've got a heart like an old washing machine/ Bounces 'round till my soul comes clean.' I said, 'That sounds more like John Prine,'" he said with a laugh. "And I'll be darned, those songs live, especially 'Boundless Love,' are really taking off. The crowd really seems to like it."

As has been the case historically, Prine moves effortlessly among songs bursting with humor to others that resonate deeply and profoundly, such as "Summer's End," an impressionistic meditation on the passage of time, loss and forgiveness.

His career is now managed by his wife, Fiona. And Oh Boy Records, the label he set up more than 30 years ago, making him one of the first musicians to go independent, is being overseen by his son, Jody, since the death in 2015 of Prine's longtime manager, Al Bunetta.

Prine's long been a critical favorite, and early on caught the attention of esteemed peers including Kris Kristofferson, who was among the first to champion the erudite songs that allowed Prine to quit his day job as a mail carrier in Chicago.

John Prine has a number of ideas of what he thinks heaven might be, all of which are the focal point of one of 10 new songs on his first album of original material in a dozen years, "The Tree of Forgiveness."

The veteran singer and songwriter, best known for such songs as "Hello in There," "Angel from Montgomery" and "Sam Stone," also is pretty well convinced of one thing he doesn't expect to find should he make it past the Pearly Gates one day.

"Surely they don't have 'No Smoking' signs in heaven," Prine, 71, said with a grin and a gravelly chuckle on a cool afternoon this week at his Hollywood hotel, a couple of days before a scheduled appearance at the Grammy Museum on Wednesday as well as his concert on Friday at the Ace Hotel downtown.

"I really miss smoking cigarettes," he said by way of explanation of the genesis of "When I Get to Heaven," a strikingly humorous take on life after death. "I gave them up the night before I had my neck surgery." (He underwent an operation 20 years ago to remove a malignant tumor.)

Bob Dylan also has sung his praises over the years, telling writer Bill Flanagan almost a decade ago that "Prine's stuff is pure Proustian existentialism. Midwestern mindtrips to the nth degree. And he writes beautiful songs."

He also has become a touchstone for a new generation of articulate and insightful country and Americana singer-songwriters including Miranda Lambert, Kacey Musgraves, Sturgill Simpson, Jason Isbell, Amanda Shires, Brandy Clark and Margo Price, among many others.

A number of them have shared concert bills with him, recorded one or more of his songs or, in the case of husband-wife team Isbell and Shires, sung harmonies with him on the new album.

In fact, one of the first things Musgraves did on arriving in Nashville from her native Golden, Texas, was to look Prine up at one of his shows and try to get him appropriately conditioned to hear a song she'd written about him.

"She and a friend of hers came to one of my shows," Prine said, "and wanted to take me out to the parking lot and get me to smoke a joint with them."

Then she played him her song, "Burn One With John Prine," which describes her ideal for the afterlife: "My idea of heaven/ Is to burn one with John Prine."

"She's really something," said Prine. "I think she's going to be really big. She seems to have that quality: She can do pop stuff too. I'm not sure how long she's going to stay with country. Of course, country sells a lot of records now."

He also expressed his admiration for an artist he otherwise might seem to have little in common with, one who is 45 years his junior, and compared with his status as a cult favorite of longstanding, she is arguably the biggest pop star in the world: Taylor Swift.

"Even her early songs, when she was just trying to appeal to other 18- and 19-year-olds, they were always interesting songs," he said. "It was there. Whether or not you're a fan or can relate to being an 18-year-old girl, right from the get-go she was fully formed, I thought."

In fact, many younger songwriters are giving Prine renewed hope about the state of pop and country music.

"What I hear in their music is that it's good," said Prine, now considered one of the deans of the folk-rooted, singer-songwriter tradition. "I hear good songs with good, grounded ideas. I didn't know if another generation was gonna come along like that.

"My music has been called so many different things over the years," he said, adding with his Cheshire cat grin, "I figure as long as it's selling, call it what you want."

SONGS FROM THE GUT: A CONVERSATION WITH JOHN PRINE

Holly Gleason | Fall 2016 | *No Depression*

What started as a message board in the earliest days of AOL, when dial-up ruled the world and people first disappeared down highly specific rabbit holes of passion and discussion, became *No Depression*, the *Sports Illustrated* of alt-country and roots music. Eventually shuttering its print publication after its final run as a heavy-stock quarterly aligned to University of Texas Press, *No Depression* survived as an online publication supported by a dedicated community of writers, readers, contributors, and posters.

Like all things old-school, *No Depression* brought a specific thrill when held in-hand and read on paper. When a decision was made to create quarterly theme issues to explore facets of the music, whether culture, creation, or subject matter, editor Kim Ruehl assigned me a lengthy Q and A with Prine for an issue about politics. John Prine, whose songs about social issues always transcended the times they were written in, was the perfect candidate. In this sweeping conversation, he considered the reality of how people treat each other, the fact that so little social progress was being made, and the power of empathy and observation to show deeper truths. —Ed.

John Prine, the original "new Dylan", has always written songs with a deep heart and strong empathy for the people who go unseen. Veterans ensnared in addiction, old people who are forgotten and alone, alienated women ignored in their marriage, strip-mining coal companies, and patriotism as First Amendment tourniquet are all part of the iconic singer-songwriter's canon—and they're all captured with a tenderness that heightens the commentary.

On the precipice of 70, the Chicago-born-and-raised Prine has always brought the political to the personal without stridency. Using his narrative story-songs to show instead of tell the way hypocrisy, cruelty, or indifference undermines our humanity, Prine has become one of America's—and Americana's—best loved artists. Having read at the Library of Congress, seen his self-titled debut inducted into the Grammy Hall of Fame, and continuing to headline major festivals and multiple nights at Nashville's Ryman Auditorium, Prine remains as vital today as he was when he was just a postman playing open mic nights in Chicago.

With the sudden death of long-time manager Al Bunetta in 2015, Prine ruminated about what he wants his music to yield going forward. Slated to release *For Better or Worse*, a second country duets album featuring Alison Krauss, Susan Tedeschi, Lee Ann Womack, Kacey Musgraves, and more this September, he's turned Oh Boy Records and his career management into "the family business" with son, Jody Whelan, at the helm. This new order to his creative life has inspired him—and he's looking at returning to the studio for an album of new songs in 2017.

After all the years and miles, Prine remains as topical as ever. For an aw-shucks guy with a candy heart, that was never the master plan. But, as Prine would tell you, "things become clichés for a reason," and his songs likewise contain so much truth they continue to resonate across the decades.

In a recent conversation, Prine and I talked about how much he's enjoying being back on the road. The Grammy winner also considered his legacy, how topical songs inform us, and why the Peabody Mining Co. is still mad about "Paradise."

Holly Gleason: With the new album on the way, are there any plans that stand out?

John Prine: Going into [the Americana Music Association conference] week, we're going to do my first album at the Station Inn, in sequence. We're going to film it, which I think will be very cool. Most of the songs we play [regularly] anyway, but three or four, we have to learn.

HG: That first album is definitive. Do you ever look back and marvel?

JP: I wish I knew the guy who was writing those songs. I think that guy left. I haven't seen him since he signed with a record company, when it all became professional. It takes a certain amount of innocence out of [the songwriting] when that happens—because you *know* you're writing songs to be recorded. Basically, I'm the same guy, but the guy who wrote those first songs, he didn't know if anyone was going to listen or hear them. He was just writing.

HG: Did you realize how much social commentary there was?

JP: I was always writing more observations. That was how I saw the way people lived. It was how it looked to me, how it felt, how it smelled. At a point, I stopped giving people names. There were so many characters it started to feel like a soap opera.

HG: But there was so much commentary.

JP: I didn't know any better. Have you ever heard any stories about guitar players who listened to Chet Atkins and Les Paul? Les Paul, especially. They would dub parts over another, and layer things up. But you'd get some guitar player out there who didn't realize [that's what they'd done], and they'd think, "Well, if they can do it. . ." And [they'd] teach themselves how to play something that was actually multiple parts.

I didn't know any better either. So I threw everything in. I went through the weight of the world and included it all when I was writing.

HG: Bob Dylan obviously set the standard, plus some of the other writers of that era.

JP: They were huge for me. If it wasn't for Bob Dylan, on the strength of wanting to play Hank Williams songs for my father, I doubt I'd have wanted to write. But Dylan opened the door. No, Dylan *built* the door, opened it, and left the door open for a whole lot of us to walk through. He cut a path through that door and forward, and long after he's gone, people will still be following that path.

HG: What was it about Dylan?

JP: I really liked his singing. I thought he phrased [things] real cool, a lot of thought went into how he did it. The way he sang really pulled you into the words, and what he was saying. That raised up what he was writing, too.

HG: And the politics of his work, did that inform yours?

JP: I didn't consider myself very political—and I didn't consider myself a folksinger. It was just the route I took, and clubs I played. But really, I liked country and rock and roll. What I learned to play was what my older brother taught me, that was a big part of the "style" I have now.

HG: You got inside some very heavy things, John.

JP: I wasn't really looking for something to write about. I was interested in words—the sounds of words, and the way words worked off each other.

HG: So you're going to sidestep the literary aspect of what you do.

JP: I enjoyed English when I had a teacher who knew enough to leave you alone and let you follow your imagination. If they wanted me to memorize verb parts, I hated that. But if the teacher wanted me to write dialogue for two characters on an escalator, I'd go to town. Get an "A," ace that.

I wasn't much of a reader. I got hooked on John Steinbeck, because of his shorter books—*The Pearl, Cannery Row, Sweet Thursday*. Then I gradually approached the longer ones, though I still haven't read *The Grapes of Wrath*. I thought the movie was so good with Henry Fonda and all; I know the book's always supposed to be better, but I can't imagine how.

Stories and Characters

John Prine's songs—whether written in his early 20s or somewhere in his 60s—have always been literary, always turned on the small details of regular lives, as well as the craggy-voiced baritone's singular metaphors and images.

'Angel from Montgomery' became the postmodern torch singer's go-to, based largely on Bonnie Raitt's recording of it, where she wailed for escape from her mundane life: "Make me an angel that flies from Montgomery / Make me a poster from an old rodeo."

Country fans know Miranda Lambert's version of 'That's The Way the World Goes 'Round', with its profession of being "naked as the eyes of a clown".

Prine's 45-year-old debut, *John Prine,* contains songs that became standards for a reason. They were miniatures of seemingly real situations, rendered with close portraits and a compassion that got listeners to lean in. [. . .]

HG: If you weren't trying to *say* something, are you surprised how topical these songs from *John Prine* remain?

JP: It's amazing to me—particularly 'Sam Stone' and 'Flag Decal'. If somebody had bet me money on their lifespan, I would've said three, four years. Vietnam was going to be over, and we wouldn't need 'em anymore. But because of the way it all went down, the war didn't just end. We brought the boys home in waves, and left some there . . . and as time has gone on . . .

HG: You mean everything in the Middle East?

JP: There's no war—just sending people to "protect your interests." You still get a ribbon if you get killed, but there's no principle being fought for or protected. And when you get back, people don't know what you were really fighting for, so it's hard.

HG: Do people tell you their stories? Is that how you know?

JP: You can feel it, Holly. Just the reaction ['Sam Stone'] gets in the show. It's not nostalgia for this song; that sadness is *right now.* It's something very real to the people who're hearing it.

HG: In 'Sam Stone', there's the matter of heroin, to cope with what can't be shared.

JP: It's a huge teenage problem now, even in the upper-class suburbs. And it's so quiet, too. I only find out when I ask my boys. They've had friends OD, kids in well-to-do families who seem well adjusted.

I don't know why people don't get the idea heroin isn't good for you. I've had friends try to talk me into it; encourage me. They only do it once a month—and they're all dead or their lives are severely damaged.

When I was writing 'Sam Stone', I didn't know too much about it then, but I thought, "Wow, heroin must be really fun or good, because why would they throw everything away for it?" People'd steal from their mother, forget about their kids, let their life go. They wouldn't even look back.

HG: Was there a 'Sam Stone'?

JP: It rhymed with "home". But I *knew* the character. He'd just got back home from the service. I knew several of those guys, and they all ended up different ways, but it was never good.

I hung out with a fairly rough crowd as a teenager. There were certain things I just wasn't there for. If they were gonna rob somebody or were hurting somebody. I didn't see the point in that, so I just didn't come around. But a bunch of us got drafted at the same time. Five of us went in on the same day; four went to Vietnam. Nobody came back the same. Even the ones who didn't see combat—it was that thing of not knowing. Being over there, you could just go for a beer, and with the landmines everywhere, your friend could step on one, and that was that.

HG: You went to Germany.

JP: I felt as lucky as when I was a little kid. When the orders came down, one in 10 maybe didn't go to 'Nam. In January of 1966, when I got called, LBJ had gone from 23,000 troops to a half million on the ground over there. So pretty much everybody who was drafted went.

They sent me to Louisiana for training, and I figured they were setting me up for a rice paddy somewhere. But when I took the aptitude test, I didn't open the quiz book, just wrote A, B, C, D, A, B, C, D over and over—and it came back I was some kind of mechanical genius.

Somebody in Germany's time must have been up, they needed that skill set. I was classified a heavy-duty construction mechanic. I always felt if I just went my way and walked down the street, if I didn't lift the hood, I'd be okay.

HG: You wrote 'Some Humans Aren't Human' on *Fair & Square*. Pretty straight commentary.

JP: You know, I thought the talking part was pretty mean [*"You're feeling your freedom and the world's off your back / Some cowboy from Texas starts his own war in Iraq"*]. Taking George Bush apart intelligently . . . but I'm not a mean person, and I don't ever want to pick on one person like that. I like to let people draw their own conclusions.

I don't want to hit people over the head, but give them something they've seen before, maybe in different colors. Or actually *show* them what they've seen, so they realize they're looking at it.

Mister Peabody's Coal Train

Prine does an exquisite job of "showing" in his song 'Paradise', also from his 1971 debut. For him, it was a tune about the place his parents came from. But the catchy campfire favourite also made a powerful environmental statement by holding a child's memory against a landscape changed forever by strip mining.

The song's lyrics place blame on the Peabody Coal Company for changing the landscape of large portions of Muhlenberg County, Kentucky. But, as Prine's song says, the company was still in business.

When, in 2013, a pair of activists were arrested protesting at Peabody's annual shareholders' meeting—which had been moved to Wyoming to avoid scrutiny—the activists' lawsuit against the coal company opened with a portion of 'Paradise.' Peabody Coal countersued two years later, trying to have Prine's song removed from the suit.

JP: All I was trying to do [with 'Paradise'] was tell the story about my mom and dad's hometown. All I was saying was if you were there, this is what you would see. You'd *see* the World's Largest Shovel, which tore up this little town. It was evidence of what was happening, you couldn't miss it.

If they hadn't made such a fuss, nobody would've even realized—or thought much about the song. But they went after me, and people started paying attention.

HG: They came after you again, too. You've just had a federal judge affirm your song.

JP: There was a federal lawsuit where they quoted a couple verses [as part of the complaint]. Peabody, when they saw my verses, they countersued and got so incensed. *That's* what [Peabody] went after, not the infraction they were being sued for.

When the federal judge finally ruled [on Peabody's complaint], he not only said my lyrics didn't defame them, [but] they were the truth. He upheld the song, and even quoted 'Blowin' in the Wind' in the summary he wrote.

A few weeks later, Peabody declared bankruptcy.

HG: That song—like so many you've written—is as timely now as ever.

JP: I guess so. It was never the plan. But it's [turning out that way] . . .

I'm gonna sing 'Paradise' at Yosemite in August for the 100th anniversary of the [National Park Service]. President Obama is going to give a speech. It's a big deal. I'm honored to be part of it.

My wife, Fiona, is a really big fan of the President. They were born on the same day, the same year. She really wants to meet him, especially while he's still in office, so this is my chance.

HG: You have empathy as a writer. It seems that's where so much of your commentary ends up coming from.

JP: I'm opinionated as anybody. I see people and envision what they're like, what they're life is—and I might be totally wrong. But as a writer, I'm trying to come up with a good story. Those stories, I guess, show things.

But I like to say I work off raw imagination and good instincts. That's why I usually turn down ideas to write songs for movies. It's somebody else's idea. I can't come to the conclusion they might want me to.

HG: 'Hello in There' is old people who're forgotten. As a young man, you saw that issue when it wasn't something you and your audience would've been plugged into. Now, well, it's not quite a crisis, but . . .

JP: I'm 69. Things in this world don't change that much. . . . I see how we treat old people, just like we did then. My audience is about my age, so if they're not thinking about themselves, they're thinking about their parents.

HG: What's to come?

JP: I write in little bunches, then I write a song that tells me which way a record's gonna go. *Fair & Square* came together with 'Taking a Walk', about a guy who's so isolated and lonely, he's just out there walking. It wasn't what the record was about, but it was the heart of it, I think, emotionally.

Right now, I don't have that song. But the songs I've got are about relationships, not so much men and women, but more man-to-man—or person-to-person. I don't know if I'm heading in the right direction yet, and I never approach anything thinking I'm gonna make a statement. I just let the songs come from my gut. That way I know they come from a pure place.

That's really the best way to do it.

JOHN PRINE REFLECTS ON THREE GRAMMY NOMINATIONS

Randy Lewis | December 12, 2018 | *Los Angeles Times*

Having tagged in from Hilburn as the *L. A. Times*' writer of record on "John Prine," Randy Lewis understood better than most the impact of *The Tree of Forgiveness*'s 2019 Grammy triple. Not only did *Tree* receive a nomination for Best Americana Album, "Knocking on Your Screen Door" and "Summer's End" were *both* nominated for Best Americana Song.

Fresh from being voted the Americana Music Association's Artist of the Year, nominated for the Rock & Roll Hall of Fame, and enshrined in the Songwriters Hall of Fame, the seventy-year-old Prine was receiving the same critical validation his friend Bonnie Raitt had received with *Nick of Time*. It had been thirteen years since his last true studio album *Fair & Square*, 2006's Best Contemporary Folk Grammy winner, sandwiched between Steve Earle's *The Revolution Starts Now* in 2005 and Bob Dylan's *Modern Times* in 2007.

Prine had stayed true to the independent path he'd started walking in 1981, and *The Tree of Forgiveness*'s recognition was a validation beyond the music. Had Prine made a different decision, taken the money offered over the years or allowed himself to be subject to "input" from people who didn't truly understand, it's unlikely he'd still have the desire to make records at all at this stage of his career—let alone records as formidable as *Tree*.

When Lewis checked in on Prine, he found the artist's wisdom tempered, as ever, by wonder. In a world of cynicism and self-interest, the award-winning critic found not only a man tickled by the recognition but also someone who still remembered everything about his Best New Artist nomination at the 15th Annual Grammy Awards in 1972.

Gratitude, love, and delight don't always exude gravitas. Lewis's instinct to assess what had been an outstanding year was also an opportunity to show Prine's humility to the *L. A.*

Times' readers. With eleven nominations and two Grammys, Prine was as concerned about winning for Oh Boy's team, especially Fiona and son Jody Whelan, as he was for himself.

The night before the Grammys, Lewis sat with Prine in the forward balcony of the Troubadour for a large portion of the Americana Music Association's all-star tribute, witnessing firsthand Prine's enthusiasm for the music community, fellow performers, and their love of his songs. Through a night of Bob Weir, Margo Price, Boz Scaggs and Sara Watkins, Iron & Wine's Sam Beam, and Bettye LaVette, the vastness of Prine's songs was on display.

Posting on the *L. A. Times*' website on February 10, Lewis noted Dwight Yoakam's choice to cover "Spanish Pipedream," the irreverent power-acoustic song, "because [Yoakam] said it often perplexed regulars at a western bar called the Corral in the northern San Fernando Valley he played upon moving to Los Angeles from his home in Kentucky. Like many who preceded him, Yoakam said Prine's songwriting provided him with a template and goal to aim for in his own development as a songwriter." –Ed.

If you think the impact of a Grammy Award nomination, or win, ever fades, try asking John Prine.

The veteran folk singer and songwriter just collected three more Grammy nods from his latest album, "The Tree of Forgiveness," yet he talks about his first nomination as though it were yesterday rather than 46 years ago.

"My first Grammy nomination? I was 24—I was nominated for best new artist of the year," Prine said recently from a tour stop in Toronto. "To still be in the game now is just great."

The Grammy love is just the latest expression of admiration and respect heaped on him over the last year. In September he was named artist of the year by the Americana Music Assn. and last month—on the same day—he was announced among the finalists for induction into both the Songwriters Hall of Fame and the Rock and Roll Hall of Fame. (Prine didn't make the Rock Hall, which announced new inductees on Thursday.)

The latter two organizations are recognizing the body of work Prine has amassed since emerging in 1970 from Chicago with an extraordinary debut album, "John Prine." That collection contained several songs that not only have become cornerstones of his own repertoire, but have been famously interpreted by other artists, among them "Angel From Montgomery" (most famously by Bonnie Raitt) and "Hello in There" (Bette Midler).

The Americana honor focuses on his newest work, "The Tree of Forgiveness," a work that was lauded by critics upon its release earlier this year. In addition to the Americana album Grammy nomination, two songs are vying for the Americana roots song Grammy: "Knockin' on Your Screen Door" and "Summer's End," both written with his frequent songwriting collaborator.

"Screen Door" applies a humorous, devil-may-care veneer to a more serious theme about growing old alone, while "Summer's End" is an achingly bittersweet portrait of someone trying to patch things up after a relationship has disintegrated.

Valentines break hearts and minds at random/That ol' Easter egg ain't got a leg to stand on
Well I can see that you can't win for tryin'/And New Year's Eve is bound to leave you cryin'

"The attention the record's gotten has really knocked me out," Prine said. "That wasn't something that was totally expected—the fact that it wasn't just an initial reaction when the record came out, but that it's stayed throughout the year, I'm really grateful. It's a good feeling to have when you're 72."

The latest nominations bring his total to 14. He's won Grammys twice, both for contemporary folk album: "The Missing Years" (1988) and "In Spite of Ourselves" (1999).

In addition to the awards consideration, Prine also has earned a place of admiration among an entire generation of literate singer-songwriters. His name is consistently at or near the top of the list of influential song-writers cited by the likes of Miranda Lambert, Chris Stapleton, Sturgill Simpson, Jason Isbell, Margo Price, Brandy Clark and numerous others.

His unofficial fan club also includes such well-regarded peers as Bob Dylan and Kris Kristofferson.

As candid in his speech as in his songs, Prine typically displays his good humor in conversation as well. And at 72, having come through several rounds of treatment for cancer and still writing, recording and touring, he sees little reason to pull any punches when discussing his hopes about the Grammy Awards ceremony that will play out Feb. 10 at Staples Center in Los Angeles.

"There are a lot of people in Americana who have never won one before," he said. "I don't want to feel like I'm being a hog, but it really would be nice to win. For Oh Boy [Records, his own label] it would be really important. It would give the label a big boost. Oh Boy is still doing great for as long as we've been around."

Prine started Oh Boy in 1981 primarily as a mail-order business. He was in the vanguard of musicians stepping away from the major label system to take greater control over their recordings. The label is now run by his son, Jody, while his wife, Fiona Whelan Prine, has been overseeing his tour bookings and career decisions since the death in 2015 of his longtime manager, Al Bunetta.

His nomination for the Rock Hall of Fame, a club that includes Elvis Presley, Chuck Berry, the Beatles and the Rolling Stones, put him in line to join one of his dearest, departed friends, Sun Records founder Sam Phillips—the man who, among other things, directed Prine to a cancer specialist in Texas three decades ago whom Prine credits with saving his life.

"I'd love to be at that party," he said with a gravelly chuckle. "To tell you the truth, the nomination for the Rock and Roll Hall of Fame totally surprised me. I had no idea that was coming. I know a lot of people like to say it's enough just to be nominated. But I've been nominated for so many things, I'd like to get this one. I think it's a long shot, considering I never had a No. 1 rock 'n' roll record.

"I don't know if it will come this year, my first time I've been nominated," he said several days before the inductees were announced. "But it sure would be nice to get there while I'm still walking."

JOHN PRINE ON USING "UNWED FATHERS" TO MAKE A STAND AGAINST ABORTION BANS

Chris Willman | May 30, 2019 | *Variety*

John Prine always had empathy for women and the unrecognized fates they faced; his songs made that much clear. There was the shipwrecked housewife from a time when divorce was not something nice people did in "Angel from Montgomery"; the aging barfly looking for love and being left behind in "The Oldest Baby in the World"; the fat girl who only dreamed of love, because no one wants a heavyset young woman, in "Donald and Lydia"; and the pregnant teenager being sent away to have her baby in "Unwed Fathers." They all demonstrated Prine's ongoing compassion for women overlooked, cast off, and treated as if they have no real value.

That empathy sparked Tammy Wynette to record "Unwed Fathers" as the opening track to and first single from 1983's *Even the Strong Get Lonely*, her twenty-fifth album. The Bobby Braddock cowrite set the perfect tone for a record that also included "A Slightly Used Woman," "I'm So Afraid That I'd Live Through It," "Still in the Ring," "Even the Strong Get Lonely Sometimes," and "Only the Strong Survive."

When it appeared that Roe v. Wade's Constitutional protection of a woman's reproductive autonomy was under assault, Prine put his music into action. He enlisted Americana force Margo Price, whose hard bar-room country packed a rock intensity, and they recorded a simple acoustic guitar–forward version. Even more Appalachian than *Aimless Love*'s original, Price's harmonies are starker and sweeter than the original, dialing up the harsh contrast between innocence of the child abandoned by the unwed father "who can't be bothered, but runs like water through a mountain stream."

Never one for proclamations, Prine let his actions speak with a single that called attention to the issue as well as benefitting the American Civil Liberties Union. According to indie retail site johnprine.bandcamp.com, *The Living Room Sessions*, recorded from May 16–18, with a Jason Isbell duet on "People Puttin' People Down" as the B-side, donated four dollars per download, a meaningful portion of the sale price.

Making sure his intentions were clear, Prine spoke to *Variety*'s award-winning music editor Chris Willman not long after Alabama passed the Human Life Protection Act. Also known as the Alabama Abortion Ban and House Bill 314, the controversial act was passed by the Alabama Legislature, and Governor Kay Ivey signed into law the statute that would make any doctor who performed an abortion guilty of a Class A felony, punishable with life in prison. More than striking down exception clauses for rape and incest, the hope was that the Human Life Protection Act would be challenged, have its case taken to the Supreme Court, and ultimately upend Roe v. Wade.

Like "Paradise" and its lingering truth about the Peabody coal company's impact on Muhlenberg County, "Unwed Fathers" offered a portrait of a young girl left by a boy and being sent off in shame to have a child without the neighbors seeing. People forget that, fifty years ago, that was a reality pre-Roe v. Wade. Prine was old enough to remember and willing to humanize the impact this legislation would have.

To Willman's credit, he saw the importance of the issue *and* Prine's gesture. Though *Variety* covers the broadest expanse of entertainment of any trade, a story for a one-off charity single—especially for an artist who's not Lady Gaga, Bruce Springsteen, or Justin Bieber—signals a strong recognition of the elements at play. —Ed.

It figures the guy who wrote "Angel From Montgomery" would care about women in Alabama. Anyone who thought the fight against state abortion bans lacked male allies can look to John Prine, considered one of the best songwriters of his or any generation since his self-titled 1971 folk-rock debut. He was outraged enough to first set up an online auction benefiting the Alabama ACLU, then raise money for the national organization by recutting "Unwed Fathers" as a soon-to-be-released single with alt-country heroine Margo Price.

Was there any personal impetus for using "Unwed Fathers" to make a stand on state abortion bans?

I'm always concerned when our civil liberties are being attacked. I believe in our Constitution. We wanted to support the work of the ACLU and invite others to do the same. That song has always been about how women are the ones who carry, birth and sometimes are left with taking care of and raising children too. Now they want to take away their right to decide if or when they do that. Women should be the ones to make decisions about what affects their lives in such a big way. It seems pretty simple to me.

You sing this remake with Margo Price. It's a powerful visual when she's being outspoken about reproductive issues while nine months pregnant.

Margo and I sing "Unwed Fathers" as a duet onstage all the time. She was the perfect fit—and she is a woman who makes her own choices! I think Margo would stand up for what's right whether she was pregnant or not. She is a woman who knows her own mind, and we love her and her family.

Your fan base skews progressive. (Jason) Isbell is a good example of an artist who still has supposed fans tweeting that they're quitting him because of his liberal politics. So do you risk losing any?

I've been singing these songs for 50 years, so if fans hear something new in them now, I'd love to hear what it is they are hearing.

You're being inducted into the Songwriters Hall of Fame June 13.

I'm delighted. It's wonderful to be included in a club like that. It'll be great to meet up with Tom T. [Hall, a fellow inductee]. We don't get to hang out too often.

Is there a Tom T. Hall song you wish you'd written?

I love "Old Dogs, Children and Watermelon Wine." Best setup for a song I've ever heard: "Sittin' in Miami, pouring blended whiskey down . . ."

There was a gap of 13 years between your previous album of all-new material and "Tree of Forgiveness." So maybe it's foolish to already be anticipating the next one?

I'm writing, for sure. The success of "Tree of Forgiveness" was very surprising to me. I'm very happy my fans from the first record (in 1971) to the most recent are now bringing their children and grandchildren to my shows. That's motivating me to write. Yeah, I'll probably bake a new record in the next couple of years.

Things You Didn't Know About John Prine

AGE: **72** BIRTHPLACE: **Maywood, Ill.** PREVIOUS JOBS: **Army, mailman** DISCOVERED BY: **Kris Kristofferson** BIGGEST FANBOYS: **Bob Dylan (calls Prine "pure Proustian existentialism"), Roger Waters ("He lives on that plain with Neil Young and Lennon")** BEST TRIBUTE SONG: **Kacey Musgraves' "Burn One With John Prine"**

MOJO: THE LAST IN-DEPTH INTERVIEW

Bob Mehr | 2020 | *MOJO*

When Bob Mehr drove from Memphis to Nashville during the days just after Thanksgiving 2019, no one would've guessed this would be John Prine's last comprehensive interview. Longtime critic at the *Commercial Appeal* and author of the *New York Times* bestseller *Trouble Boys: The True Story of the Replacements*, Mehr had long been a contributor to *MOJO*, the acclaimed British music magazine.

Beyond Prine's sense of irony and humor, it's remarkable the consistency in so much of what he said over the years. In this retrospective reflection on half a century of music, Prine had the fullness of a career, the recent acclaim, and a sense of timelessness to much of his catalogue to inform his answers. He also had insight that unpacked record-business practices for what they were—as well as the common sense to bet on himself.

Interview done, Mehr returned home. Prine played two concerts in Florida, then a New Year's Eve stand at the Ryman Auditorium with the Secret Sisters and Marty Stuart. In 2020, he played Sweden, then Norway, closing the run February 13 at Paris's Café de la Danse.

To read Mehr's interview is to see a man at peace with himself. Having gone through years of slight, years of wild acclaim, years of rocking hard, and years of battling cancer, Prine had found what seems like bliss: three wonderful boys, his Irish bride who was now his manager, making music, and finding an even broader audience. —Ed.

JOHN PRINE IS DEEP in thought, discussing the craft of songwriting, when suddenly his gaze is diverted to the big bay windows of his dining room. His eyes suddenly widen with excitement.

"It's starting to snow," he says, his voice rising. "Hey Fi! It's snowing!"

It's the start of the holiday season, and Prine is holding court in his Georgian-style manor in this quiet south Nashville neighborhood. The singer and his manager wife Fiona moved here a couple years ago, in part because their old house had become a stop on a country music celebrity bus tour. "You'd be carrying out your garbage and there's people taking pictures with flash bulbs," chuckles Prine. "Very glamorous."

In a black sweater and slacks, with prodigious cheeks and twinkling eyes, Prine cuts a genial figure. He talks with his head cocked slightly to one side, the result of a neck cancer and surgery that threatened his voice and career two decades ago (he's since survived a second bout of lung cancer). Sipping from a glass of iced tea, he ponders plans to stock the vintage Wurlitzer jukebox in the corner with a selection of Christmas 78s. "I gotta get it fixed first though," he notes. "Last time I tried to use it, Elvis Costello was over for dinner, him and Joe Henry, and I tried to play them some Bing Crosby songs and the thing started pouring out smoke."

In a previous life as a US army mechanic, the Illinois-born, Kentucky-rooted Prine might have took a shot at repairing it himself. As it is, songwriting proved a more persuasive calling than the military, or the mail route he famously trudged for many years. Discovered and championed by Kris Kristofferson while playing the folk clubs of Chicago, then signed to Atlantic Records, Prine launched his recording career in 1971 with *John Prine*: a collection of singular story songs that his longtime admirer Bob Dylan once hailed as "pure Proustian existentialism . . . Midwestern mindtrips to the nth degree."

Prine's most recent album, 2018's Grammy-nominated *The Tree of Forgiveness*, testifies to enduring skills, although he admits "I write mostly out of fear now. I have to have a deadline." More surprising, perhaps, is the growth of his audience, including a crop of acclaimed young artists—starring Jason Isbell and Kacey Musgraves—plus continuing support from the old guard, including Led Zeppelin's Robert Plant who, it turns out, Prine's wife has just run into shopping in nearby Green Hills.

"Robert's a fan of mine," says Prine. "So is Roger Waters. A lot of the big English rocker guys from the '70s like me. I don't know why they weren't fans in the '70s. But I'm glad everyone's come around."

What was your earliest exposure to music?

Me and my brothers were all born and raised in the Chicago area, but my parents were both from Western Kentucky. So there was country music playing in our house all the time: Roy Acuff, Hank Williams. Every night my dad would have the radio tuned to the local country station, or sometimes he could pick up WSM down in Nashville on weekends. He didn't play music. He couldn't sing either, but that didn't stop him. (laughs) When he'd had a couple too many he'd stand on a chair or a table and sing The Wabash Cannonball.

Was there a sense that you were Southerners in exile?

Oh yeah. My dad had come up north for work, but he was deeply connected to Kentucky. I remember in second or third grade we were supposed to go home and ask our parents where we were from, what our heritage was. The kind of thing where kids in class would stand up and say they were Irish-German or Scandinavian or whatever. My dad, after he had a couple beers, said, "Remember, son: you're pure Kentuckian, the last of a dyin' breed."

I gather you weren't much of a student.

I was lucky just to finish high school. I promised my dad I would graduate and it took me five years to get out. I just didn't hear what they were saying, y'know? I was a daydreamer. The only thing I would ace was if there was an English class or something where you didn't have to hit a book, but just use your imagination and write. It seemed easy to me to write dialogue and situations that I thought of. I started writing songs to Carter Family melodies. But by the time I got done with the melody it didn't sound like one of theirs. I was writing a lot up until I was about 16. Then I guess I got busy being a juvenile delinquent. I can't remember having any serious ideas of becoming a songwriter then. I thought it was so far away that it was not anything you should even dream about.

You ended up becoming a mailman instead.

Yeah, I did that for six years, before I got drafted in the army, then again after I got out. The pay was good, but the work was awful, between the elements and the dogs chasing you. Plus, I was low man on the totem pole so they gave me the worst mail route—it had over 500 houses on it, all with steps. I eventually whittled it down to 450—it took me four years to do that.

You were drafted at the height of Vietnam war, but caught a break and ended up stationed in Germany.

In boot camp, I was in in Fort Polk, Louisiana. They were training us to crawl through the swamps and kill the Vietnamese. We were all sure we were getting sent over there. Everybody got their orders and I'd say 85 percent of the guys went to Vietnam. When I got the orders for Germany, my father was really happy. Actually, so was I. That's where I started playing and writing again. I had my mom and dad ship over my guitar and I'd play in the barracks.

You returned to the States in the midst of the whole countercultural revolution.

I got back just before Christmas of '67. So much had changed in that time, '66 and '67. When I went away most of my buddies that didn't get drafted, they were greasers, with slicked back hair and leather jackets. When I came back they all had long hair and bell bottoms. I got married while I was in the army, married my high school sweetheart. So I was an old married man at 21. My buddies were still finding themselves when all that hippie stuff hit. I was never really a hippie. I was more like a retired greaser. That's probably why I never got into writing songs about "let's get together" or "we can save the world." I was more of an observer of this new world, because I was kinda removed from it.

You would write songs while working on your mail route, like Sam Stone, Hello In There and Paradise off your first album. Did you realise how good they were?

I thought there was a possibility they could be really good, or just plain awful. They were really different; they had nothing to do with regular songs. So I had mixed feelings. I was proud of them because they were mine, but I wasn't sure they were gonna connect with other people. I do remember around that time, Bob Dylan was on the first "Johnny Cash Show." When I saw the two of them singing together I thought the music I was playing and writing, it'd fit right straight in between the two of 'em. I thought, that's exactly where I want to be.

You made your first appearance on stage at an open mike night, basically on a dare, right?

It was just a little club in Chicago, not even 20 people in there when I got up. I wasn't the type to heckle, but I'd had a few beers and wasn't really impressed with what I was hearing, said so under my breath. Someone at the next table said, "Well if it's so easy, why don't you get up and do it?" So I said, "Well, maybe I will." I got up and sang Sam Stone and the audience just sat there. They looked at me, looked at each other, looked at me again . . . seemed like an eternity. Finally, they started applauding. The owner of the club came up afterwards and offered me a job singing there. I couldn't believe it. The thing I really remember was that I was more comfortable than I'd ever felt. I felt like that's where I belonged.

It wasn't long before your friend and fellow Chicago singer-songwriter Steve Goodman brought Kris Kristofferson to see you play.

That was huge. I mean, Kris was it. He was the biggest thing to come along in the way of lyrics since Bob Dylan. There was nobody in the place when Kris got there. I sang seven songs and got off the stage. Kris brought me a beer and asked me if I would get back up there and sing those same seven songs and anything else I had. He was interested in everything I'd ever written. That was enough validation right there.

Your connection with Kristofferson led to a deal with Atlantic Records.

Paul Anka had been hanging out with Kris the night in Chicago when he came to see me. I think Paul just saw the excitement that Kris had and thought, I should get in on this. Anka wanted to manage me and Goodman so he ended up buying us plane tickets to New York. I wasn't gonna go but Goodman talked me into it. We got to New York and picked up a copy of the Village Voice at LaGuardia [Airport]. We look at it, and Kris is playing at the Bitter End; Carly Simon was opening. We took a cab on down there. Just as we got out, Kris and his band are walking down the street—they'd been at the bar next door between shows. Kris see us and says, "I'm gonna put you guys up onstage, you're gonna do some songs tonight." We didn't know it, but the second show was for record company people. They were coming to see Kris 'cause he was the new world wonder. It was full of label people; Jerry Wexler was sitting down front. He came and talked to me after I got offstage. Asked me to show up at his office at Atlantic at 10 the next morning. I showed up; I had a record contract waiting for me. I hadn't been in New York City 24 hours! If you'd put that in a movie people would have thought it was too corny.

Pretty early on in your career you made a connection with Bob Dylan, who's been a vocal fan of yours.

It was before my first record came out. Me and Goodman were back in New York doing press and getting our pictures taken. Kris was in town and he said to come over to Carly Simon's apartment: "I got a surprise for you guys." We're over there about a half hour and there's a knock at the door. It's Bob Dylan. Nobody had really seen Bob anywhere for a while. I sang Far From Me off my first album; when I got to the chorus Bob started singing along. The record wasn't even out! It almost stopped me in my tracks. I found out later that Wexler had sent him an advance copy. Dylan said when he first heard my voice he thought I'd swallowed a Jew's harp. (laughs)

With your fourth album, 1975's Common Sense, you made more of a rock record with former Stax guitarist/producer Steve Cropper. It seemed like you were searching for a sound.

Things happened pretty fast for me, so I was still finding my way musically. I took a full band out for the Common Sense tour, a band I wasn't ready for. But [Cropper's] production was such that I had to take some kind of band to perform the songs. But every gig was like torture for me. Now it's a different thing—I'm uncomfortable without my band.

You also asked to leave Atlantic around this time and moved over to Asylum. You seemed increasingly uncomfortable with a major label existence.

My contract with Atlantic was a five-year contract for ten albums of self-written material. Every six months I was supposed to put out a record. In retrospect, the whole singer-songwriter thing was mainly a way for labels to get publishing on some really great songs. They promised all these songwriters, "Oh, you're going to be a big recording artist." They'd put a couple of records out, then ignore them or they'd drop them, but they'd own the publishing forever. They still have the publishing on my first album, and it's almost 50 years. You'd think I could get it back by now.

You ended up making your first Asylum album, Bruised Orange, with Steve Goodman producing. The album was a success, but then you did an about face with a rockabilly record, Pink Cadillac.

Bruised Orange did really well and Asylum was happy. So I decided now I want to make a noisy record—a live record with a band, and I want all the noise to stay. I didn't want to use Dolby on the thing. I was big into being anti-Dolby at the time. (laughs) It was suggested I go to Memphis and talk to Knox Phillips and Jerry Phillips at the Phillips Recording Service.

Which is how you ended up working with their father, Sun Records founder Sam Phillips. You're probably the last artist he ever produced.

We would go into the studio at six every evening and play till six in the morning. We did that five nights a week for a good three months.

Eventually, Sam drove by one night and saw the lights were on and came by to check out, see who was in his studio. The way Sam told it my voice sounded so awful he thought he'd stick around and see if he could fix it. (laughs) And so he produced a couple things: Saigon and How Lucky Can One Man Get.

Was the experience working with him as intense as one might imagine?

It was crazy and incredible all at the same time. Sam was like a fire and brimstone preacher. He didn't ever talk about the music, he talked about the way you did things. He would speak in parables. It was a total experience. I didn't know he hadn't produced anyone in years and years. He'd turned down McCartney! Said he didn't want to do the Beatles. Whatever roads I went down, to actually cross paths with him, I wouldn't give it up for nothing.

You moved to Nashville in 1980. Once you got there you started writing some country hits and then started your own label, Oh Boy.

I was spending all my time here when I wasn't on the road, and my marriage was falling apart [in Chicago], so I figured I'd move down here. I got in with some good people, like Roger Cook, who I wrote Love Is On A Roll with and that went to Number 1 [Country] for Don Williams. Then I wrote Unwed Fathers with Bobby Braddock and Tammy Wynette cut that. One day, I heard those songs back to back on WSM and I thought, Man, I have arrived. I'm gonna go out and buy a Cadillac and I did. (laugh) As far as my own career, I was getting fed up with the majors. I told my manager Al Bunetta, Let's start our own record company, let's just sell records to the people who come see us. I thought it would be more honest that way. That's why we started Oh Boy. A lot of people figured we were shooting ourselves in the foot. But the '80s were terrible—when I heard Warner Brothers dropped Van Morrison, Bonnie Raitt, and Little Feat, they dropped a bunch of them in one month, I thought, What's going on? This is crazy. Why would I try and get another major label deal?

The years that followed saw you growing your cult following out on the road, leading up to your "comeback" with The Missing Years.

In areas where we had busted through to playing concert halls, we were back in the clubs in the mid-'80s. But as long as I was having a good time on the road and sold the records to fans, I thought that was enough. We had two albums, *Aimless Love* and *German Afternoons*; they both did good for our core audience. By [the early-'90s], we got an offer from Columbia, a good-sized offer, like half a million bucks, which I turned down. I figured if there was that much interest we should kick it up ourselves, which is when we did The Missing Years. We were making a concentrated effort to make a record that could compete. I didn't have to be an island and just make music for my fans. That's where [Tom Petty & the Heartbreakers bassist] Howie Epstein came in to produce. He pulled that record out of me like a dentist with a sore tooth. We were recording at Howie's house in the Hollywood hills. I was singing in the bathroom; there were microphone cables up and down the hallways. We were cutting one instrument at a time, one song at a time. A song would take us over a week, sometimes two or three weeks. But, boy, when he played stuff back to me I couldn't believe how good it sounded.

You won a Grammy for The Missing Years, married Fiona, started a family—then were diagnosed with neck cancer. After your surgery, were you worried you wouldn't be able to sing again?

I was more worried about just living and seeing my kids grow up, honestly. I couldn't sing for about a year afterward, just didn't have the power. I remember finally booking a show in Johnson City, Tennessee. I figured it was far enough in the sticks that if it didn't go well people wouldn't hear about it for a while. (laughs) About 800 people showed up, and I made it through the show. Afterwards, I stayed and shook hands with everybody that came out. I didn't know how much I'd missed it. That was the night I realized I can go back out and do this again.

You've been enjoying a pretty amazing run over the last few years. Your last album became your highest charting LP and got several Grammy nominations. You've been playing to big crowds. . . .

Seems I can't do any wrong these days. About five years ago, I was thinking about, not retiring, but just kicking back, doing fewer shows. But ever since I brought out [The Tree of Forgiveness] we're doing everything we can just to keep up with it. It's still selling after 18 months. I'm getting a lot of young kids coming to the shows, and in turn they're going back and listening to my old stuff.

Do you feel vindicated for having done things your own way this whole time?

Everything I was doing all those years on the road, I thought I was just doing to get enough money to pay the bills, to put one foot in front of the other. But it's all coming back to me now in the best way possible. I always believed in what I was writing, but I never expected a bigger audience. If you're out there day after day, going around playing the same places, you pretty much think you've reached your audience. But there's more people finding my music every day. So I feel extremely lucky, I really do.

PART X

Gonna Smoke a Cigarette That's Nine Miles Long

"WHEN I GET TO HEAVEN": A CANDID CONVERSATION WITH JOHN PRINE

Benjy Eisen | April 9, 2020 | *Relix*

Relix shows the breadth of Prine's reach. Having provided the world "Illegal Smile," Prine always had a subtle counterculture appeal. But Benjy Eisen, a longtime contributor, realized that as much as he knew Prine's surface truths and obvious hits, he didn't understand the man.

With the blessing of his editors, Eisen set up a forty-five-minute call in March 2018. The conversation went swimmingly. Genuine camaraderie was achieved; questions were considered. Prine even acknowledged doing some European dates, working *Tree of Forgiveness* through 2020, taking some time to see the world with Fiona.

As with many people locked down as the pandemic hit, the isolation made Eisen more introspective. When the news broke that Prine had been admitted to Vanderbilt University Medical Center in early April 2020, Eisen's sense of what might be in their conversation deepened. The complete transcript of the interview—with Eisen's personal ruminations included—was one of many tributes posted in the days following Prine's April 7 passing.

John Prine was a part of so many people's lives over the years. Here, someone who came to him later and found the same truths and joys speaks to his endurance. —Ed.

Most mornings, since being asked to shelter-in-place due to a global pandemic, I've been getting in the shower, turning on John Prine's version of "Clay Pigeons," and quietly singing along. It's been the perfect quarantine song. "*Count the days and the nights that it takes to get back in the saddle again.*"

A longtime fan of Prine's greatest hits—the surface stuff—I overlooked his cover of Blaze Foley's "Clay Pigeons" until my Spotify algorithm introduced it to me on a road trip from Los Angeles to San Francisco in the fall of 2017. I had to pull off at the next exit, take out my iPhone, and look up everything I could find on it while playing the song a second, then a third time in a row.

It was at that moment I realized I knew nothing about John Prine. I knew his songs and his characters, his protagonists, his icons, the angel from Montgomery and the father with a hole in his arm where the money goes. But I knew nothing about the man behind these towers of song.

I became determined to write a piece as I sought some kind of answer to my question "Who is John Prine?" At the time I expressed naively but out of genuine enthusiasm: "I want to find some part of his story that has never been told and then tell it."

In March of 2018, I was able to have a fantastic 45-minute conversation with him about all the things I wanted to know—all the things he hadn't been asked before and also all the things that may have changed since he's been asked them last. Some topics are worth revisiting: Does he feel the need to take a stand, politically, now that Trump is President? What young songwriters are inspiring him these days? Does he have any plans to retire?

But as with every piece of art and conversation, everything changes when the artist dies. Things mean something different, other things mean something more. After it was reported that John Prine was in critical condition a couple weeks ago, having contracted COVID-19, I refreshed my news feed on him regularly, looking for hopeful updates. He had just returned from a European tour; he talked about that very tour at the end of our interview two years ago, when it was still in the future—he planned on celebrating by taking the rest of this year off and traveling the world with his wife.

I recalled our unusual interview and looked up the transcript, only to find that so much of it is still relevant for right here and now. I wanted a portrait and I got a candid.

I still don't know who John Prine is. But I know we'll all miss him.

Do you ever miss being a mailman?

Never, no.

Do you have a plan B if your music career doesn't work out?

No. When I left the post office and I told them I was leaving to go into show business, the superintendent, the Postmaster said, "Don't take your retirement money." And I said, "Why?" He said, "You'll be back." I said, "You don't understand, if it doesn't work out I'm not coming back."

You've had a long and impressive career, during which—sadly—you've seen some of your peers come and go. Who do you miss most?

Steve Goodman. We were like blood brothers—we got thrown into the fire at the same time and were both Chicago guys. We went to New York, and got record contracts within 48 hours of each other, so there was this bond. Goodman was the reason I went to New York. When I got the record contract, I wasn't gonna go. And Stevie also was the one that made Kris Kristofferson come over to listen to me.

The last thing in the world Kris Kristofferson wanted to hear was another singer-songwriter and Goodman made him get in a cab at 1 o'clock in the morning, after he'd done two shows, and dragged him over. And nobody was in the club; I was waiting for my paycheck and the chairs were on the tables. We pulled four chairs down and I sang 7 or 8 songs for Kris. He asked me to go back up there and sing everything I'd ever wrote. He championed my stuff after that. And that was supposed to be Goodman's shining hour and Goodman wouldn't hear about it—he wanted everybody to see his buddy from Chicago.

There are entire essays written about some of your songs, including attempts to analyze certain lyrics. Do you have any anecdotes about anyone wildly, if accidentally, totally misinterpreting your lyrics and what you mean to say?

[Laughs] Actually, there have been quite a few over the years. But I kind of figured, better than correct them, I thought there's kind of like there's no such thing as bad press as long as people are talking about your lyrics. Also, I've gotta say, unless it was totally out of the ballpark, I like to leave a lot of interpretation to the listener. They may interpret it totally different than what you meant, but it still means something to them. So I wouldn't want to bust their balloon.

I think maybe that's actually the secret of a good song—everyone finds their own meaning in it and it works for all of them. I'm sure even for you, some of these songs must have changed their "true" meaning over time.

That's true. I'm surprised, actually, at how many of the songs have worn as good as they have. That's something you really don't have any control over once you get it out there.

I was surprised when I learned that "Clay Pigeons" was a cover because it sounds so much like one of yours. What inspired you to cover that song in particular?

I love when Merle Haggard finally did his version of "If I Could Only Fly," 'cause I love the song. And man, that killed me. Haggard did the song before, with Willie [Nelson]—and it was nice. But it didn't pull the fullness of the song like it did the second time.

Haggard actually went back and did the song again. That tells me he had been sitting around for years with the song, probably singing it in hotel rooms. And I went back and listened to the rest of Blaze Foley's stuff and "Clay Pigeons" stuck out to me like I had written the song myself. And so it was natural for me to cover it. It felt relatable, you know.

In an interview with Rolling Stone, you talk about a gift that Johnny Cash gave you, and it's interesting because it's Johnny Cash. But what's the strangest gift that you've ever received from a fan?

There was a fan up in St. Paul, Minneapolis and the guy was an amateur taxidermist. His name was Professor Beardsley. And his wife was with him and the wife told me that there was no rodent or anything on their property that didn't get stuffed. He said they even have little mice stuffed on the wall. The guy brought me a chicken hat with earmuffs built into it. It was a chicken that he stuffed with its legs hanging out from the back. And the chicken head up the front like a damn ornament. I wore that for years, only for special company.

Let me guess, you're wearing it right now.

No, I evidently gave it to an ex-brother-in-law. I couldn't figure out who on earth I would give that chicken head to, but it was Eddie, my ex-brother-in-law.

***Tree of Forgiveness* is a very evocative image, but before I heard the album or could read the lyrics, I was wondering what you meant by that exactly. Let's start with: What does a tree of forgiveness look like?**

Sounds like a Christmas tree, I would guess.

Of course you're gonna say that. The lyric comes from the song "When I Get to Heaven," which is your comedic take on what you're looking forward to in your vision of the afterlife. It strikes the match of humor to hold a light to all those unknowns about the divine: "When I get to heaven/I'm gonna have a cocktail."

Originally, I just wrote the chorus and that's all it was. It was kind of my own private happy hour song—like uh oh, it's time for a cocktail, you know. I had the thing about smoking a cigarette nine miles long and I thought, 'I can't do that; I had cancer twice, I had to give up smoking twenty years ago and I still love it. I like to watch people smoke. I like to go stand next to them when they fire up, so that first whiff I could kind of get that secondhand smoke they warn you about, you know.

I'm an ex-smoker myself. I still dream about smoking.

When I wrote the song "When I Get to Heaven," I'm trying to figure out where can I go get a cigarette, and it's not gonna be anywhere "here." If I could smoke, it's not at the bar where you'd have to stand outside like an animal, like you're pissing on the fire hydrant or something. I thought, 'The only place I would be able to smoke is heaven.' They wouldn't have cancer up there and probably they wouldn't have "no smoking" signs.

Not in my heaven, anyway.

And that was the last song I wrote for the record—"When I Get to Heaven." I still hadn't referenced "the tree of forgiveness." So I had to stick it in. That's it—it's a nightclub in heaven!

So the title of the album came before the lyric?

Years before. I knew five years ago I was gonna make a record sometime called *Tree of Forgiveness*. I didn't know why—I tried to write a song a couple of times called "The Tree of Forgiveness" and it just seemed too whatever. It didn't work, not with the original what I had in mind. And I still wanted to get the title in the record, so I ended up calling the nightclub in heaven The Tree of Forgiveness—which is not a bad name for a bar.

The album opens with the song "Knockin' On Your Screen Door." Were you thinking of a specific and actual screen door, when you wrote those lyrics, or was it just something you thought everyone could relate to?

No, I co-wrote that with a good buddy Pat McLaughlin. He came up with the title. I'm not sure what he was thinking of. Pat is a happily married man but I knew him in his bachelor days and he really got around, if you know what I mean. And I have a feeling whenever he comes up with an image like "Knockin' On Your Screen Door," it has something to do with an old flame. He's gonna look up her number and knock on her screen door, or whatever. So I just took it at face value that that's where it was. Me and him are so familiar with each other, we could finish each other's sentences; we just go from one image to another until we have something we can tie a bow around.

That's a great idea—there's a few screen doors I wouldn't mind knocking on.

There you go, now you're catching on.

"The Lonesome Friends of Science" is another song that really stood out. I was wondering, apart from the possibility now that you're going to accidentally start a real movement to have Pluto back as a planet—is it an actual pushback at modern science or do you think it's more of like a satiric, tongue-in-cheek look at these doomsday pundits?

I don't know why, but it really ticked me off when they did that. I thought, how dare them! When I was a fifth grader, I had to sit in a boring science class and memorize those planets—then they tell me forty years later that Pluto's not actually a planet. I was kidding, you know. But it really ticked me off. So much so that it stuck with me all these years and I decided to write something about it. I had this idea that "The Lonesome Friends of Science" was like a secret society of scientists that sit around and drink together and decide, 'What can we do to really throw everybody off? We'll get rid of Pluto!' Just 'cause they're bored, or something.

They need to stay relevant with a new headline.

[Laughs] Exactly.

In "No Ordinary Blue," there's the lyric, "Leave the past behind. . . ." Certain songs tell stories that are like postcards from the past. Do those songs make you dwell in the past? When you're singing them night after night, decade after decade, do they still take you back to that place in time?

On "No Ordinary Blue," I thought we were writing about two lovers that were having a hard time communicating with each other. So I thought it was good advice for the guy to give to himself at the time, to leave the past behind and not bring it up, whether it was an argument or something—one of them kept bringing it up. With a song, I think it would take a different connotation; I don't wanna leave the past behind if I'm still making royalties from it.

That's the pull quote, right there. Talking of quotes, did your dad really say "When you're dead, you're a dead pecker head," or did you make that up for "When I Get to Heaven"?

He said it a thousand times. I had three brothers—no sisters, no girls. Four boys. His only piece of advice about religion was when you're dead, you're a dead pecker head. He would say it Sunday morning, he would say it late at night when you're drinking beer. If the conversation ever came to religion, that was his entire outlook. His other piece of advice was, "Don't bullshit the bullshitter," and what I remember at his funeral [was] me and my brother sitting there, in our ties and suits looking at each other, going, "Don't bullshit the bullshitter!" [laughs] When you're dead, you a dead pecker head—he ain't going nowhere, this guy; just the funeral home.

At this stage in your career, when working on an album, how involved do you like to be with the production and post-production aspects, from the players to the final mix?

I get a wave on the mixing part, I'm no good at that. So I don't know anything about that. I was there for all the overdubs and stuff, but Dave Cobb was so good at using just minimal stuff in the background. I cut it with just my guitar. We had bass and drums and he pretty much just would go out one time, tell the bass player and drummer what he wanted; never told me to change anything. I just sang what I sang, how I wrote the song. I thought what he gave me back for a record was a real fuel.

I'm sure by now you've heard early feedback from your friends, your team and the press. Since artists and fans often disagree about favorites, I'm wondering—are you surprised at the songs that have become the most popular, the most loved?

Yeah, and the record's not even out yet. I was real surprised about the one that me and Phil Spector wrote, "God Only Knows." A lot of people really love it. I wouldn't have recorded it unless I thought it was really good, but it surprised me how many people really like it. My favorites [on *Tree of Forgiveness*] were the one about Pluto—"The Lonesome Friends of Science"—and the song "Summer's End." I'm partial to those.

"Summer's End" is my favorite. You've been enjoying a cultural revival lately where you've been mentioned a lot in the press, especially in interviews with a younger generation of established artists. Not all of them are on the same musical branch as you, but they still point to you as an influence and a hero. Mike Gordon from Phish, for example. And also Sturgill Simpson. Do you hear these shout outs? Did any of them influence you in return? Have you discovered or even befriended any of these younger-generation songwriters?

Yeah, I've become good friends with Sturgill and Jason Isbell, Amanda Shires; Margo Price is a good buddy. Kacey Musgrave is a good buddy, too. The thing I like besides them being as talented as they are is they're good people. Throughout the years, I don't especially hang out with famous people—I've got good friends and they're also songwriters. That's, like, secondary. But to like somebody's music and find out that they're real earthbound, their feet are on the ground—I think that's probably the most admirable trait that I see when I meet another performer or songwriter. I like to see somebody that's really grounded. I like nuts, too; I like people that are floating around like a balloon. But I also like it when they're genuine.

Totally. Do you still listen to music for fun? What was the last concert you went to?

The last concert I went to just for fun? I don't like being around a lot of people. Believe it or not, I'm probably going hard of hearing. I got this thing where I'm sitting in the audience and when people applaud really hard, it really hurts my ears. And funny enough, it doesn't hurt them when I'm standing on stage. I prefer to go to a concert when I can walk around and not have to sit next to people who applaud too loud. I guess the last concert I was at was Jason Isbell at the Ryman. My wife and I just sat in the audience and enjoyed the show.

You've never shied away from the three things they tell you not to bring up at the party—religion, politics, and money. With the current state of American politics being such a divisive hot button, are you inspired to write about what's been going on? Do you ever feel any responsibility as an artist to address certain things?

First of all, anything I ever wrote that came out, even sideways sort of protest songs, I never really thought about it as such when I was writing the song. Even "Your Flag Decal Won't Get You Into Heaven Anymore"—I was a mailman, I was delivering *Reader's Digest*, and all of a sudden everybody and their brother was sticking flag decals on all their stuff and I was the guy delivering to their doorstep. I thought it was a funny song; it turned out to really kind of stick it to people that are really ultra-patriot.

When things are like they are right now, you can hardly not write about it. I also gotta say with that nut we've got in the White House there was a couple of times when I went, 'This guy's fuckin' nuts;' I go to myself, 'I've gotta write a song about this.' I tried a couple of times but he is such a cartoon that it's difficult to write something.

I saw in an article where Randy Newman was answering that question; he had a difficult time writing about Trump, 'cause from day-to-day, the guy's a joke himself. You feel you're just reporting the news to write about him.

Laughing is usually better than crying, but there's a lot to be angry about, either way. You've always been great at being able to tow that line, presenting a sentiment that's poignant and meaningful—or needs to be discussed—while framing it in a way that's humorous. A spoonful of sugar. I think that's one of your trademark elements.

Yeah, for me it stemmed from my childhood. You'd run into a bully, and if you could make them laugh before he clenched his fist to punch you, it was harder to punch you if he was laughing. You have to be quick on your feet and make a humorous incident out of it.

You've been a songwriter for a long time now. The creative process is different for everyone, but surely there are times when new songs just flow and other times when writing a new song is like pulling your own tooth. What makes you say, 'Hey, I wanna write some songs and put out a new album?' What starts up the songwriting engines in your little steam engine?

Well the reason I did the record at the time I did it, this new record, is my wife is my manager now and our son is running the record company and they came to me last summer and said, 'It's time for a record.' I didn't have any recourse except to finish what I was doing. I was writing songs, but I was writing at my own pace. I thought when I got ten good songs, I'd go looking for a producer. Well, they said I needed a record then. They didn't say why, they just said, 'It's time for a record.' So I went to this hotel for a week with a bunch of boxes of unfinished lyrics, and I took the songs that I'd already written and pieced everything together really fast, just 'cause my family threatened me.

You have your own record label. People are always talking about how the record industry has changed, but it's always been changing. And always in big ways. What have been the biggest changes and surprises for you since your first album?

This might be the first record where social media is such a huge thing, right in your face. It's the norm right now, whereas 13 years ago I put out a couple of collections of country stuff that weren't original material—and I'm just saying that 'cause we knew we've got the records out there—but each time there was a little bit more social media than the last time. And now, it's the biggest part. Selling the actual CD's . . . is a thing of the past. The numbers aren't there, so it's all about the social media now. I don't fight that. Especially with my son running the record company—he's experienced the end of that and he embraces it. And Oh Boy Records has lasted 45 years now.

It has, which is rare and awesome.

I know. I think a lot of majors have gone by the side of the road.

Enough about the past, let's talk about the future. You have this new album coming out, then you're going on tour behind it. There's the album cycle, then the tour cycle. How far in advance do you plan, and do you have a plan for 2018? 2019? Do you ever plan to take a break or retire?

We're touring till the end of the year, then we go to Australia in February of next year. We're gonna do a big European tour in 2019; we'll be working this record up till 2020—and then I think my wife and I are gonna take a year off and try and go see the world.

AFTERWORD

Second-generation hillbilly expat. Proud union man's son. Apple of his mama's eye. Little brother. Make-it-work kid. Stare-out-the-window dreamer.

Guy from the neighborhood. Old Town School of Folk Music denizen. Postman. US Army veteran. Songwriter in a mail shelter. Joker. Car lover.

The first new Dylan. Journeyman maker of songs. Fan of Sun Records, bluegrass, and home cooking. Writer for the unseen, voice of the unheard. Sardonic social contrarian. Romantic of the highest order. Believer in what people can be.

Trailblazer. DIY before DIY was done. Independent label operator. Troubadour. *Austin City Limits* regular. Secret handshake among those who know. Sorta movie star. Duet singer, especially with girls. Keeper of "Sam Stone," "Donald and Lydia," "Angel from Montgomery."

Lover of Fiona; father to Jody, Jack, and Tommy. Cancer survivor. Jaunty dancer. Inspiration for next wave after next wave: Kacey Musgraves, Sturgill Simpson, Margo Price, Tyler Childers, Jim James, Bon Iver, Drive-By Truckers, Conor Oberst, Justin Townes Earle, the Avett Brothers, Jason Isbell, Amanda Shires, Brandi Carlile, and his own signings, Kelsey Waldon, Arlo McKinley, Tre Burt, and Emily Scott Robinson.

Americana Icon. Grammy winner. Grammy Hall of Famer. Savorer of all that life offers and affords. Man of passion. Fountain of compassion. Loyal friend. Poet of the common man. Champion of the underdog.

Speaker of truths in his songs and in his actions. Lover of children, other people's happiness, and the irony of the moment.

Those are a few of the titles that define John Prine, the kid from Maywood, Illinois, who found so much about fame goofy and so much about the hypocrisy of the world heartbreaking. He didn't set out to be a big shot—just thought he could write better songs than the guy at the open mic—but he made friends with Steve Goodman, and the two ended up on the rocket ride of the less-than-superstar strivers.

He evolved over the years, but he never changed his core truths. He was willing to scrape away the hubris and rhetorical build-up he saw around him to write what felt like basic songs that sucker punched transgressors with a wink or a child's innocence.

That was his magic. You can see it in these interviews, tracing the arc of where he started, where he went, the frustrations and boldness— again, *nobody* with a shot started their own label—that anchored how he navigated the world and protected those songs.

He liked living so much, whether it was a fishing trip in the Ozarks or sneaking into Barneys New York to buy Fiona some shoes. He wasn't slavish about getting the next record done, but he always knew when it was ready, when it was time to seek something else. He was fearless about following his muse, whether it meant Memphis's royal Phillips family, Howie Epstein, or Dave Cobb.

That's part of what made Prine so singular among writer-artists. He never shied away from an unthinkable notion, never churned out albums just to have a reason to tour. He was mindful about what he said. But he also had a mind that turned on childlike spindles of how he saw right and wrong, that always summoned up something so basic and true, how could the rest of us miss it?

His sense of metaphor, comparisons, and language was unmatched. He could draw connections and show you the tenderest emotions without seeming to reach. That's to say nothing of his whimsy; this is a man who not only rhymed "polaroid photo" with "exactly-odo, Quasimodo" but also built a whole song ("The Sins of Memphisto") to pay off his new slang rejoinder.

As marvelous as the worlds he created around himself were, one has to wonder about the world between his ears. With his sense of decency and fair play, his fascination with *Weekly World News* tabloid headlines, his ability to be still but also to create joy around countless people across myriad moments, John Prine's mind must've been three kinds of amusement parks that were just the right size, with wooden rollercoasters, foot-long hotdogs, and homemade cotton candy—a place where people fell in love or fell into better than they deserved.

Following the death of Al Bunetta, his longtime manager and co-owner of Oh Boy, Prine found new joy in his little record company. Installing his wife as manager, their oldest boy Jody as label head, and a young woman from Thistle Farms as the marketing pivot, he was—in his seventies—writing songs that rivaled his best work. Sharing the stages with deserving younger artists, he passed on his wisdom and helped lay the foundation for the next few waves of Americana artists who will propel the genre-defying, songwriting-driven country/folk/blues/rock oeuvre well into the twenty-firstcentury.

When you hear a quirky lyric, a yearning melody, a flicker of a scene from some young songwriter or artist you can't quite pin down, think of John, a man who was as consistent as he was quixotic, as committed to the values he learned in Paradise, Kentucky, with his grandmother and grandfather as those he found in Chicago taverns with his union-man father. Prine dedicated himself to a wide range of people and humanitarian causes. These undertows flowed throughout his music: free speech, women's rights to their bodies, helping the homeless, a landmine-free world, protecting the environment, and just basic common sense and kindness.

Will there ever be another John Prine? Unlikely. The forces that shaped him, the cultural realities and clashes he lived through, the love he was basted in, those things seem to be lost in our fast and furious world. It's why young artists found him so electric and new generations clamored for more—and why these songs may be even more vital today than when they were written.

Maybe knowing how he came to be, how he evolved, and what he meant to so many great writers, artists, poets, thinkers—it's a bridge to

CREDITS

I gratefully acknowledge the help of everyone who gave permission for material to appear in this book. I have made every reasonable effort to contact copyright holders. If an error or omission has been made, please bring it to the attention of the publisher.

"Singing Mailman Who Delivers a Powerful Message in a Few Words," by Roger Ebert, originally published October 9, 1970, in the *Chicago Sun-Times*, reproduced on RogerEbert.com. Reprinted with permission from Chaz Ebert, president, The Ebert Company, Ltd.

Radio interview by Studs Terkel, broadcast in 1975 on *The Studs Terkel Show*, WFMT-FM. Printed with permission from Chicago History Museum and WFMT.

"The Postman Sings Twice," by Cameron Crowe, published February 9, 1973, in the *Los Angeles Free Press*. Reprinted with permission from Cameron Crowe.

Excerpt from *In Their Own Words: Twenty Successful Song Writers Tell How They Write Their Songs*, by Bruce Pollock, 1975. Reprinted with permission from Rock's Backpages.

"*Bruised Orange*: Prine Gets His Second Wind," by Robert Hilburn, published 1978 in the *Los Angeles Times*. Reprinted with permission.

"John Prine Is So Fine," by Jay Saporita, published January 21, 1975, in the *Aquarian Weekly*. Reprinted with permission.

"Ten Years of Folks: 20 Years of the Earl," by Dave Hoekstra, published November 1981 in the *Illinois Entertainer*. Reprinted with permission from Dave Hoekstra.

Interview by Dave Wallace Jr., published December 1980 in *Hot Rod*. Reprinted with permission from Dave Wallace Jr.

"John Prine: How Do You Label Him?" by Robert Hilburn, published 1982 in the *Los Angeles Times*. Reprinted with permission.

Bobby Bare and Friends excerpt, aired March 28, 1985, on The Nashville Network. Printed with permission from the Country Music Hall of Fame and Museum.

"John Prine Starts from 'Zero' Again: Looking Ahead and Looking Back, Singer-Songwriter Sees the Light," by Dave Hoekstra, published July 20, 1986, in the *Chicago Sun-Times*. Reprinted with permission from the *Chicago Sun-Times*.

"John Prine Turns Meat and Potatoes into Music," by Bob Millard, published 1985 in *Country Song Roundup*. Reprinted with permission from Bob Millard.

Excerpt from *Shuck Beans, Stack Cakes, and Honest Fried Chicken: The Heart and Soul of Southern Country Kitchens*, by Ronni Lundy, 1991. Reprinted with permission from Ronni Lundy.

Biography written for release of *German Afternoons*, by Holly Gleason, for Oh Boy Records, 1986. Printed with permission.

Shooting script for *German Afternoons* feature, by Mike Leonard, broadcast August 1, 1986, on *The Today Show*, NBC. Printed with permission from Mike Leonard.

"Not Exactly Missing in Action," by Gil Asakawa, published February 1992 in *Pulse!*. Reprinted with permission from Gil Asakawa.

"Special Delivery: Ex-Mailman John Prine Proves He Can Still Carry a Message," by Cynthia Sanz, published April 1992 in *People*. Reprinted/translated from OhBoy! and published with permission of Time Inc. Reproduction in any manner in any language in whole or in part without written permission is prohibited.

Shooting script for *The Missing Years* feature, by Mike Leonard, broadcast 1991 on *The Today Show*, NBC. Printed with permission from Mike Leonard.

"Hometown Hero: John Prine Comes Home to Give Back," by Dave Hoekstra, published May 9, 2010, in the *Chicago Sun-Times*. Reprinted with permission from the *Chicago Sun-Times*.

Excerpt from *More Songwriters on Songwriting*, by Paul Zollo, 2016, reproduced on bluerailroad.wordpress.com. Reprinted with permission from Paul Zollo.

"*Lost Dogs and Mixed Blessings*," by Michael McCall, published 1995 in the *Nashville Scene*. Reprinted with permission from Michael McCall and the *Nashville Scene*.

Script excerpt from *Daddy and Them*, by Billy Bob Thornton, 2001, Free Hazel Films/Industry Entertainment/Miramax/Shooting Gallery. Printed with permission.

"How to Survive on an Apple Pie Diet," by Robert Christgau, originally published October 5, 1999, in the *Village Voice*, reproduced in *Is It Still Good to Ya?: Fifty Years of Rock Criticism, 1967–2017* (Duke University Press Books). Reprinted with permission.

"The Voice of Experience," by Randy Lewis, published April 30, 2000, in the *Los Angeles Times*. Reprinted with permission from Randy Lewis.

"John Prine—To Believe in This Living," by Lloyd Sachs, published May 1, 2005, in *No Depression*. Reprinted with permission from Lloyd Sachs.

"A Literary Evening with Ted Kooser and John Prine," March 9, 2005, retrieved from the Library of Congress. Printed with permission from Ted Kooser.

"John Prine: Fair and Square," by Jesse Kornbluth, published January 1, 2005, on HeadButler.com. Printed with permission from Jesse Kornbluth.

Interview with John Prine and Mac Wiseman, by Andy Ellis, 2007. Printed with permission from Andy Ellis.

"BackTalk with John Prine," by Alex Rawls, published December 1, 2002, in *OffBeat Magazine*. Reprinted with permission from *OffBeat Magazine*.

"John Prine: For Better, or Worse, or Better, & Better," by Holly Gleason, published September 12, 2016, in the *Contributor*. Reprinted with permission.

John Mellencamp speech at PEN Award Presentation, September 19, 2016, John F. Kennedy Presidential Library. Reprinted with permission from John Mellencamp.

"John Prine: Innocent Days," by Holly Gleason, published November 23, 2011, in *Paste*. Reprinted with permission.

Tree of Forgiveness album release special with Dave Cobb, broadcast April 2018 on *Outlaw Country*, SiriusXM. Printed with permission from SiriusXM.

"John Prine Is Still Singing About Heaven and Mortality—and Sounding as Vital as Ever," by Randy Lewis, published May 16, 2018, in the *Los Angeles Times*. Reprinted with permission from Randy Lewis.

"Songs from the Gut: A Conversation with John Prine," by Holly Gleason, published in the fall 2016 issue of *No Depression*. Reprinted with permission.

"John Prine Reflects on Three Grammy Nominations," by Randy Lewis, published December 12, 2018, in the *Los Angeles Times*. Reprinted with permission from Randy Lewis.

"John Prine on Using, Unwed Fathers," to Make a Stand Against Abortion Bans," by Chris Willman, published May 30, 2019, in *Daily Variety / Variety.com*. Reprinted with permission from Steven Gaydos.

"*MOJO*: The Last In-Depth Interview" or "John Prine: The *MOJO* Interview," by Bob Mehr, published 2020 on *MOJO*. Reprinted with permission from Bob Mehr.

"'When I Get to Heaven': A Candid Conversation with John Prine," by Benjy Eisen, published April 9, 2020, in *Relix*. Reprinted with permission from Benjy Eisen.

INDEX